34.95

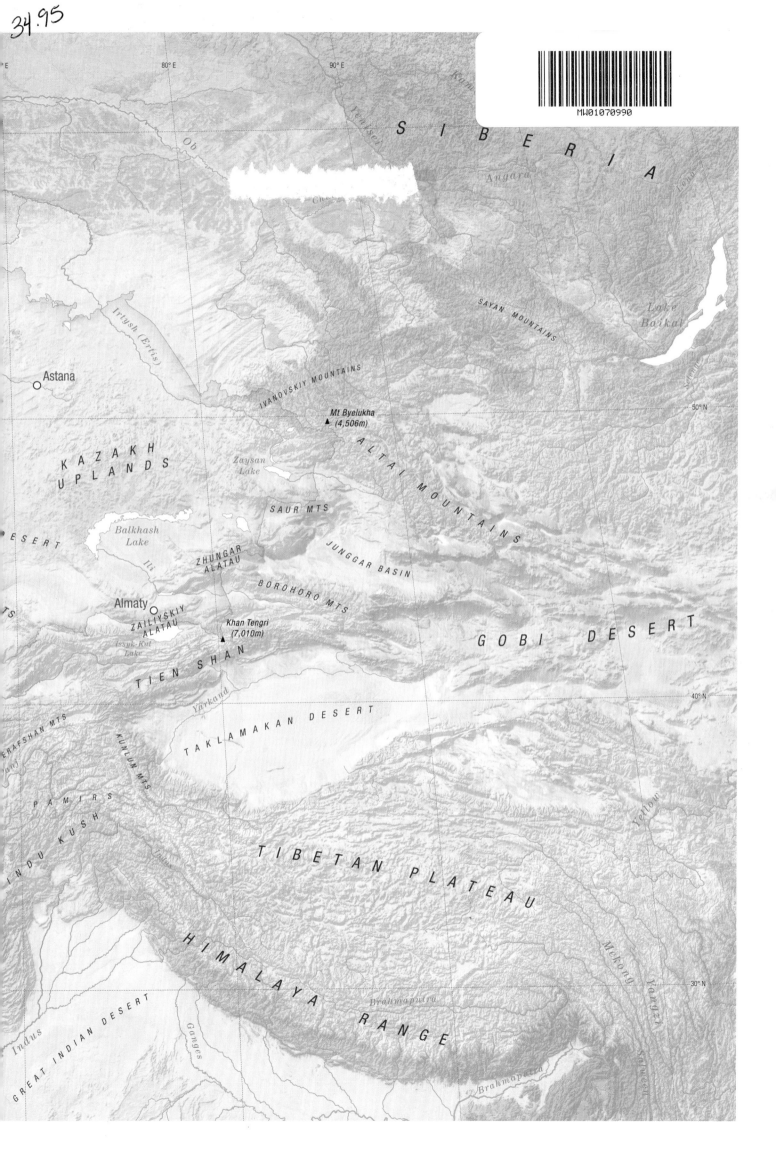

E · 80° E · 90° E

S I B E R I A

Ob

Yenisei

Angara

Lena

Lake Baikal

SAYAN MOUNTAINS

Irtysh (Ertis)

Astana

KAZAKH UPLANDS

50° N

IVANOVSKIY MOUNTAINS

Mt Byelukha
(4,506m)

A L T A I   M O U N T A I N S

Zaysan Lake

SAUR MTS

Balkhash Lake

Ili

ZHUNGAR ALATAU

JUNGGAR BASIN

DESERT

BOROHORO MTS

Almaty

ZAILIYSKIY ALATAU

G O B I   D E S E R T

Issyk-Kul Lake

Khan Tengri
(7,010m)

TS

T I E N   S H A N

Yarkand

40° N

T A K L A M A K A N   D E S E R T

ERAFSHAN MTS

anj

KUNLUN MTS

P A M I R S

Yellow

INDU KUSH

T I B E T A N   P L A T E A U

Mekong

Yangtze

H I M A L A Y A   R A N G E

30° N

GREAT INDIAN DESERT

Indus

Ganges

Brahmaputra

Brahmaputra

Salween

# An Illustrated History of
# KAZAKHSTAN

## Asia's Heartland in Context

Jeremy Tredinnick

# FOREWORD BY MINISTER ERLAN IDRISSOV

Kazakhstan is a very young nation. In less than a quarter of a century we have become a stable nation with a fast-developing economy, rising middle class and high aspirations for the future. Our multinational population, which is a product of our rich history, is fundamental to the development of the country and our confidence that we will achieve the nation's ambitious goals.

We are located, however, in an area which, for decades, was seen both as remote and, frankly, of little global importance. Therefore, it comes as no surprise that the few books written about Kazakhstan in English have been largely academic studies focusing on the ancient history of the Silk Road or the former Soviet Union. There has been very little in print for the general reader.

But as Kazakhstan has grown in prosperity and influence, and economic and political forces have pushed Central Asia up the global agenda, we have seen a new appetite for learning about our country. That is why this new story of Kazakhstan and its place within the broader Central Asian, Eurasian and global spheres could not come at a better time.

This book has a number of very valuable characteristics. Firstly, academic experts in each historical field have been invited to participate to make it both comprehensive and accurate. But great care has also been taken to make this research accessible for the general reader who will find a great deal to interest them.

Given my role, for example, I found it fascinating to read about the diplomatic genius of Ablai Khan, who can be seen to be one of the founders of the present-day multi-vector foreign policy of Kazakhstan. His story emphasizes the truth in the saying that wisdom from the past must always guide us today, something which has particular importance as we face the major challenges of the modern world.

Secondly, this book has been written and edited by someone who possesses deep personal knowledge of Kazakhstan. Over the last 10 years, Jeremy Tredinnick's many visits and meetings with a wide variety of people have given him a perceptive insight into the history and modern life of our country.

He is also the author and editor of *An Illustrated Map of Kazakhstan*, which brings to life our Silk Road heritage, Tourism and Cultural sites, Energy and Infrastructure. I believe strongly that geography shapes the life of nations, their economy, culture and mentality. So this experience makes his contribution even more valuable.

Lastly, the diversity of images which illustrate this book underlines how far-reaching and noteworthy Kazakhstan's past has been. They have been sourced from museums, organizations and individuals throughout the world and add greatly to the value of the book.

Kazakhstan's fascinating history, presented in this book in vivid colour and great detail, has shaped our open approach to the world. I am proud that Kazakhstan is known as a good neighbour and reliable international partner, committed to fostering peace and understanding. The values that we cherish and promote in the name of global progress come from our forefathers and our history. I hope this new book will increase understanding about our country and what makes it unique.

I hope – and believe – that every reader will find this new narrative both enjoyable and rewarding.

**Erlan A. Idrissov**
**Minister of Foreign Affairs of**
**the Republic of Kazakhstan**

Above: A golden snow leopard leaps from mountain peaks in a classic example of Scytho-Siberian animalistic art created by the Iron Age Saka culture. Opposite: A nomadic Turkic *khagan* (ruler) holds friendly discussions with the Sogdian official An Jia in this panel from the sixth century CE An Jia sarcophagus. Previous page: An exquisite golden plaque from the Zhalauly treasure depicts two deer with interlocking antlers

**ODYSSEY BOOKS & MAPS**

Odyssey Books & Maps is a division of Airphoto International Ltd.
1401 Chung Ying Building, 20–20A Co nnaught Road West, Sheung Wan, Hong Kong
Tel: (852) 2856 3896; Fax: (852) 3012 1825
E-mail: magnus@odysseypublications.com; www.odysseypublications.com
Follow us on Twitter—www.twitter.com/odysseyguides

Distribution in the USA by W.W. Norton & Company, Inc. 500 Fifth Avenue, New York, NY 10110, USA.
Tel: (800) 233-4830; Fax: (800) 458-6515; www.wwnorton.com

Distribution in the UK and Europe by Cordee Ltd. 11 Jacknell Road, Dodwells Bridge Industrial Estate,
Hinckley, Leicestershire LE10 3BS, UK. Tel: (1455) 611-185
info@cordee.co.uk; www.cordee.co.uk

Distribution in Australia by Woodslane Pty Ltd. Unit 7/5 Vuko Place, Warriewood, NSW 2012, Australia.
Tel: (2) 9970-5111; Fax: (2) 9970-5002; www.woodslane.com.au

*An Illustrated History of Kazakhstan: Asia's Heartland in Context*, First Edition
ISBN: 978-962-217-852-6
Library of Congress Catalog Card Number has been requested.
Copyright © 2014, published by Airphoto International Ltd.

Managing Editor: Jeremy Tredinnick
Cover designer: Ng Kin Man, Alex
Designer: Au Yeung Chui Kwai
Maps: Mark Stroud (except pages 28, 31, 41 and 43, ©Labgeoarch)

Cover photography: Jeremy Tredinnick
Back cover photography from top: Library of Congress, Prints & Photographs Division; Karl Baipakov;
Shaanxi Provincial  Institute of Archaeology; Jeremy Tredinnick x2 (bottom and inside back flap)

Production by Twin Age Ltd, Hong Kong. E-mail: twinage@netvigator.com
Manufactured in Hong Kong

Opposite: Portraits of a Kazakh man and woman taken during the Imperial Russian era.

The gorgeous ribbed dome of the Mausoleum of Khoja Ahmed Yasawi in Turkistan, one of Kazakhstan's greatest cultural treasures.

# CONTENTS

Above: A *balbal* (an anthropomorphic stone figure) stands guard over a Turkic burial site in the Merke region of the Tien Shan
Opposite: The Holy Ascension Cathedral in downtown Almaty – constructed entirely of wood, it has survived major earthquakes and has been beautifully renovated

An *akyn* (a type of Kazakh minstrel – a highly respected position) sings for a captivated audience (©MAE (Kunstkamera) RAS No 2035-213)

# EDITOR'S NOTE

The research and preparation of this book has been a journey of discovery wholly in keeping with the exciting subject matter within its pages. Whilst delving into the reams of material – both print and online – that represent our ever-increasing knowledge of human history in the Central Asian region, it became clear that in many instances our understanding of early periods of human movement and civilization is far from complete, and more often than not in dispute to varying degrees. There is still much for us to discover.

I have come to the conclusion that most Central Asia researchers – whether their field is in palaeontology, archaeology, ancient or medieval history, anthropology or linguistics – are never happier nor more animated than when debating or disputing the theories of their peers or forebears. Such disagreements are not malicious, they merely serve to highlight the passion with which the protagonists strive to reconstruct the past – never an easy task when clues are thin on the ground and sources are contradictory.

There will no doubt be those who disagree with certain aspects of the historical tale told in this book – that is an inevitable consequence of any attempt to cover a region infamous for its historical complexity. However, we were lucky to be assisted in its production by many world-renowned experts in their various fields. Each chapter contains an essay by an expert on that period, and their findings and conclusions are backed by many years of detailed and authoritative research.

Of course this book is not intended to be an academic publication, despite the scholarly credentials of its contributors – to present an illustrated history of Kazakhstan dating from the evolution of man through to the present day in only 200 pages necessitates a significant amount of summarization and paraphrasing. Instead, it aims to tell the story of this fascinating country and the broader region within which it is set in a comprehensive but accessible manner, augmented by attractive images and informative maps.

Mark Twain once said that "History doesn't repeat itself, but it does rhyme". Nowhere is this more apparent than in the vast steppe lands of central Eurasia.

Top: A late 19th century image of nomads on the move, their yurts and other belongings neatly packed onto camels (©MAE (Kunstkamera) RAS No 119-168). Above: A golden plaque of a horned deer with folded legs, part of the Zhalauly treasure discovered in the Almaty region and dating to between the seventh and sixth centuries BCE

**A note on spellings:** The English spelling of both place and people's names in the mass of historical literature related to Central Asia is confused and often contentious. As well as different methods of transliteration (think Dzungar/Djungar/Zhungar/Junggar or Genghis Khan/Jenghis Khan/Chinggis Khaan), the diverse cultures who wrote about the region – from Chinese to Greek, from Persian to Russian – used greatly differing languages and forms of writing, and indeed often had entirely dissimilar words to describe the same tribe or state (the Kipchaks were called Polovians or Polovtsy by the Russians and Cumans by the Byzantines, while the Xiongnu or Hsiung-nu were later known in the West as Huns).

Rather than allow ourselves to become bogged down in a quagmire of semantic pedantry, we have wherever possible used spellings that appear to us to represent common usage in International English, often offering alternative spellings in brackets after the first use in each chapter. There may at times, however, be inconsistencies, for example where a specific spelling or preferred name fits the historical context within which it is being used alongside related spellings. For this we do not apologize; rather, you should look at it as a valuable lesson in preparing for the many different spellings you will come across if you choose to undertake further literary exploration.

**A note on dates:** In deference to Kazakhstan's diverse religious demographic, the traditional use of "BC" (Before Christ) and "AD" (*Anno Domini*) has been replaced with the equivalent but more neutral "BCE" (Before Common Era) and "CE" (Common Era), whereby "Common" simply pertains to the most frequently used modern international timeline reference, the Gregorian Calendar.

# ACKNOWLEDGEMENTS

A book of such geographical, cultural and historical scope requires the assistance of a wide range of people. The publisher and editor would like to gratefully acknowledge the following individuals and organizations for generously donating their time and resources, thereby making a valuable contribution to this book:

The Embassy of the Republic of Kazakhstan to the United States, Washington, D.C.

Aktayeva Lyazzat Suleimenovna and Saule Satayeva of the Central State Archive of Cinema-Photo Documents and Sound Recording of the Republic of Kazakhstan

Karl M. Baipakov of the Institute of Archaeology of the Republic of Kazakhstan

Meruyert Kh. Abusseitova and Napil Bazylkhan of the R.B. Suleimenov Institute of Oriental Studies

Aiman Dossymbayeva of the Nazarbayev Center in Astana

Jennifer Chi of the Institute for the Study of the Ancient World at New York University

Altynbekov Krym of the Scientific Restoration Laboratory Ostrov Krym

Zainolla Samashev of the Astana branch of the A. Kh. Margulan Institute of Archaeology

Didar Kassymova of KIMEP University, Almaty

Zhanat Kundakbayeva of Al-Farabi Kazakh National University

Olga Vasilyeva, Nina Zabcova and Alexey Alexeyev of the National Library of Russia

Wang Weilin and Sun Zhouyong of the Shaanxi Provincial Institute of Archaeology

Lisha Bai of the Shaanxi Cultural Heritage Promotional Center

Dmitriy A. Voyakin of Archeological Expertise LLC

Roy Bolton of Sphinx Fine Art (www.sphinxfineart.com)

Berik Barysbekov of CAPro (Central Asia Production, www.capro.kz)

Assel Kozhakova of the Astana EXPO-2017 National Company

Aigul Saduakassova

Alan Aydakhar

**Rakhmet! / Spasibo! / Thank you!**

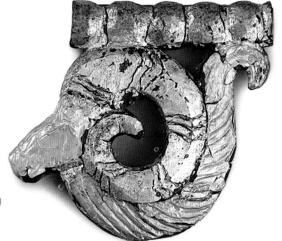

Above: A wooden argali head covered in gold and tin foil, part of the horse tack excavated from a kurgan in the Berel Valley of eastern Kazakhstan's Altai Mountains

# INTRODUCTION

Telling the "story" of Kazakhstan through the ages illustrates its many significant roles in human history: it served as a fulcrum for early human migration throughout Eurasia and the wider world; it was one of the most important centres of bronze metallurgy during the Bronze Age; its steppes were the crucible for Iron Age nomadic warrior societies that would change the world order; and its bustling southern cities were vital links along the many trade routes of the classical Silk Road of antiquity.

In more recent times, the territory of modern-day Kazakhstan was home to successive waves of Turkic peoples who subsequently spread out to occupy vast regions and new countries stretching from the Mediterranean Sea to eastern Siberia; it was a vital central portion of the great Mongol Empire; and was seen by Imperial Russia as intrinsic to its empire-building plans. As a republic of the Soviet Union, the Kazakh territory suffered many atrocities but none more heinous than the use of its eastern steppe as

overland trade. The future looks promising, but as Kazakhstan drives towards modernization and progress, it is fully aware of the importance of understanding and learning from its past, in order to ensure old mistakes are not made anew, and to maintain the myriad cultural links that, through time and across continents, have been woven together to form the rich fabric of Kazakhstan's society today.

This book represents an opportunity to bring together the discoveries and conclusions of a variety of academics from a range of disciplines that span epochs, each chapter detailing a significant period in the history of Kazakhstan and the broader Central Asia region, but together providing a balanced and comprehensive chronicle of human existence stretching from hundreds of thousands of years ago until the modern day. In the process, we hope to dispel a few myths, put right some common but erroneous preconceptions, and present some little-known but fascinating nuggets of information that will help the reader to appreciate more fully this complex but richly rewarding part of the world.

For example, in the early chapters we learn of the significance a changing climate had on the initial movement of man's evolutionary ancestors, then humans themselves, as the Eurasian landmass dried out and humid, swampy savannahs were replaced by sweeping grasslands more conducive to Stone Age man. Human cultures in the Stone Age and Bronze Age were defined by their environments, and when that changed they were forced to either adapt or migrate, a process that rewarded creativity (imagine the huge advantage the early metallurgists had with their copper and bronze tools), created interaction between communal groups and allowed new cultures to blossom.

The origins of the horse-borne nomadic warrior tribes that emerged during the Iron Age have been debated for centuries, but new archaeological evidence is beginning to

a testing site for hundreds of atomic bombs during the Cold War – a period of appalling suffering for its people that left a traumatic and lingering legacy, and which led directly to Kazakhstan becoming one of the leading voices in the global movement for nuclear disarmament and nonproliferation.

Today, as a relatively young and dynamic nation Kazakhstan is mirroring the significance of its past: its natural resources are exported to a number of neighbouring countries, it has become a hugely important strategic partner for all the major world powers, it is a regional leader and role model within Central Asia, and is a pioneering member country on a new "Silk Road" of intercontinental

Top left: A Kazakh eagle hunter and his magnificent bird in Nura near Almaty during a festival in 2013. Above: Petroglyphs at Tamgaly, a UNESCO World Heritage site renowned for its wealth of rock art dating back to the Bronze Age unravel the mystery, shedding light on the vital role played by the broad Eurasian forest-steppe belt, across which tribes spread and communicated in both directions. The earliest known "Scythian" burial mound, or *kurgan*, is Arzhan, situated in Russian Siberia's Tuva Republic beside a tributary of the Yenisei River and dating to the ninth or early eighth century BCE. Kazakhstan's earliest excavated kurgan is located at the Shilikty burial complex in the Zaysan region of East Kazakhstan and is dated 810-750 BCE, but kurgan sites far to the west in the Pontic Steppe date from about a century later, leading to the conclusion that the epicentre of the equestrian warrior elite societies was in the Tuvan and Altai region, from where it spread out – albeit swiftly – as far as the Black Sea and Crimea.

Cultural exchange – and to a degree a blending of bloodlines – took place throughout northern Eurasia during the Bronze and Iron Ages. A common and often visceral argument throughout Central Asia and the many ethnic groups that populate the region is the ethnic root of their predecessor tribes and states. Were they Mongoloid or Caucasian? Modern genetics is helping to clear up some of these issues, but frankly the question is moot, given the nature of Central Asia's human interaction over the last half-dozen millennia, characterized as it was by massive migrations, tribal movements and conquering armies.

The Scythians (and Saka) are now considered to have been mainly Europoid (Caucasian) in feature, but with a progressive mingling of Mongoloid traits the farther east they lived, until by central Mongolia the nomadic tribes were purely Asiatic. Repeated forced migrations and invasions by tribes from the east – starting with the Wusun in the second century BCE – has resulted in a genetic mix that today shows incredible diversity in facial type throughout Central Asia, and this can only be a good thing in the modern world of multiracialism and multiculturalism.

What is most relevant from the Scythian period is not ethnicity but cultural connectivity – environmental conditions were the main driver for cultural and societal development, and thus it was that the steppes and mountain foothills from the Black Sea to Lake Baikal and from the

Siberian taiga forests to the Tien Shan became home to tribal groups who were otherwise unrelated but who followed a remarkably similar way of life and were therefore grouped together as though they were a single entity by the contemporary states that bordered their lands, such as the Achaemenids, the Greeks and the Zhou dynasties of China.

The Scythians' shared way of life was based on nomadic pastoralism – the breeding of livestock, in particular horses and sheep, but also goats, cattle and camels – that required frequent movement to new pastureland. The term "nomad" is one that is often misinterpreted, thought to mean that its proponents simply wandered the land looking for good grazing. This could not be further from the truth: the true nomads of Central Asia had well-organized and seasonally determined patterns of movement that took them from rich summer pastures to winter camps, where they hunkered down to survive the extremes of that season.

Each tribe used its own traditional pastures and camps, moving along well-known migratory routes between them, and they would defend these lands vigorously from encroachment. Depending on a group's geographical location, nomadism could involve moving great distances across flat steppe, or making much shorter journeys between high alpine meadows and lower piedmonts (in the mountain regions of Tien Shan or the Altai), a form known as vertical nomadism.

Other false perceptions regarding the Central Asian nomads include the idea that their way of life represented merely a stage of human development between hunter-gatherer societies and the sedentary agriculturalists that followed. This has been categorically disproven; as Sören Stark and Karen Rubinson write in their introduction to *Nomads and Networks*: "On the contrary, nomadism should be seen as a highly sophisticated subsistence strategy that coexisted as an alternative to the sedentary cultures of agricultural and urban societies."

Ongoing archaeological exploration and greater research into ancient literature has also shown that the nomads were not the uncouth barbarians so often depicted, but in fact operated under a highly developed socio-political system, did in fact practise some agriculture where conditions merited it, and created an artistic tradition – the Scytho-Siberian animalistic style – that produced some of the most refined and beautiful metalwork of the age.

Below: The interior of a yurt in the museum of the Presidential Cultural Centre in Astana. Bottom left: A close-up of the superb craftsmanship of the myriad golden objects and detailing on the Golden Man's jacket and belt (from a replica located in the same museum)

The relationship between nomadic groups and the sedentary communities and urban dwellers along the ancient trading routes was also far more complex than many imagine. Interaction between the towns and cities and the nomadic warrior clans could of course be violent, but more often it was based on mutual trading of goods, or on an overlord-vassal basis, whereby the nomads ensured peace and safety from attack in return for tributes in the form of both essential goods and luxury items. It was a symbiotic association for many centuries, especially during the golden period of the Silk Road, when southern Kazakhstan boasted dozens of major trading centres, from caravanserais and small towns to large, opulent cities.

The significance of the ancient cities in the territory of southern Kazakhstan should not be overlooked. Long thought of as a region full of nomadic tribes but devoid of any noteworthy settled civilization, only in recent decades has it become fully clear just how important the trading routes of the northern Tien Shan and the banks of the Syr

Darya were to the merchant caravans that plied their wares between East and West. Cities such as Taraz, Ispidzhab, Otrar, Sauran and Yangikent were major hubs of commerce and civilization, rivalling the power and influence of more globally renowned cities like Samarkand and Bukhara. The era of the Turkic Khaganate and the Karakhanids (6th-13th centuries CE) was their heyday, when cities boomed under the protection of nomadic federations and everyone profited from the immense trade passing through Central Asia between the Mediterranean, northern Europe, the subcontinent and dynastic China.

The coming of Genghis Khan's hordes at the start of the 13th century heralded rapid and momentous change in Central Asia, but while the destructive power of the Mongol military forces was trumpeted across the world, less well known was the fact that if a city or region's inhabitants offered no resistance, acquiesced and paid obeisance to the "Unbending Lord", then Genghis would hold off his plundering troops and forbid pillaging, sometimes even

allowing a city's ruler to remain in power. Such was the case for much of Zhetisu (Semirechye) – although the Syr Darya cities fared much worse, foolishly standing against the all-conquering Mongols.

The Mongols did much damage, including the incidental destruction of much of the sophisticated agricultural and urban network of southern Kazakhstan over the coming centuries, but they also created the foundation for future states based on the concept of a strong, centralized power. The minting of coins helped to facilitate trade, which continued and remained robust in the region despite the opening of the Maritime Silk Route between Asia and Europe, but a pattern of internecine warfare between a variety of clans and rulers all claiming Genghisid descent took its toll, resulting in the breakaway of two sultans – Kerei and Janibek – from Abulkhair Khan's "Uzbek" horde in the mid-15th century, and the creation of a new state: the Kazakh Khanate.

As with so many of its predecessors, the Kazakh Khanate was a confederation of many tribes, both Turkic and Mongol, and during the height of its power it controlled almost all of modern-day Kazakhstan's territory and substantial regions beyond, both north and south. The Kazakhs boasted diplomatic relations with neighbouring states in all directions, from Imperial Russia to Mughal India, from the Qing Dynasty to the Ottoman Empire. However, internal power struggles once again were an affliction, and the ascendancy of the Dzungar Empire in the lands to the immediate east, followed by their invasion of Kazakh territory and the "Years of Great Distress" in the early 18th century, drove the Kazakhs to seek help from the mighty Russian Empire, becoming a vassal state and thereby sealing their doom as an independent nation for more than 200 years to come.

The colonization of Kazakh lands by Imperial Russia initially seemed relatively benign, but its insidious nature and the deliberate corrosion of Kazakh cultural beliefs inevitably led to insurgencies and outright rebellion. These were mercilessly put down by the far stronger Russian forces, but when, at the start of the 20th century, Tsarist Russia imploded and the Communist Soviet Union was born, there was a brief moment of hope that an independent Kazakh republic might also now be possible.

This was not to be; Russian Central Asia was split into Soviet Socialist Republics (SSRs), and the Kazakh SSR was to suffer through decades of Soviet "experimentation", with misguided collectivization schemes that destroyed the traditional Kazakh way of life, forced mass relocations of numerous ethnic groups from every region of Soviet Russia, purges of "undesirables" and the creation of horrific prison labour camps. The infamous "Virgin and Idle Lands Project" that caused the shrinking and virtual destruction of the once mighty Aral Sea is now considered one of the world's greatest environmental disasters, while the egregious testing of atomic bombs in the eastern Kazakh steppe has been condemned on a global scale.

It is worth noting, however, that despite the deplorable list above, the Soviet era did also allow for a blossoming of Kazakh art, literature and music, while industry, science and education were all developed to a relatively high degree as well. Thus, when in 1991 an independent Republic of Kazakhstan was finally declared, the country's immense wealth in natural resources, combined with its multiracial, literate population, gave hope that it could make a successful transition to becoming a sovereign, democratic state.

Kazakhstan's first decade was a difficult one, with the creation of a free market economy facing many obstacles and pitfalls. However, President Nazarbayev's strategy of focusing on fast economic progress while maintaining strong centralized power – to ensure political stability – proved to be astute and successful. Substantial foreign investment was attracted to the country's phenomenal energy and mining sectors, and since the turn of the 21st century its modernization and economic progress has made Kazakhstan one of the world's fastest developing countries.

Having succeeded in building a strong economy, President Nazarbayev and his government have begun to accelerate the process of democratization that is essential to the country's aspirations on the global stage. In 2012 the president set out his Kazakhstan-2050 Strategy, designed to make it one of the 30 most advanced nations in the world by the year 2050. This is an ambitious dream, but one that can become reality if the people of Kazakhstan draw strength from their past, learn the lessons of history and fulfil their great potential.

Opposite: Portrait of a wealthy Kazakh family in eastern Kazakhstan in the late 19th century (©MAE (Kunstkamera) RAS no 106-86). Above: President Nursultan Nazarbayev at work in his office

# PRE-HISTORY: HUMAN MIGRATIONS AND THE STONE AGE

Kazakhstan's role in the history of mankind is significant, stretching far back to the beginning of our ancestors' colonization of the planet. Although there are varying theories about exactly when and where the first human precursors left the continent of Africa, and which routes the successive waves of migrating hominids took, clear archaeological evidence has shown that first *Homo habilis* and *ergaster*, then *Homo erectus* and *Homo Neanderthalensis*, and finally *Homo sapiens* all moved from the Near East into Central Asia and made their homes there. Modern-day genome testing has subsequently shown that the colonization by humans of both northern Europe and Siberia – and from there North America – began in Central Asia and the territory of Kazakhstan.

When considering how and why early man took up residence in this region, it is important to understand that Central Asia's topography and climate were wildly different – and in constant flux – during the Palaeolithic era that lasted from 2.5 million years ago right up to the Mesolithic period (12,000-7,000 years ago). The Palaeolithic – along with the Mesolithic, Neolithic and Eneolithic – are terms used by archaeologists to categorize stages of human evolution, primarily related to their development of increasingly sophisticated tools. These periods roughly parallel geological terms that describe the changes in climate and geology that resulted in very different landscapes and environments through time. Thus the Palaeolithic and its different phases (Early, Middle and Late) tie in with the Pleistocene era, while the Holocene era – lasting from 12,000 years ago to the present day – corresponds to the Mesolithic, Neolithic, Eneolithic and Bronze Ages and beyond (see Table on next page), when humans took advantage of the stable, more liveable environment to take huge strides forward in social development.

The essay that follows explains their connection in greater detail, but in short, when the first hominid, *Homo habilis*, ventured into the region and made its home by the shores of the Caspian Sea and in the foothills of the Karatau mountains (a spur of the Tien Shan), Central Asia was a hot, humid savannah under the influence of a monsoonal climate from the south. These early ancestors of man made basic tools from stones and lived near reliable water sources.

Very slowly, as tectonic movements raised the Tien Shan to truly mountainous proportions, the climate changed to become influenced from the Atlantic; the Caspian Sea, which had been far larger then, retreated and the savannah turned into grasslands and deserts under a continental climate. Long periods of glaciation were an additional problem for the new waves of hominids (*Homo erectus* and Neanderthal man), who were forced to adapt to the changing climate, more arid environment and new animal species. They also needed water as a priority for survival and therefore lived beside rivers and lakes, but they required access to suitable rock materials as well, from which they could fashion tools and weapons. A more advanced form of tool making developed with the Neanderthals, who struck large flakes from core stones and created tools from these.

When the first true humans, *Homo sapiens*, migrated into Central Asia approximately 40,000 years ago, they mingled with Neanderthal communities that had already spread out through most of Kazakhstan's territory. One of the great anthropological questions is whether modern man interacted peacefully with Neanderthal man, even

The vast expanse of Kazakhstan's central steppe was slowly inhabited by mankind over many millennia

# Kazakhstan in Pre-history

| ANTHROPOLOGICAL ERA | DATE (APPROX) | HUMAN ANCESTRY | TRADITIONS AND CULTURES | GEOLOGICAL ERA |
|---|---|---|---|---|
| EARLY (LOWER) PALAEOLITHIC | 2.5 million-130,000 years ago | *Homo habilis* *Homo ergaster* *Homo erectus* | Oldowan (Proto-Levalloiso-Acheulean) Acheulean (Levalloiso-Acheulean I) Core-tool industries | EARLY PLEISTOCENE (1.6 million-800,000 years ago) MIDDLE PLEISTOCENE (800,000-130,000 years ago) |
| MIDDLE PALAEOLITHIC | 130,000-40,000 years ago | *Homo Neanderthalensis* *Homo sapiens* (from 40,000-50,000 years ago) | Mousterian (Levalloiso-Aceulean II) Flake-tool industries | LATE PLEISTOCENE (130,000-12,000 years ago) |
| LATE (UPPER) PALAEOLITHIC | 40,000-12,000 years ago | *Homo sapiens* *Homo sapiens sapiens* (Modern man) | Blade-tool industries | LATE PLEISTOCENE (130,000-12,000 years ago) Last Glacial Maximum (25,000-12,000 years ago) |
| MESOLITHIC (EPIPALAEOLITHIC / MIDDLE STONE AGE) | 12,000-7,000 years ago | *Homo sapiens sapiens* | Hunter-gatherers Microlith industries | HOLOCENE Boreal period (9,000-7,500 years ago) |
| NEOLITHIC (NEW STONE AGE) | 5,000-3,500 BCE | *Homo sapiens sapiens* | Kelteminar Atbasar Early animal husbandry | HOLOCENE Atlantic period (7,500-5,000 years ago / 5,500-3,000 BCE) |
| ENEOLITHIC / CHALCOLITHIC (COPPER AGE) | 3,500-2,000 BCE | *Homo sapiens sapiens* | Botai Yamna Afanasevo Horse domestication and pastoralism | HOLOCENE |
| BRONZE AGE | 2,000-900 BCE | *Homo sapiens sapiens* | Srubna Andronovo Karasuk | HOLOCENE |

interbred with him, or whether their relationship was antagonistic, with *Homo sapiens'* more advanced tool-making skills (they made blade-like tools from more refined stone flakes as well as bones and antlers) allowing them to overwhelm and wipe out the Neanderthals. Nobody knows, but what is clear is that the more advanced humans swiftly superseded the Neanderthals, who became extinct relatively quickly after their arrival.

Men next began to use microliths, or tiny sharpened flakes, to make composite tools such as spears and arrows (for newly invented bows), and by the Mesolithic era a hunter-gatherer culture had emerged, with communities boasting

nascent social systems. It had taken around 1.8 million years for humans to evolve to this stage, but from around 5,500 BCE onwards the rate of human development soared. This coincided with the Atlantic period of the Holocene era, when the arid Boreal period ended and Kazakhstan's landscape became far more amenable to human existence, with a gradation from south to north of desert, semi-desert, dry steppe and forest steppe, much as it is today.

This mixed landscape allowed the development of Neolithic cultures that were homogenous across wide areas – the Kelteminar culture in the drier southern regions and in the north the Atbasar culture. The hunter-gatherer communities had now expanded into larger and

Facial reconstructions of man's ancestors, from *Homo habilis* (top left) to *Homo erectus* (bottom left) and Neanderthal man (above)

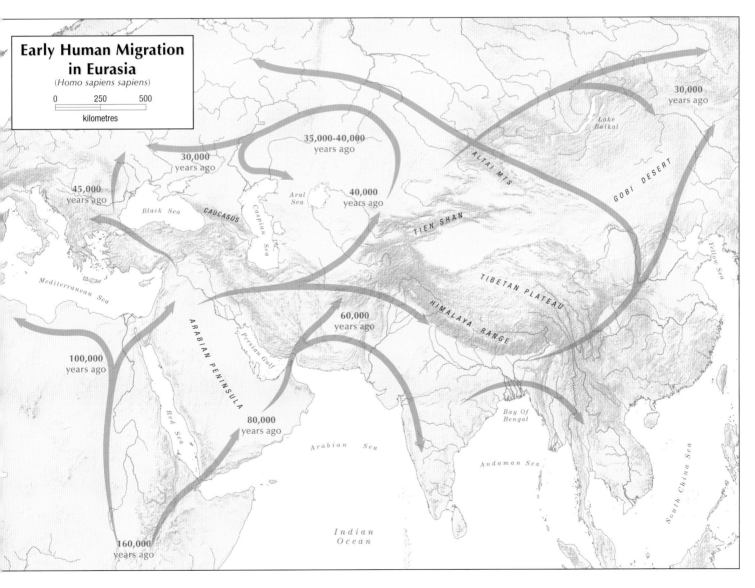

## Early Human Migration in Eurasia
*(Homo sapiens sapiens)*

0    250    500
kilometres

30,000 years ago

35,000-40,000 years ago

30,000 years ago

45,000 years ago

*Black Sea*    CAUCASUS    *Caspian Sea*    *Aral Sea*    40,000 years ago    ALTAI MTS    *Lake Baikal*    GOBI DESERT

TIEN SHAN

*Mediterranean Sea*

ARABIAN PENINSULA    *Persian Gulf*    60,000 years ago    TIBETAN PLATEAU    HIMALAYA RANGE    *Yellow Sea*

100,000 years ago

*Red Sea*    80,000 years ago    *Arabian Sea*    *Bay Of Bengal*    *Andaman Sea*    *South China Sea*

160,000 years ago    *Indian Ocean*

more complex societies where animals were becoming domesticated, basic agriculture took place and earthenware pottery was made. The Kelteminar people were more settled and were based along rivers such as the Amu Darya and Syr Darya, and in the foothills of the Tien Shan, but the Atbasar in the lush grasslands and forest-steppe of the north were semi-nomadic, ranging out from their home bases to hunt prey such as the enormous herds of horses that proliferated right across the vast Eurasian Steppe.

A very significant development now occurred, as human colonies in Europe and the Urals began to mine copper and create basic metal tools. This was the beginning of what is variously called the Eneolithic, Chalcolithic or Copper Age; exponents of this new metallurgical industry spread into Central Asia and a new culture emerged that took a vital step towards the dominant characteristic of Kazakhstan's future steppe dwellers. This was the Botai culture – the earliest known humans to have domesticated the horse.

The domestication of horses was a key factor in the development of human societies. It allowed them to revolutionize transport, communication and warfare.

Exactly when and where horses were first domesticated has been much debated; it was originally thought to have happened in Mesopotamia's agricultural Fertile Crescent during the 3rd millennium BCE, but archaeologists excavating the Eneolithic villages near Botai in the Kokshetau region of northern Kazakhstan in the 1980s postulated that horse pastoralism existed here around 3,500 BCE – 1,000 years earlier than previously thought.

In 2008 an international team brought to light three lines of evidence demonstrating that the Botai both harnessed and milked horses in large numbers. These included studies of the metacarpal (forelimb) bones that showed closer resemblance to domesticated horses of the Bronze Age than wild horses; forensic study of the premolars, which showed banding from bit-wear that occurs only in bridled animals; and organic residue analysis of multiple pots that showed processing of mare's milk (specifically from summer milking), indicating that it was stored in large quantities for later consumption.

Other studies also showed that the Botai communities had a stable economy based primarily on sedentary horse

pastoralism. The Botai settlement boasted 158 or more pit-houses that could have supported a population of 400 people. The design of the village was more complex than previous cultures, with buildings aligned in rows along avenues and arranged around plazas, suggesting advanced social organization. Such a high population density could not have been supported by hunting wild herds alone, and tools used for working hides and producing leather straps were far more abundant than projectile points or other hunting tools.

The fact that 99 percent of bones discovered belonged to horses is telling as well, and the skeletal remains provide valuable information about the distance between large game kill sites and home bases: if hunters were on foot they needed to minimize the weight carried home by efficient field processing of large game, so only the most valuable meat and carcass products were culled from a wild animal, and a horse's heavy vertebral column would be left behind. However, people who had horses to ride and/or use as pack animals did not need to worry about weight and distance, and the presence of whole carcass remains in the villages point to their use of horses for either one or both purposes.

The lifestyle of sedentary horse herders would have been very different from that of their predecessors, who did not have a dependable source of meat and milk, rapid transport for hunters, or pack animals to carry heavy loads. A regular food supply, the stability and social development inherent in larger communities, and the ability to travel great distances and gather materials not locally available, was a huge step forward for human development.

It is possible that other, even older sites may exist, waiting to be discovered, but for now Botai stands out as the earliest known place where man first mastered the horse, a momentous partnership that would swiftly carry us towards civilization and dominance of the world. With this new ability – and the subsequent discovery that adding tin (or zinc) to copper created a harder, more durable metal – a whole new world order was about to begin: the Bronze Age.

The abundance of horses in northern Kazakhstan's steppe land led to a human culture that preyed heavily on them, eventually domesticating and mastering them – a momentous occurrence for mankind

# The Stone Age in Kazakhstan

By *Zhaken K. Taimagambetov* and *Jean-Marc Deom*

The Palaeolithic era, commonly known as the Early Stone Age and split into Lower (Early), Middle and Upper (Late) periods (see Table on page 22), spanned a vast time period that lasted more than two million years. Central Asia during this time underwent great climate change, which engendered a shift in the region's environment from warm, humid savannahs with plentiful water to slowly increasing aridity, giving rise to different types of grassland and desert landscapes. It also saw the first colonization of the Eurasian landmass by humans and their forebears.

The territory of modern Kazakhstan was a very different place 1.8 million years ago, when the first hominids migrated out of Africa and arrived in the region. The landscape was mostly wet savannah, the Caspian Sea was more than twice its current size, the Tien Shan mountains reached only a third of their current height, and the Aral and Balkhash lakes did not exist.

Kazakhstan has great geographical importance as a crossroads for human migration around the world – it was from Central Asia that humans moved both west towards Europe and east into Siberia during the Palaeolithic periods (traces of human presence here during the various Palaeolithic phases precede those in Europe, Siberia, Mongolia and northern China by several thousand years).

The Katon-Karagay region of the Altai Mountains. Rich in biodiversity, mountain foothills were excellent sources of water and food for the hunter-gatherers who first moved into Kazakhstan's territory

First, however, around 1.8 million years ago *Homo habilis* (and/or *Homo ergaster*) came out of Africa as far as the Caspian Sea, where they manufactured basic stone chopping tools on its shores. *Homo erectus* followed, a more advanced hominin who performed the more sophisticated "Levallois technique" of "preparing" a stone core (nucleus) in order to extract a single large flake from which a tool was produced – they did this earlier in this region than anywhere in Eurasia.

A third important influx came around 130,000 years ago, when *Homo Neanderthalensis* (Neanderthal man) arrived in Kazakhstan and mastered different flake-tool techniques for the production of more diversified tools of smaller size. During this period, the Karatau mountain range saw the early stages of sophisticated blade techniques that would become characteristic of Aurignacian man (the earliest Upper Palaeolithic culture in Europe). Finally, *Homo sapiens* (and its subspecies *Homo sapiens sapiens* or "Modern man") migrated into Central Asia from the Near East, initiating the colonization of Europe and Siberia from Kazakhstan's territory during the Late Palaeolithic period characterized by the blade-tool technique (the many open-air sites and quasi absence of caves and human skeletons makes dating sites and their contents a difficult and contentious matter).

The Mesolithic (Epipalaeolithic) period that bridged the Palaeolithic and Neolithic eras (approx 12,000-7,000 years ago) began when the largest mammals – such as mammoths, giant deer and rhinoceroses – had retreated northward at the end of the Last Glacial Maximum period. The arid continental climate that followed depopulated the central parts of the region, but some cultures remained around the water basins of the south and in the moister areas of the north, where they merged with migratory groups. Together they developed hunter-gatherer techniques adapted to this Early Holocene environment, including a new stone industry for making microliths (tiny, shaped flints used in composite tools such as spears).

When the Neolithic period (also called the New Stone Age) began around 7,000 years ago (5,000 BCE), the physical environment of Central Asia had become much as it is today, and human communities progressively domesticated wild animals and cultivated plants. Horse domestication, which would ensure the military supremacy of humans on the Eurasian steppes until the invention of artillery, was achieved in northern Kazakhstan during the final stage of the Neolithic – the Eneolithic period or Copper Age around 5,500 years ago (3,500 BCE).

## CLIMATE CHANGE AND NEW ENVIRONMENTS

When discussing time in a geological sense, one must remember that geographic conditions, climate and landscapes are extremely variable. Over the course of the last two million years, our ancestors, the genus Homo (*habilis, erectus, neanderthalensis* and *sapiens*), witnessed extreme geographical change throughout the world. In Central Asia these changes included a process of increasing aridity as the Tien Shan mountains were uplifted by tectonics, causing a switch from a southern monsoonal climate to Atlantic-influenced atmospheric circulation. Additionally, in the last million years extreme fluctuations in climate between glacial and interglacial stages occurred, provoking deep anomalies in landscape zones and the flora and fauna within them.

From about 12,000 years ago (the early Holocene) the modern desert and semi-desert zones of Kazakhstan became established, and later the semi-desert regions were reduced and replaced by the dry steppe and forest-steppe zones we see today. This landscape evolution is categorized in four phases: the Early Pleistocene, Middle Pleistocene, Late Pleistocene and Holocene (see Figure 1 on page 28).

During the Early Pleistocene (from 1.6 million to 800,000 years ago) the Caspian Sea flooded the huge area of the Pre-Caspian and Turgai depressions (the Apsheronian period). At this time the climate was warm and humid and most of Kazakhstan was covered by savannah vegetation. The first colonization by early hominins occurred at this time; Lower Palaeolithic campsites have been found near the Caspian shore on the Apsheronian terraces (Shakhbagata), as well as in the Karatau mountains (Arystandy) located along stream terraces just above the plains, and offer the best clues as to life for our ancestors at this time.

Around a million years ago the Caspian Sea regressed, leaving behind a huge clay plain, and the Tien Shan mountains rose to the snow line (above 3,000 metres), resulting in the first and largest period of glaciation, and the formation of three vegetation belts in the Kazakhstan region: forest-steppe in the north, steppe in the centre and desert in the south. The wildlife of the Early Pleistocene (called Odessian and Tamanian fauna) featured the southern mammoth, ancient horses (*Equus stenonis* and *sussenbornensis*), the Etruscan rhinoceros (*Stephanorhinus*), gazelle and bison (*Eobison*).

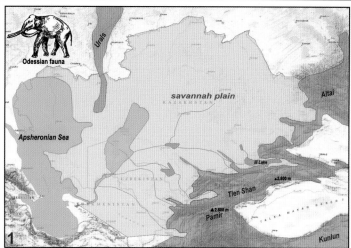

EARLY PLEISTOCENE (1,6 Ma BP): Apsheronian transgression

EARLY MIDDLE PLEISTOCENE (800 ka BP): Tien Shan heights reach the snow line

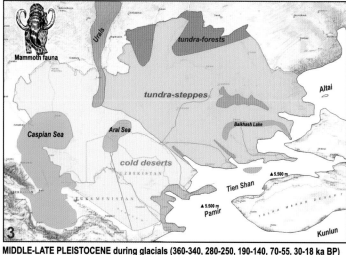

MIDDLE-LATE PLEISTOCENE during glacials (360-340, 280-250, 190-140, 70-55, 30-18 ka BP)

MIDDLE-LATE PLEISTOCENE during interglacials (330-310, 240-230, 220-190, 130-115, 105-70, 55-30 ka B

Figure 1: The four phases of Kazakhstan's Quaternary landscapes, from 1.6 million years ago (1.6 Ma BP) until the Late Pleistocene around 30,000 years ago (30 ka BP)

The Middle Pleistocene period (800,000-130,000 years ago) was characterized by a succession of pluvial (rainy) and arid climatic phases linked to the fluctuations between glacial and interglacial stages. Around 500,000 years ago the Tien Shan mountains reached heights above 5,000 metres, thereby blocking the Indian monsoon and its influence on Central Asia and enhancing an arid continental climate; an enlargement of the desert expanses followed, and a division into northern desert (or semi-desert), central and southern desert occurred. Then, during the Shirta interglacial period (245,000-170,000 years ago), tectonic events coupled with an increase in glacial deposits and water runoff resulted in the establishment of new water bodies such as Lake Balkhash.

In this new environment *Homo erectus*, using Acheulean stone tools such as hand axes, was able to take advantage of the favourable climate during the seven interglacial periods between 800,000 and 180,000 years ago, settling in the steppe zones (and in extreme arid zones like the Pre-Balkhash during the glacial pluvial phases). They lived among a faunal complex that slowly changed along with the climate. The early stage was the Koshkurgan fauna (Tiraspol in Europe)

comprising the giant rhinoceros (*Elasmotherium*), giant camel (*paracamelus gigas*), a new genus of horse (*Equus mosbachensis*), ox, bison, wild donkeys and ostriches. The second stage is called the Irtysh fauna (Khazar fauna in Europe), consisting of steppe mammoths that became woolly during glacial periods, saiga antelopes, cave lions, giant deer and steppe bisons.

The Late Pleistocene era (130,000-12,000 years ago) began with the favourable conditions of the Riss-Wurm or Eemian interglacial period (130,000-115,000 years ago), and this encouraged the coming of a new wave of human colonization. This was the introduction of Neanderthal man, who brought with him the Mousterian stone tool industry which signalled the start of the Middle Palaeolithic period. The Eemian was followed by the extreme climate of the Last Glacial period (115,000-12,000 years ago), which saw a steep drop in temperature around 90,000 years ago, followed by a worsening around 65,000 years ago, and the final, coldest period (the Last Glacial Maximum) between 25,000 and 12,000 years ago, when huge ice deposits filled the mountains and permafrost covered the arid plains.

Within that harsh period, a relatively warm, wet interglacial stage occurred around 40,000-32,000 years ago, allowing the immigration of *Homo sapiens* and the establishment of Late Palaeolithic cultures (blade industry). However, the cold, dry conditions of the Last Glacial Maximum marked a hiatus in the development of Palaeolithic cultures. It is therefore not surprising that the territory of Kazakhstan is characterized by a high number of Neanderthal sites but very few Late Palaeolithic sites. The wildlife typical of this era is the mammoth faunal complex, including typical mammals of the "glacial fauna" group: mammoths, woolly rhinoceroses, bisons, Baikal yaks, eland-like antelopes, aurochs and cave hyenas.

The Holocene interglacial era (12,000 years ago until the present day) began with a long arid continental phase that persisted until the end of the Boreal period (9,000-7,500 years ago) – the mountain foothills were covered by tundra steppe vegetation and the plains by desert and dry steppe. This environment was scantily inhabited, although some Epipalaeolithic groups held out and Mesolithic communities moved in from the south and north. It was only when the Atlantic period (7,500-5,000 years ago) began that the territory of Kazakhstan saw the establishment of its modern vegetation belts (forest-steppe, two types of dry steppe and three types of desert). This much more inviting landscape quickly became densely populated by Neolithic cultures: their sites are abundant throughout Kazakhstan, found almost everywhere in the proximity of water resources.

## STONE AGE CULTURES

Stone Age Kazakhstan was inhabited in stages: at first the early hominins arrived in the southern Karatau range and on the Aral and Caspian shores; later influxes spread out to the northern deserts and semi-deserts of the Pre-Balkhash region, the dry steppe of

The Karkaraly region of the Kazakh Uplands (Highlands) clearly shows the tectonic movement of millions of years ago. Uplifting rock resulted in changing landscapes and climates throughout Eurasia

Central Kazakhstan and the Pre-Irtysh, and the piedmont steppe of the Tien Shan and Altai ranges; and during the Neolithic practically all areas of this huge territory were colonized.

Industrial traditions and techniques developed over time and with increasing sophistication: the core-tool techniques characterized by the early Oldowan and Acheulean cultures involved working on a core until it was reduced to the desired tool. The flake-tool technique (called Levallois) whereby a flake was detached from a core and refined as a tool was already used by *Homo erectus* but became widespread with the Mousterian culture of Neanderthal man. By the Late Palaeolithic humans were preparing cores for the detachment of a series of homogeneous long blades (blade-tool technique), and in the Mesolithic-Neolithic era modern man began to use much harder materials for the production of miniaturized blades (microlith-tool technique).

Different raw materials were often used for making Palaeolithic tools, depending on what was most accessible from region to region: from the Pre-Caspian to the Pre-Irtysh (Figure 2, zones 1 and 4) flint tools were most common; chalcedony was found in the Karatau range of South Kazakhstan (zone 2); and siliceous siltstones (aleurolite) and quartzite sandstones in the Pre-Balkhash (zones 3 and 5).

The five industrial stages of the Stone Age in Kazakhstan are: Oldowan and Acheulean (both core-tool industries, respectively characterized by choppers or bifacial hand axes), Mousterian (flake-tool industry), Late Palaeolithic (blade-tool industry) and Mesolithic-Neolithic (microlith-tool industry). The variance in industrial development across Eurasia is largely attributed to an abundance of excellent raw materials in the west, as opposed to their relative scarcity in the east. Of course, Kazakhstan's central location between West and East Eurasia – characterized by Acheulean (hand axe) and Pebble (chopper-chopping) stone tool industries respectively and geographically separated by the so-called Movius Line – allowed it to be exposed to a mix of influences and led to the earliest development of a local Levallois industry.

Oldowan, the earliest lithic industry (2.5-1.2 million years ago), mostly consists of roughly flaked choppers (unifacial) and chopping (bifacial) tools, and a few primitive axes with poorly knapped sides. It is often called the Pebble tool industry as the hominins who made them often used pebbles or at least rocks with the same basic shape. In Kazakhstan

Oldowan tools have been found in two areas: on the shore of the Caspian Sea and in the Karatau mountains. On the Caspian they appear together with some bifacial tools made using a Kombewa-Levallois technique (a flake is used as a core in order to remove a single smaller flake), and this industry is called the Proto-Levallois. In the Karatau range a culture appeared known as the "Core-and-Flake" or Arystandy culture. The inhabitants here removed small flakes from large pebble-like nucleuses, suggesting analogies with pebble tool industries found in the western piedmonts of the Tien Shan and Pamirs and influences from East Asia or from the Soan valley in North Pakistan. Both the Proto-Levallois and the Core-and-Flake industries constitute the foundation of two respective uninterrupted traditions: the Proto-Levallois technique developed into the Levallois, which influenced the entire Palaeolithic development in Kazakhstan territory; the more localized Core-and-Flake would influence the continuous development of the Karatau cultures.

The Acheulean Early Palaeolithic industry began around 1.4 million years ago in Tanzania's Olduvai Gorge with the appearance of *Homo erectus*. This was an evolutionary step forward from the Oldowan industry of chopper tools, whereby cores were worked directly into bifacial hand axes (ovate or elongated), splitting axes, cleavers or adzes. This led to the introduction of the "prepared-core" Levallois technique, which consisted of preparing a core (nucleus) in order to extract a single large flake from which the tool would be produced.

In Kazakhstan a pure Acheulean industry has been discovered only in central Kazakhstan and northern Pre-Balkhash, where it possibly appeared during the pluvial phase connected with the Mindel glaciation period (750,000-675,000 years ago). The rest of the country developed a hybrid industry using the Levallois technique which is called the Levalloiso-Acheulean-I. Meanwhile, in the Karatau range the Acheulean period saw the establishment of the Levalloiso-Acheulean technique together with a transformed version of the former Core-and-Flake industry.

The Middle Palaeolithic era heralded the emergence of a new industry, the Mousterian, which lasted from 130,000 to 30,000 years ago and was characterized by an assemblage of more diversified tools of smaller size like small hand axes, scrapers, knife scrapers, denticulates, triangular points, etc. These were now being produced by a number of different techniques: the Mousterian-Acheulean tradition for hand

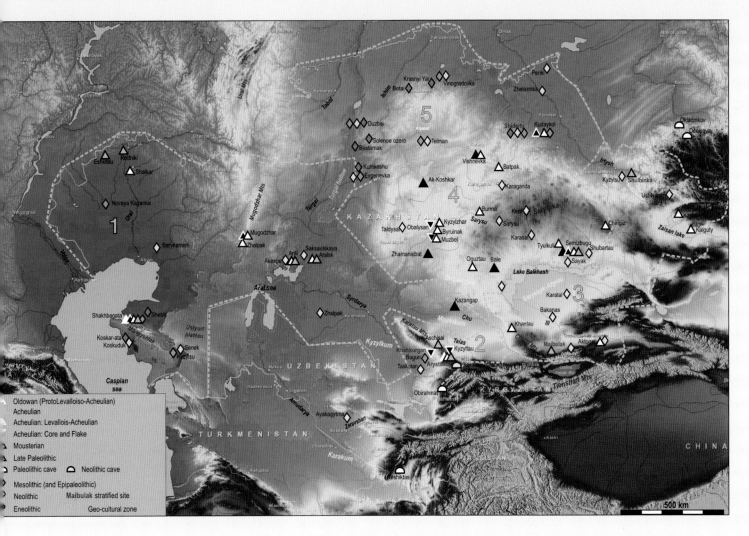

axes and backed knives, and the Levallois-Mousterian technique for flake tools. The Mousterian cultural industry is linked to the colonization of Eurasia by Neanderthal man.

The Upper Palaeolithic industry (40,000-12,000 years ago) is associated with *Homo sapiens sapiens* or modern man. They used harder rocks such as flint for the production, by refined prepared-core techniques, of a large variety of tools of small size, in particular of flake-and-blade type (from which comes the term blade-tool industry). These Stone Age men further refined the flakes and blades by chipping their cutting edges (denticulate or serrated) or by creating notches, often by pressing the edges with an antler tool. The most typical tools of this period are knives and narrow-bladed flints called burin, graver or chisel. Stone was now not the only material used; bone and antler were also worked into useful tools, and at this time rock art and stone figures began to appear in Europe and southern Siberia.

The Mesolithic and Neolithic periods developed during the interglacial Holocene climate. The environment in Kazakhstan was still cool and continental during the Mesolithic era (12,000-7,000 years ago), but around 5,000

BCE the climate became wetter and more productive for humans, sparking the start of the Neolithic era. By the end of the Neolithic (2,000 BCE) Kazakhstan's territory had become more arid – essentially the same as the present day. Central Asia's fauna changed during this time from glacial to Turanian, supporting the introduction of a new tool industry – the making of microliths, small sharp pieces of flint (or other hard rock) that were used in composite tools for hunting or domestic use. Mesolithic populations were scanty, but with the Neolithic Age came more productive economies that encouraged a settled lifestyle and the use of ceramics.

## KAZAKHSTAN'S MAIN STONE AGE SITES

The majority of the Stone Age sites discovered in Kazakhstan's territory are open surface findings, with only a few of the buried (stratified) type. Among the open-air sites, the regional centres of the three main traditions – the Caspian shore, the northern Pre-Balkhash and the Karatau valleys in South Kazakhstan – suggest longstanding occupation almost without discontinuity from 1.8 million years ago until Neolithic times, whilst all the buried sites excavated so far show continuity lasting only one or two periods.

Figure 2: This map shows the main Stone Age sites located in Kazakhstan and the five geographical regions that categorize use of different raw materials for making tools

The important Early Palaeolithic sites are divided by the dominant industrial tradition. The site of Shakhbagata in the Sarytash Gulf of the eastern Caspian Sea is situated on the terraces of the Pliocene transgression of the sea. Here archaeologists discovered cores, massive flakes, bifaces, splitting axes and spalls of the Proto-Levalloisian type. The site of Arystandy on the terraces of the upper course of the eponymous river in the Karatau range revealed roughly knapped flakes of chalcedony hidden within Early Quaternary conglomerate rock. Both sites are dated to around 1.8 million years ago, which puts the start of human activity in Kazakhstan at around the same time as neighbouring countries (Dmanisi in Georgia, with a skeleton dated to around 1.85 million years ago, and Nihewan in northern China with stone tools dating back 1.36 million years).

The main Acheulean sites are likewise classified according to their leading tool industry. Levalloiso-Acheulean sites, mostly in the central and northern part of the country, include Shakhbagata, Kumakape and Onezhek in the Sarytash Gulf on the Caspian shore, where flint bifaces and hand axes were uncovered (Figure 3, B4-5); Mugodzhar in the south Ural-upper Emba region with Levallois-Acheulean bifaces of quartzite-sandstone; Semizbugu in the northern Pre-Balkhash, and Kudaykol in the Pre-Irtysh in East Kazakhstan also with bifaces of quartzite-sandstone (Figure 3, B3).

Pure Acheulean artefacts (hand axes of quartzite siltstone) have been found in Semizbugu and Bale in the northern Pre-Balkhash region, but other sites have also disclosed Acheulean hand axes, including Kazangap on the lower course of the Chu River, and Ak-Koshkar and Vishnevka in the Ishim (Esil) basin south of Astana.

The workshop complex of Kyzyltau (dating to 800,000-600,000 years ago) within the lacustrine depression in the southeast Karatau range (Borykazgan, Tanirkazgan, Kemer, Akkol) is a Core-and-Flake industry site where the black flint raw material was selected and prepared *in situ*. A wide range of heavily abraded flakes and cores have been found, mostly irregular orthogonal cores, core-like products and modified flakes, but also bilateral chopping tools (Figure 3, B1) and choppers forming the earliest stage of the Pebble culture of Karatau. The subsequent phase is marked by a technique of primary flaking of the core and its preparation for producing a single blank; this is regarded as an early manifestation of the Levalloisian technique. Similar stone tool findings in Mongolia and the Gobi-Altai (Flint Valley) have raised the theory that "the early human colonization of Mongolia occurred, apparently, from Kazakhstan".

The oldest dated buried site in Kazakhstan (around 500,000

Figure 3: Illustrations of the main Palaeolithic tool traditions in Kazakhstan

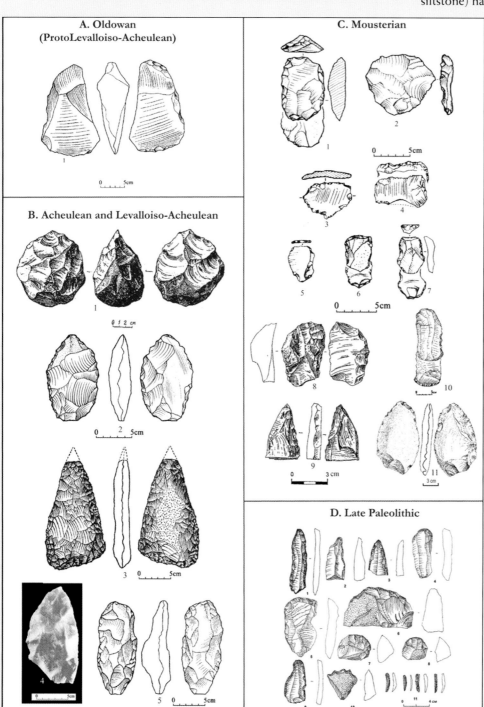

A. Oldowan
(ProtoLevalloiso-Acheulean)

B. Acheulean and Levalloiso-Acheulean

C. Mousterian

D. Late Paleolithic

years old) is Koshkurgan, located on the western slopes of the Karatau range. Koshkurgan is one of a complex of three Palaeolithic sites – the others are Shoktas and Kotyrbulak – found in areas fed by springs and small marshes 20 kilometres northeast of Turkistan. The lowest layers of cultural and animal remains were dated to between 500,000 and 430,000 years ago, although the majority of the stone tools belong to a later Mousterian industry dated to around 130,000 years ago. The large majority of the tools found belong to a "micro-industry" dominated by scrapers and with an average tool size of 2.5-3cm. This type of small tool industry shares analogies with Kuldara, the oldest site in Central Asia (Tajikistan, 900,000-800,000 years ago), the Chinese site of Zhoukoudian I (Peking man, 500,000-200,000 years ago), as well as the travertine sites of Hungary (Vertesszolos), Germany (Bilzingsleben) and Italy (Isernia La Pineta).

Kazakhstan's Middle Palaeolithic sites reveal the various Mousterian flake-tool industries that developed as Neanderthal man spread throughout the region. Levallois-Acheulean II tools (Figure 3, C10) are found at sites located in the Aral-Caspian and Pre-Irtysh regions, including Shakhbagata, Zhalpak, Shalkar, Mugodzhar, Aralsk and Kudaykol. Levallois-Mousterian sites of East Kazakhstan and Semirechye, such as Kanai, Kalguty and Aktogai, reveal pre-shaped cores that were themselves used as tools.

The Mousterian of Acheulean tradition (MTA) of Levallois facies was spread through sites in the northern and western Pre-Balkhash area – Semizbugu, Khantau and Oguztau are examples (Figure 3, C1-2). In South Kazakhstan, several dozen sites with typical Mousterian artefacts boast similar assemblages as those in Koshkurgan (Figure 3, C8-9) and the Arystandy river basin.

The technique called Denticulate Mousterian for producing denticulate and notched flake tools is represented at the sites of Burma and Kyzylzhar in the upper Sarysu river basin in central Kazakhstan and Tyulkuli in the north Pre-Balkhash (Figure 3, C3 and 7). Finally, in the middle Sarysu river basin, the Muzbel and Byruinak sites are examples of Mousterian Soanian, a Pebble-culture industry dominated by trimmed flint flakes chipped off cores from alternate directions, with the core itself finally used as chopper (Figure 3, C11).

The main Late Palaeolithic sites of Kazakhstan are found in the Aral-Caspian region at Eshkitau and Rodniki near Uralsk, Shakhbagata I-II in the Sarytash Gulf, and Aral and Aralsk in the Pre-Aral; in South Kazakhstan at Valikhanov (Arystandy), Aschisai, Ushbas and Koshkurgan (final stage); in the Pre-Irtysh and upper Irtysh at Kudaykol (final stage), Shulbinka and dozens of sites close to Zaysan Lake; in central Kazakhstan at Tuymoinak in the Sarysu basin and Batpak (final stage) in the upper Ishim (Esil); in the northern Pre-Balkhash at Sayak; and in Semirechye at Maibulak.

The most important site of this period is the stratified campsite-workshop named after Chokan Valikhanov in the Karatau mountains. Located on the third river terrace of the river Arystandy, in proximity to exposed raw materials, it consists of a cluster of around 20,000 chalcedony tools disseminated across a surface of more than a hectare. The site comprises six cultural layers including worked stones, animal bones and charcoal separated by layers of loam.

Late Palaeolithic sites did continue into the Holocene period of the Mesolithic era, with finely flaked blades, often with new technical developments like retouched backs, but without geometric micro-blades (Shakhbagata and Kudaykol are examples). This transitional period is often called the Epipalaeolithic.

The few Mesolithic sites so far discovered in Kazakhstan are poor in artefacts, testifying to the mobile and ephemeral nature of the campsites used by the human groups inhabiting the region. The beginning of the Mesolithic cultures occurred on two fronts: from the southwest (Iran and Turkmenistan) and from the northwest (the Volga and trans-Ural regions). The former spread into southern Kazakhstan where Mesolithic sites are located in the western and eastern foothills of the Karatau range along the streams of the rivers Bugun, Berkutty and Ushbulak. The latter developed in the Urals and Aral-Caspian region with sites like Novaya Kazanka, and in the Ustyurt Plateau (Kyzylsu).

Probably belonging to the same expansion from the northwest, the best-known sites are located further east in northern Kazakhstan: in the Pre-Tobol region at sites such as Evgenevka and Duzbai; in the Ishim basin (the future Neolithic Atbasar culture) with sites like Telman 14 (12,000 years old) and Vinogradovka; and in the Pre-Irtysh with the best stratified site of the period, Shiderty 3. The migratory Stone Age groups would have slowly come into contact and possibly merged with those settled communities of humans who had survived near reliable water sources, and as the climate improved the scene was set for a blossoming of human culture.

## HUMAN DEVELOPMENT IN THE NEOLITHIC AND ENEOLITHIC ERAS

More than 800 Neolithic sites have been found throughout Kazakhstan, but the majority are in areas that were already centres of Mesolithic culture. These can be divided into two groups according to the dominant cultural traits of the time: the Kelteminar in the oases of the south, and the Atbasar in the forest-steppes of the north.

The Kelteminar culture (6,000-3,000 BCE), born on the riparian edges of the Syr Darya/Amu Darya interfluvial deserts (Karakum and Kyzylkum), was made up of semi-sedentary hunter-gatherer-fishermen who progressively domesticated camels, aurochs and possibly horses, developed a fine microlithic industry typified by arrowheads and geometric blades, and started to manufacture crude pottery with geometric ornamentation. This culture spread into southern Kazakhstan, to the delta of the Syr Darya and the Aral-Caspian region.

The culture of northern Kazakhstan, often referred to as the Atbasar culture (5,000-3,000 BCE), developed a similar semi-nomadic economy in the forest-steppe environment near lakes and streams, hunting and corralling mainly horses before domesticating them during the Eneolithic period.

Kelteminar sites include Karaungur cave, with its stratified layers and rich artefacts dating back 7,000 years (see Figure 4), Karatau, the Ili River basin, Janadarya, the Pre-Aral and Ustyurt region. Of the Atbasar sites (and their

subcultural variants), foremost are Mahandzhar (in the upper Turgai with Duzbai as its centre) and the important Pre-Irtysh sites of Shiderty, Penki, Zhelezinka, Kyzylsu and Ust-Narym. In central Kazakhstan and Bekpakdala there are interesting sites such as Sayak, Shubartau and Kent that share elements of both traditions, illustrating that communication was already taking place between communities and cultures.

The Eneolithic or Chalcolithic (Copper-Stone) culture that lasted roughly from 3,500 to 2,000 BCE marked the initial spread of copper throughout Central Asia. This important technological advancement resulted in cultural changes that varied according to each region. In the south an impoverishment of the lithic (stone tool) industry occurred, while in the north there was considerable social refinement, with the evolution of well-defined housing complexes and development of new types of flat-bottomed and richly ornamented earthenware pottery.

Eneolithic sites are found in both northern and western Kazakhstan, the latter including two clusters of sites in the Mangystau region. One is located on the Buzachi peninsula near the village of Shebir and was influenced by the Khvalynsk culture of the Volga-Ural region – a proto-Indo-European culture (5,000-3,500 BCE). The other is located on the Mangyshlak peninsula north of the city of Aktau, with sites like Koshkar-ata 4 and Koskuduk 1 where artefacts specific to the final stage of the Kelteminar culture are mixed with the Shebir culture. This gives an idea of the progressive influence of the Ural-Volga stockbreeding

Figure 4: A northern view of Karaungur Valley in the Karatau region; the cave in the background was home to humans of the Kelteminar culture – at right are illustrations of artefacts discovered there

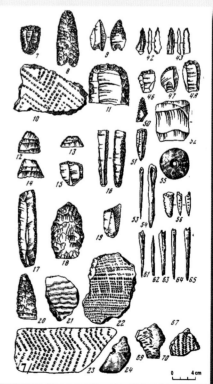

economy and mobile pastoralism spreading through the region at this time.

In northern Kazakhstan, the wet climate of the post-Atlantic pluvial phase (around 3,000 BCE) favoured the growth of the steppe lands. The increase in grassland and forests attracted populations of large mammals, and this environmental context enabled the development of the Botai-Tersek culture that steadily spread through the entire Ural-Irtysh region. Born out of the Atbasar Neolithic culture, with added western influences coming from the Pre-Caspian and southern Urals, these Eneolithic settlements are divided into two regions: the Tersek culture (around 3,700 BCE) of the Tobol, Ubagan and upper Turgai river basins, whose sites include Bestamak, Solenoe Ozero, Linovka, Kumkeshu and Duzbai; and the Botai culture in the Ishim (Esil) and Chaglinka river basins, whose main sites are Botai, Krasnyi Yar and Vasilkovska.

Located in a hilly woodland and lake environment 100 kilometres west of Kokshetau, Botai (3,500-2,500 BCE) represents one of dozens of similar permanent settlements where the earliest horse domestication has been documented. This village was made of 160 semi-subterranean dwellings with wooden roofs covered by clay plaster. Their Neolithic cultural heritage is expressed by the large amount of flint tools, microliths and spears

discovered, and by the animal bones that reflect an economy based on hunting and fishing. The overwhelming majority of equine bones has led to the supposition that the Botai people had a diet almost exclusively based on horse meat and that this specialized economy led to horse domestication.

The Botai village culture and its contemporaries were followed by the arrival of mixed cattle and sheep stockbreeders who were also metallurgists. This hugely significant new technology heralded the start of the Bronze Age, which, in combination with the mastery of horses, would allow human civilization to leap forward.

*Zhaken K. Taimagambetov is a professor in prehistoric archaeology and the Dean of the Department of History, Archaeology and Ethnology at Al-Farabi Kazakh National University in Almaty. He is a member of the Petrov Academy of Science and Art of the Russian Federation, and a member of the National Academy of Sciences of the Republic of Kazakhstan. He is the author and co-author of 45 books and teaching aids on the history and archaeology of Kazakhstan, as well as more than 350 scientific articles published worldwide in eight languages.*

*Jean-Marc Deom is a Belgian researcher at the Laboratory of Geoarchaeology of the Department of History, Archaeology and Ethnology at Al-Farabi Kazakh National University.*

The increase in fertile grassland steppe around 5,000-6,000 years ago provided rich grazing for huge herds of horses – and men were quick to take advantage, first hunting then domesticating and riding them

# EARLY CIVILIZATIONS:
# THE BRONZE AGE CULTURES

Man's discovery that copper ore could be transformed into a metal that was far superior to the stone tools he had used for many thousands of years was a defining moment in human evolution, but arguably an even greater step towards man's dominance of the world came when he learned to combine copper with other metals to form the alloy bronze. This new metal was both hard and durable; it could be worked into a host of useful everyday tools and objects, as well as deadly weapons for hunting or warfare.

The coming of the Bronze Age redefined human society and drove an expansion across Eurasia by new tribal groups searching for metal deposits, thereby broadening human interaction between disparate communities. Where resources were abundant, settlements grew into early fortified towns; bronze became a valuable commercial product and metallurgic centres were formed in various locations throughout Kazakhstan's territory. In the Urals copper was mixed with arsenic to make bronze, but when groups in the Altai region began to manufacture the far superior tin bronze, they initiated a metallurgic network that would spread across the majority of the Eurasian landmass and engender some of the ancient world's most intricate and exquisite bronze weaponry.

Above: A hunting scene, dating to the Late Bronze Age, located at Kuljabasy in the Chu-Ili region. A wild bull is being attacked from the left, but worshipped by a man, woman and child on the right. Opposite: Mobile pastoralism as a way of life developed because of man's mastery of the horse throughout the vast landscapes of the Eurasian Steppe belt, from Mongolia (pictured here) to the Ukraine

Climatic changes also affected the cultural development of human groups, causing mass movements of proto-Indo-European peoples from the plains of modern Ukraine and Russia to the forest-steppe region of western Siberia and then south into Central Asia. The first major group were the protagonists of the Afanasevo culture, followed by those of the Poltavka and Abashevo cultures, from whom developed the settled, agro-pastoralist Sintashta-Petrovka and the far-ranging bronze traders of the Seima-Turbino complex. Around the start of the second millennium BCE two new cultures came on the scene: from north of the Caspian came the Srubna (or Srubnaya), while from western and southern Siberia came tribes that collectively are known as the Andronovo. Culturally similar, these included the Alakul and Fedorovo, the former more settled, the latter more mobile, both spreading out through Central Asia in search of new metal deposits but also good water and pasture, essential for their livestock.

Where in the north environmental conditions favoured a settled lifestyle, in the drier steppe, semi-desert and desert of central and southern Kazakhstan it was necessary for tribal groups to move regularly to feed their animals.

This was the start of nomadism as a way of life, and it was improved and fine-tuned throughout the second millennium BCE, as hardier species like sheep, goats and horses took precedence over cattle. Around 1500 BCE a new tribal culture emerged in the Altai and eastern Kazakhstan: the Karasuk. Well organized and powerful, they took over control of the bronze trade and spread both east and west, spawning the Dandybai culture of central Kazakhstan.

But a game-changing innovation was on the horizon, as a new metal – iron – swept through the human sphere beginning around 1200 BCE. In the territory of Kazakhstan the easy availability, high quality and sophistication of bronze allowed it to continue as the dominant metal, but there would be no denying the great superiority of this new, harder and stronger grey metal, and when in the eighth century BCE tribal confederations of mounted nomadic warriors armed with iron weapons began to sweep into Central Asia from the north, the Bronze Age had finally run its course and a new world order was about to begin.

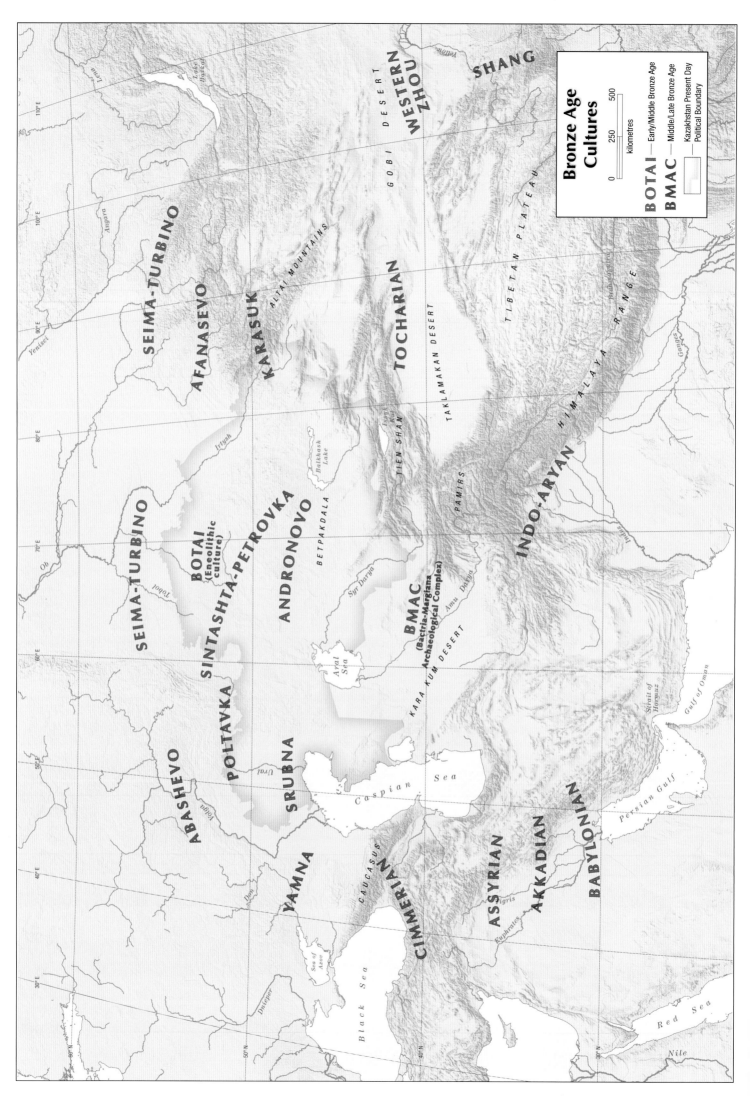

**Bronze Age Cultures**

BOTAI — Early/Middle Bronze Age
BMAC — Middle/Late Bronze Age
Kazakhstan Present Day
Political Boundary

kilometres
0    250    500

SEIMA-TURBINO

AFANASEVO

KARASUK

ALTAI MOUNTAINS

SEIMA-TURBINO

BOTAI
(Eneolithic
culture)

SINTASHTA-PETROVKA

ANDRONOVO

BETPAKDALA

POLTAVKA

ABASHEVO

SRUBNA

YAMNA

CIMMERIAN

CAUCASUS

GOBI DESERT

WESTERN ZHOU

SHANG

TOCHARIAN

TAKLAMAKAN DESERT

TIEN SHAN

Issyk Kul

PAMIRS

TIBETAN PLATEAU

HIMALAYA RANGE

INDO-ARYAN

BMAC
(Bactria-Margiana
Archaeological Complex)

KARA KUM DESERT

Amu Darya

Syr Darya

Aral Sea

Balkhash Lake

ASSYRIAN

AKKADIAN

BABYLONIAN

Strait of Hormuz

Gulf of Oman

Persian Gulf

Caspian Sea

Black Sea

Sea of Azov

Red Sea

Nile

Lake Baikal

Angara

Yenisei

Ob

Irtysh

Tobol

Ural

Volga

Don

Dnieper

Euphrates

Tigris

Indus

Ganges

Brahmaputra

Yellow

# The Bronze Age in Kazakhstan

By *Renato Sala*

The use of moulded copper by Neolithic communities signalled the beginning of the Eneolithic Age, also known as the Chalcolithic or Copper Age. Usually thought of as a final Neolithic stage that transitioned into the Bronze Age, today many archaeologists and researchers consider it rather as an early stage of the Bronze Age. The first documented proof of copper used to make tools comes from the Balkans and dates to 5,500 BCE; 500 years later it had spread to Anatolia and the Urals.

A seminal moment for mankind came with the discovery that combining a natural or artificial copper alloy with arsenic or tin – and more rarely with lead or zinc – would create bronze, a substance that could be worked into tools that were much harder, more durable and sharper than stone. This represented a major technological advance that ultimately led to the forging of iron and the phenomenal human development that ensued.

The appearance of bronze tools represented a major cultural revolution, changing the social structure within Neolithic communities where previously every household produced its own tools and weapons. Unlike stone, bronze required considerable skill to produce

and so a specialized class of metallurgists and smiths emerged, thereby establishing a structural division of labour. The need for different materials from distant regions to create this new alloy also meant that interregional communication and trade began in earnest, opening human communities to their surrounding world. Commercial operators now appeared, and with them wheeled vehicles, draft animals, writing and seals with which to facilitate trade.

Equally important was the fact that bronze items instantly became of great value, and whether in unfinished, finished or used form represented the best means of exchange between groups. Accumulation of wealth in

Figure 1: A selection of images and drawings of metal weapons and jewellery dating to the Late Middle, Late and Final Bronze periods in western Central Asia

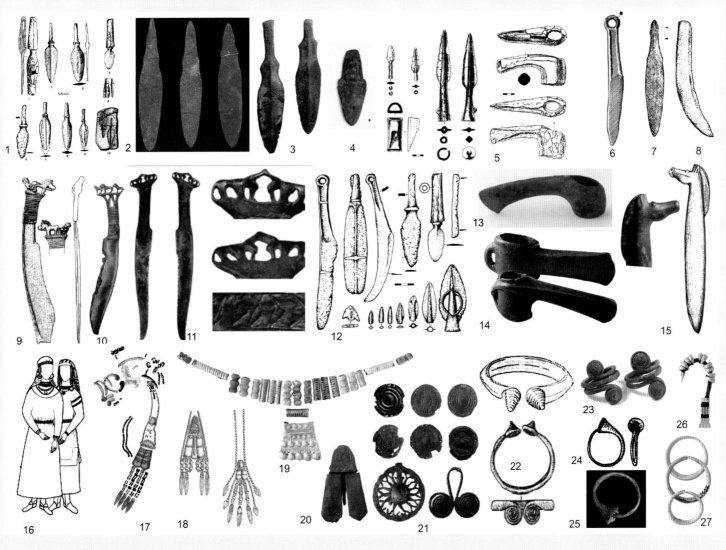

hoards of these new "capital goods" created a male-dominated, layered society, and throughout Eurasia a gradual but inexorable change now began from semi-settled, egalitarian Neolithic communities to highly mobile new societies characterized by patriarchal social stratification.

The Bronze Age can be split into three periods correlating with the locations of successive mining and metallurgic provinces and the expansion of the bronze markets. First is the Early Bronze period between 3,800 BCE and 2,900 BCE, when the production of bronze – created with arsenic, which often naturally contaminates copper ore – started in the rich copper mines of Anatolia, the southern Caucasus and the Danube region. This area is known as the Balkan-Carpathian Metallurgical Province (BCMP), and proto-towns using bronze developed here – as well as in the Near East, Aegean and Egypt – within a landscape where stone tools were still widespread.

The Middle Bronze period (2,900-1900 BCE) was a time of generally peaceful expansion to regions such as the northern Caucasus, Iranian plateau and the Indus Valley, and a new metallurgical province known as the Circumpontic Metallurgical Province (CPMP) was established connecting the Caucasus with the mines of the Carpathians and the western Urals. At this stage, possibly in Anatolia, a new type of bronze was developed that used tin in its composition. This was harder and non-toxic, and was therefore highly prized (Mesopotamian tablets report tin values 10 times higher than silver), but due to the rarity of tin deposits and incorrect tin proportions it was not widely used.

The Late Bronze period lasted from 1900 BCE until 1200 BCE, during a time when the climate was becoming drier and populated land was becoming relatively overcrowded. Metal resources became scarcer, driving the quest for new deposits of copper and tin, and competition for fresh land led to conflict and turmoil – though it also resulted in the greater diffusion of bronze use throughout Eurasia and immense economic progress. A vast swathe of northern Eurasia stretching from the Carpathians to Lake Baikal – known as the Eurasian Metallurgical Province (EMP) – became a major bronze-producing region. It was split into the West Asian Metallurgical Province (WAsMP, 2,200-1100 BCE) centred in the Urals, where arsenic bronze was produced, and the East Asian Metallurgical Province (EAsMP, 1900-800 BCE) centred

around the Altai Mountains, which developed the production of higher-quality tin bronze. It was the EMP that had the most impact on the cultures within the territory of Kazakhstan.

Kazakhstan's Bronze Age lasted from around 2000 BCE to 800 BCE, and being subject to migrations and influxes from all points of the compass, inevitably the development of bronze culture here was complex, with significant cultural diversity. The exploitation of both the rich copper deposits of the Urals and central Kazakhstan and the tin mines in the Altai led to the creation of the most important metallurgic province in Eurasia, which monopolized the most advanced bronze metallurgy, with the best alloy, the most sophisticated moulding techniques and consequently the most beautiful bronze weapons in the ancient world. Combine this with the development of highly successful stockbreeding techniques and it is easy to understand how this economic, social and military background could favour the rise – at the end of the Bronze Age – of the great horse-riding nomadic confederations that would rule northern Eurasia for 2,500 years.

## THE CLIMATIC AND ENVIRONMENTAL CONTEXT

Around 3,200 BCE the climate of the Northern Hemisphere entered a cool dry period (known as the Subboreal) that would endure for almost 2,500 years, spanning the entire Eneolithic and Bronze Age periods. Within that time frame fluctuations occurred between pluvial and arid continental phases; particularly arid continental peaks have been documented spanning 3,200-2,900 BCE (preceded by the first sharp cold peak of the Holocene), 1700-1500 BCE (particularly arid) and 1100-900 BCE (preceded by an even sharper cold peak). This affected the human populations of the central areas of Eurasia: in the Don-Volga region pastoralist communities were able to adapt to the changing climate, but in western Siberia and Kazakhstan's territory the conditions changed so much that entire vegetal bands, together with humans, were forced to migrate – from south to north during the arid phases, and north to south during wetter, colder periods, mostly because of the need for good pastures for livestock.

It is difficult to say just how influential climatic changes were to the movement and formation of these new cultures. What does seem clear is that in the third millennium BCE increasing aridity and overpopulation in the Pontic Steppe north of the Caspian Sea resulted in the displacement of local pastoralist-metallurgist proto-Indo-European tribes towards the lush pastures and copper deposits of the forest-steppe zone of western Siberia and the steppes and highland regions of Kazakhstan's territory; that latitudinal changes in landscape zones and vegetation resulted in regular interaction between the Proto-Indo-Iranian inhabitants of steppes and forest-steppes and the proto-Finno-Ugrian inhabitants of the northern forests; and that the arid phase of 1700-1500 BCE and the cold peak of 1200 BCE can be correlated respectively with the start and end of the Late Bronze Andronovo cultures in Kazakhstan.

## THE ENEOLITHIC FOUNDATION

Before the advent of bronze, around the fifth millennium BCE, several Neolithic communities made an appearance in western Central Asia. They have been categorized as the Kelteminar culture in the deserts of Transoxiana, and the Bolshemys culture in the forest-steppe and steppe regions of north and central Kazakhstan.

In the fourth millennium BCE, the southern and northern borders of this vast territory began to witness migrations of Chalcolithic tribes; they were the first to exploit the mineral deposits of western Central Asia and they became the foundation of the subsequent Bronze Age cultures here.

To the south, between the fourth and third millennia BCE the foothills of the Kopet-Dag mountains (in modern Turkmenistan) and the middle reaches of the Amu Darya river basin (Bactria) saw the immigration of proto-Dravidian peoples from the Iranian Plateau and the Indus Valley, and possibly of Proto-Indo-Europeans from west of the Caspian. They were communities with a mixed farming and pastoralism economy who, at the end of the third millennium BCE, gave rise to a Middle Bronze Age culture based on irrigation farming and proto-towns, with wide interregional trade and all the hallmarks of civilization: this is referred to as the Bactria-Margiana Archaeological Complex or BMAC (2,300-1700 BCE).

In the north, the green corridor of forest-steppe between the Urals and the Altai had represented an easy route for migration and cultural exchange since the earliest times. The fourth millennium BCE saw a wave of migration from the western Don-Volga region by an Eneolithic Proto-Indo-European group of nomadic pastoralists called the Yamna (Pit-grave or Kurgan culture). They spread eastward with wagons, cattle and sheep, reaching the Altai and the middle Yenisei River basin where they established the Afanasevo culture (3,600-2,400 BCE) – a period contiguous with the development of the horse-breeding Botai culture in northern Kazakhstan.

They mingled with local populations of Ugric and Asiatic type and, after the introduction of

This map shows the ranges of cultures, metallurgic provinces and copper and tin mine sites during the Middle Bronze period

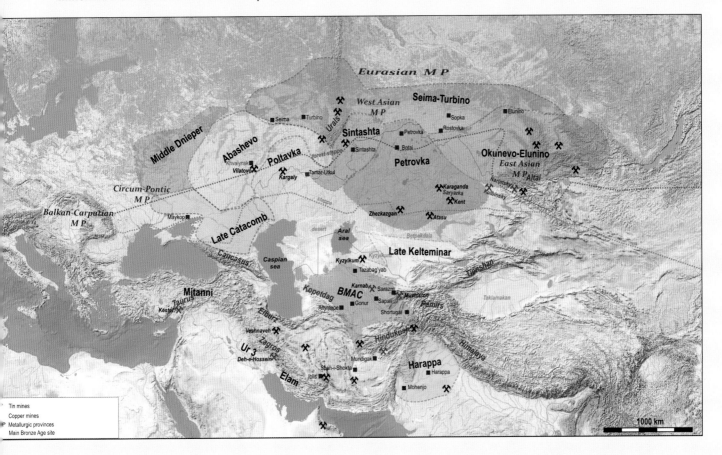

bronze metallurgy, evolved into the Middle Bronze cultures of Okunevo in the Yenisei (2,400-1800 BCE) and the Elunino in the Altai region (2,300-1700 BCE), who practised a hunting-herding economy and mined copper in the Altai and central Kazakhstan.

A second eastward wave of migrant tribes happened in the third millennium BCE, consisting of Middle Bronze Age cattle herders and metallurgists converging and mixing from two areas: Indo-European tribes from the Don-Volga steppe belt (Late Yamna cultures) and Baltic- and Uralic-speaking tribes from the forest belt (Corded Ware cultures). They settled in fortified villages along river valleys close to copper deposits and developed two distinct Middle Bronze Age cultures – the Poltavka in the steppes and the Abashevo in the forest-steppe zone. They produced arsenic bronze and traded it to the west. These two cultures in the Urals and the Elunino culture of the Altai region were the respective progenitors of two Middle-Late Bronze metallurgic phenomena: the Sintashta-Petrovka culture of the south and east Urals, territorially stable and ethnically homogenous; and the trans-cultural Seima-Turbino phenomenon, originating in the Altai, that covered long-distance trade in metal right across the forest zone between the Baltic and Mongolia. Together they represented the beginning of the western (WAsMP) and eastern (EAsMP) elements of a vast new metallurgical zone: the Eurasian Metallurgic Province (EMP).

## THE SINTASHTA-PETROVKA AND SEIMA-TURBINO CULTURES

The Sintashta culture, located in the southern and eastern Urals, dates to between 2,200 BCE and 1800 BCE, and is considered the core of the West Asian Metallurgic province (WAsMP) centred in the Urals and the first manifestation of proto-Indo-Europeans in Central Asia. The economy was based on metallurgy (arsenic bronze) and settled agro-pastoralism, and its people traded horses and metal products in the west but also in the south with the BMAC proto-towns. Life was settled and their society was well structured, their settlements located in river valleys and fortified against intertribal clashes.

Up to 100 houses were arranged in two concentric circles, each house with a smelting furnace. Cemeteries in the surrounding area contained large *kurgans* (burial mounds) covering tombs filled with weapons, silver and gold ornaments, spoked wheels, sometimes entire chariots with up to eight sacrificed

horses. The richest tombs highlight impressive burial rituals that are similar to the ones described in the Rig Veda (a sacred early Indo-Aryan Sanskrit text), thus supporting the hypothesis about the Indo-Aryan Iranian tradition of the Sintashta tribes.

The earliest examples of spoked wheels and light, swift war chariots have been found in Sintashta excavations; together with the mastery of horse riding, they conferred formidable power on these tribes, allowing for more efficient transport and travel, and far greater military capability. It is no surprise therefore that in a short time this new technology had been imitated across the ancient world. As D.W. Anthony writes in his book *The horse, the wheel and language*, "When a squadron of javelin-hurling charioteer warriors wheeled onto the field of battle, supported by soldiers on foot and horseback with axes, spears and daggers, it was a new, lethal style of fighting that had never been seen before, something that even urban kings soon learned to admire".

The Petrovka culture (1900-1750 BCE) emerged from that of the Sintashta, but spread farther eastwards into northern and central Kazakhstan in its search for metal resources. A transitional culture that led to the two main Late Bronze Andronovo cultures of the west Central Asian steppes, the Alakul and Fedorovo, it is differentiated by its less-fortified settlements and fewer chariots, weapons and horses in its funereal mounds, pointing to a progressively more peaceful environment at this time. More sheep and fewer cattle were now kept, showing adaptation in the pastoralist activity. The most important distinguishing element, however, is that the Petrovka villages mined tin and produced the superior tin bronze to trade (Petrovka tin mines have been located as far south as the Zeravshan Valley in modern Uzbekistan and Tajikistan).

This new activity was most likely influenced by the Seima-Turbino phenomenon, a cultural link created purely through the mining, production and trade of metal (mainly tin bronze) and weapons during the Late Bronze Age in the forest belt of northern Eurasia. It was centred in the Altai and developed into a broad geographic corridor stretching from Lake Baikal to the Baltic Sea (an ancient trade route for nephrite), but also south across Central Asia (again an old trade route, this time for lapis-lazuli and turquoise). The significance of the Seima-Turbino complex is its focus on tin bronze (rather than arsenic bronze), which had arrived in northern Eurasia possibly from Bactria, where tin bronze items appeared around 2000 BCE.

The early Seima-Turbino proponents lived around copper and tin mines and understood the superiority of the optimal form of this new alloy, ie the combination of 89 percent copper with 11 percent tin: it had no toxicity, was much stronger than other bronze, and had a lower melting temperature making it easier to process and cast. They invented seamless thin-walled casting forms, and used advanced lost-wax and hollow-mould casting methods to produce highly resistant weapons and the most beautiful ceremonial items of the time, from socketed spearheads, daggers and knives with horse figurines cast on the butt, to hollow-core axes decorated with triangles.

However, contrary to the settled Sintashta culture, the Seima-Turbino phenomenon became a trans-cultural metallurgical and social network featuring original metal and commercial styles emulated by various operators emerging along the road: nomadic metallurgists and warriors travelling on two-wheeled chariots. Characteristic artefacts have been found in the Carpathians and Urals, in Mongolia, China and Thailand, in Kazakhstan and Bactria, and analogs appear in Mycenaean arsenals. The Seima-Turbino phenomenon is synonymous with the East Asian Metallurgic Province (EAsMP), which, alongside the WAsMP, finally broke the longstanding monopoly of the Caucasus metalworking traditions (CPMP) and signalled the start of the Eurasian Metallurgic Province (EMP) and the Late Bronze period.

The Sintashta-Petrovka cultures and the Seima-Turbino metallurgic network are the two original sources of the Bronze Age on Kazakhstan territory, and the main factors in the formation of ethno-linguistic Indo-Iranian cultures in western Central Asia. The Sintashta provided a powerful industrial and military social structure, while the Seima-Turbino metallurgists developed the most advanced technological and commercial metal products of the time; the former were settled in compact areas near good pastures and mineral resources, the latter were highly mobile as they searched for and traded in metal. Both were heavily armed.

These northern miners, metallurgists and pastoralist groups were drawn towards the south by copper and tin deposits, markets for the metal trade (and potential booty), new pastures and freshwater springs. As they went, they colonized the existing Eneolithic tribes until they came into contact with the BMAC

A map showing the major sites and copper and tin mines of the Late Middle to Final Bronze periods, and their relation to the various cultures of the time

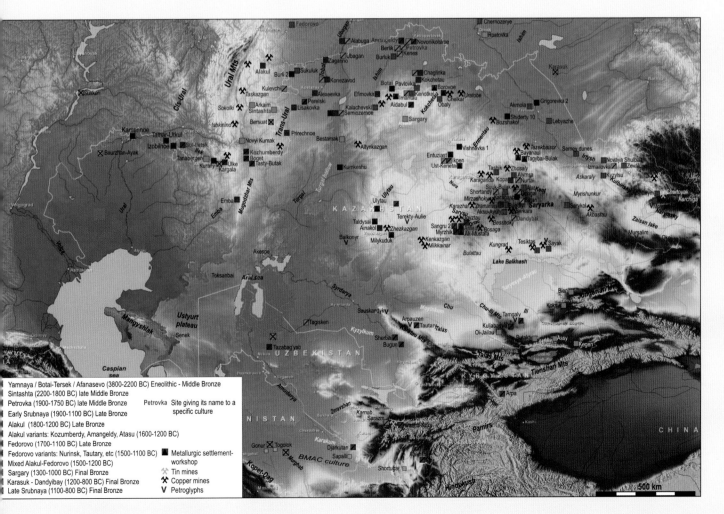

Yamnaya / Botai-Tersek / Afanasevo (3800-2200 BC) Eneolithic - Middle Bronze
Sintashta (2200-1800 BC) late Middle Bronze
Petrovka (1900-1750 BC) late Middle Bronze    Petrovka   Site giving its name to a specific culture
Early Srubnaya (1900-1100 BC) Late Bronze
Alakul (1800-1200 BC) Late Bronze
Alakul variants: Kozumberdy, Amangeldy, Atasu (1600-1200 BC)
Fedorovo (1700-1100 BC) Late Bronze
Fedorovo variants: Nurinsk, Tautary, etc (1500-1100 BC)    ■ Metallurgic settlement-workshop
Mixed Alakul-Fedorovo (1500-1200 BC)
Sargary (1300-1000 BC) Final Bronze    ☼ Tin mines
Karasuk - Dandyibay (1200-800 BC) Final Bronze    ✖ Copper mines
Late Srubnaya (1100-800 BC) Final Bronze    V Petroglyphs

civilization of the Amu Darya. There, some groups blended with the local population, intermarrying and adopting their cultural traits but also possibly contributing to the dismantlement of the prevalent urban system. From there the route to the southeast followed a well-watered mountain corridor lined with tin and gold mines to the Indus Valley and the Aravalli polymetallic district. At some point they started to call themselves "Arya" (hospitable or noble), from which the term Aryan comes.

These Bronze Age pioneers also spread west to southeast Anatolia where, between 1500 BCE and 1300 BCE, as charioteers and horse training elite they constituted the aristocratic ranks of the Hurrian Mitanni state, challenging the Assyrian empire and controlling the tin mines of the region and the Middle East metal trade.

Around 1500 BCE the WAsMP began to degrade as a result of renewed copper mining in Europe, and control of the EAsMP passed into the hands of the Karasuk culture, an aggressive, highly mobile people based in southern Siberia and mainly oriented towards the east.

## THE ANDRONOVO CULTURAL TRADITION

Around 1900 BCE two widespread cultural complexes appeared in the Ural region, both indirect descendants of the Poltavka and Abashevo cultures. In the Don-Volga-Ural river territory was the Srubna (Timber Grave culture), while in the trans-Urals, southern Siberia and throughout Kazakhstan as far as the Syr Darya and Amu Darya basins –

across the Sintashta-Petrovka area – was the Andronovo cultural complex. They intermingled around the copper mines of the pre-Urals, which represented a mixed zone between the two; both groups were stockbreeders and metallurgists, but where the Srubna followed the tradition of arsenic bronze typical of the Sintashta, the Andronovo made tin bronze, which the Petrovka had adopted from the Seima-Turbino metallurgists.

Andronovo is the conventional name for an archaeological horizon that incorporated a number of very similar cultures at this time throughout a large area of Central Asia, in particular the Alakul and Fedorovo. The term comes from a 1914 study of a Bronze Age cemetery near the village of Andronovo in the middle Yenisei River in Siberia, dated to the 15th century BCE and today considered to be the easternmost extent of the Fedorovo culture.

The Andronovo cultures were genetically related, shared common characteristics and often interacted on the same territory, making clear distinction between them difficult. From the Petrovka culture in the forest-steppe of northern Kazakhstan and the southeast Urals emerged the Alakul (1800-1200 BCE), whose oldest monuments can be found in the region previously inhabited by the Botai culture, and the Fedorovo (1700-1100 BCE), who appeared a century later in the same region. The Alakul people were possibly the latest incarnation of existing Petrovka communities, but the Fedorovo were a mobile group and probably migrated into the region. Both cultures are thought to have spoken a common proto-Indo-Iranian language with Ugrian influences, and lived in independent family groups with tribal affiliations.

The common traits of the Alakul and Fedorovo traditions included subsistence strategies, settlement patterns, funerary rituals and material culture (ceramics, metal objects, jewellery) as well as their penchant for petroglyphs (rock art). This justifies their grouping under the term Andronovo – their distinctions are based on secondary elements detected by archaeologists in their dwellings, burial sites and ceramics.

For the Andronovo cultures the main priorities were to find metal deposits, water and good pasture for their livestock – ideally all three in close proximity. Metallurgy and pastoralism were in fact complementary: they each required mobility and expansion, and both copper and tin deposits and rich pastures are found together in the mountainous, well-

A Bronze Age well in the Kumai archaeological complex east of Astana, part of a large settlement that has yet to be properly excavated

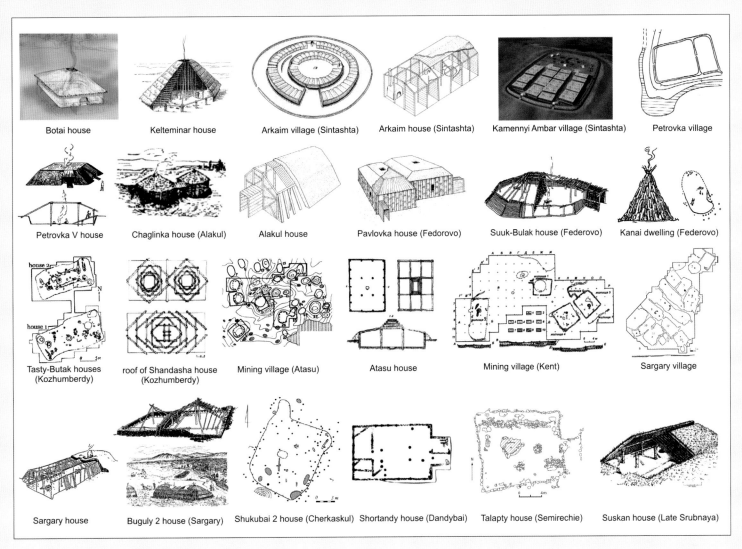

Botai house · Kelteminar house · Arkaim village (Sintashta) · Arkaim house (Sintashta) · Kamennyi Ambar village (Sintashta) · Petrovka village

Petrovka V house · Chaglinka house (Alakul) · Alakul house · Pavlovka house (Fedorovo) · Suuk-Bulak house (Federovo) · Kanai dwelling (Federovo)

Tasty-Butak houses (Kozhumberdy) · roof of Shandasha house (Kozhumberdy) · Mining village (Atasu) · Atasu house · Mining village (Kent) · Sargary village

Sargary house · Buguly 2 house (Sargary) · Shukubai 2 house (Cherkaskul) · Shortandy house (Dandybai) · Talapty house (Semirechie) · Suskan house (Late Srubnaya)

Figure 2: These illustrations show the variety of settlements and houses at different stages of the Bronze Age and in different regions

watered landscapes of the Urals, Altai, Tien Shan and Pamir ranges, as well as the low-mountain chains of Ulytau and the Kazakh Highland area, Kulbinsky in East Kazakhstan, and Karatau and Chu-Ili in South Kazakhstan. These areas were also the most populated by Eneolithic communities, who could be used as workers and integrated as a different caste.

Andronovo pastoralism was initially of the East European type, which lacked pigs and at first used a majority of cows, before gradually changing to sheep and goats as the mainstay of life. Horses were used in the north and Bactrian camels in the south, each comprising 30 percent of a group's herd. The arid climatic conditions required specific husbandry techniques, with migration between winter and summer camps involving multiple seasonal dwellings, a herd composition made of mobile and resistant species like sheep, goats and horses, horse riding, water management and clan cooperation.

In northern latitudes, where bronze metallurgy started, the abundant snow cover meant stockbreeding required the cutting and storing of fodder, leading to large, stable residential communities that favoured social cooperation

and tribal confederation. In the southern deserts, though, stockbreeding relied on year-round migration, which promoted higher mobility and nomadism by more independent groups. Tribal organization and nomadism were the main innovations in the pastoralist world of the second millennium BCE, and prepared the ground for the formation of rich and powerful pastoralist societies.

Their settlements consisted of houses aligned on the first terrace of streams, beside lakes or near springs, and where possible sheltered from northern winds. The largest villages, covering more than one hectare, developed in proximity to mineral deposits, while in the open steppe they were much smaller. On average they consisted of 10-20 family houses, each with 6-8 people who owned 12-18 head of livestock requiring one square kilometre of pasture. It is estimated that the population of Kazakhstan during the Late Bronze Age grew from 30,000 to more than 100,000 people.

Their houses were usually constructed in semi-subterranean fashion, the floor area dug a metre down into the earth with surrounding walls made of muddy clay or stone. They were square or rectangular in shape and quite large – from

100 to 300 square metres – with pyramidal, gabled or stepped pyramid roofs covered by reeds and clay and supported by wooden poles; an external roofed corridor served as a hallway. The interior floor was compacted clay with between one and eight fireplaces; it often also housed a furnace. Fedorovo settlements were lesser in number and smaller, sometimes just single houses, and never in the form of specialized metallurgical centres.

Two Bronze Age grave sites, one in Tamgaly in Zhetisu, four hours' drive from Almaty (top), the other more than 1,000km away in the Kumai archaeological complex two hours east of Astana

Burial rituals shared many basic features typical of all the Andronovo cultural horizon, but there were variations across the sub-cultures. Cemeteries were located around settlements (Alakul) or near water basins (Fedorovo). Tombs consisted of kurgans with kerb or flat stone arrangements inside rectangular or oval fences: kurgan tombs with diameters ranging from five to 80 metres characterized the Petrovka culture and the central parts of the Alakul cemeteries; flat-fenced tombs are found in the periphery of large Alakul kurgans and are characteristic of Fedorovo cemeteries.

The actual graves were pit chambers with the walls and roof built of timber (in forested areas) or stone (in desert regions, and more frequently in Fedorovo sites). Burials were mostly of individuals (although couples and couples with a child have occasionally been found); the Alakul mostly buried the bodies of the dead, but the Fedorovo practised cremation as well. The skulls and legs of sacrificed animals were placed in the grave along with jewellery, ceramics, metal objects and horse tack, apparently useful tools for the deceased's coming "journey"; weapons however were rare, and chariots and sacrificed horses, frequent in Petrovka burials, decreased with the Alakul, were almost never found in Fedorovo kurgans, and had practically disappeared by 1500 BCE.

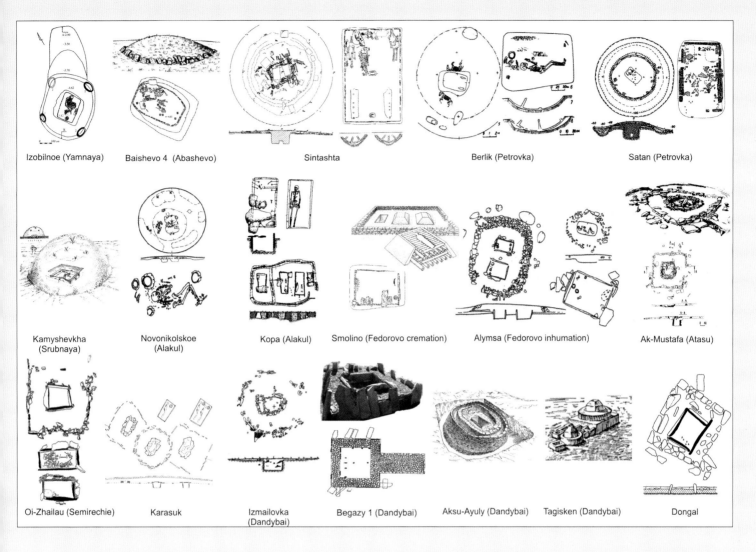

Izobilnoe (Yamnaya)    Baishevo 4 (Abashevo)    Sintashta    Berlik (Petrovka)    Satan (Petrovka)

Kamyshevkha (Srubnaya)    Novonikolskoe (Alakul)    Kopa (Alakul)    Smolino (Fedorovo cremation)    Alymsa (Fedorovo inhumation)    Ak-Mustafa (Atasu)

Oi-Zhailau (Semirechie)    Karasuk    Izmailovka (Dandybai)    Begazy 1 (Dandybai)    Aksu-Ayuly (Dandybai)    Tagisken (Dandybai)    Dongal

Figure 3: Burial types from the cultures of the Late Middle to Final Bronze periods

## ANDRONOVO METALLURGY, HANDICRAFTS AND ART

Andronovo metallurgy developed as part of the Eurasian Metallurgical Province (EMP) and inherited the traditions of both its western and eastern variants, the WAsMP and EAsMP. The mines were round pits or narrow trenches around 100 metres long and 10-15 metres deep. The most productive copper mines were in north and central Kazakhstan; they offered up pieces of native ore weighing several tons and provided 80 percent of total Andronovo production. The richest of these deposits (such as the mines at Kenkazgan near Atasu or Dzhezkazgan in the Ulytau) produced a total of between 500,000 and one million tons of ore, which translates to 30,000-80,000 tons of copper. The richest tin mines were located in the adjacent Kulbinsky and Narymsky ranges of northeastern Kazakhstan.

Ore was processed in furnaces consisting of underground wells shaped like an inverted cone 1.5 metres deep by two metres wide. The walls were of fired clay with a few spiralling ventilation ducts, and the upper mouth was connected to a few horizontal chimneys 7-12 metres long. Tin bronze was the predominant

metal produced. The most common metal objects were arrowheads, spearheads and knives, with longer daggers and axes created less frequently. The knives and daggers had handles of bone, wood or metal, the latter boasting a simple mushroom-shaped or horse-figurine butt.

Hoards of metal objects have been found in Kazakhstan dating from 1300 BCE. Some contained metal, moulds, blanks and serial objects; these are thought to have been hidden during times of crisis ready for later exchange and trade. Other hoards contained domestic equipment and are thought to have been hidden by families during times of turmoil. The rich assemblages of metal objects in burial sites are thought to have been sacrificial hoards for the dead; they of course were regularly robbed within a few decades or centuries of the burials, which is why modern-day finds of untouched treasure are very rare and met with great excitement.

The jewellery of this age was of exquisite elegance. It was fashioned from gold, silver, bronze or copper and has mainly been found in burials of women dressed in ceremonial attire. Andronovo women wore round or rhombic palmate pendants, collar rings lined with gold leaves and strings of bronze pellets, trumpet earrings, and bracelets and rings with conical spirals (see Figure 1 on page 39). Glass beads lined the cut of the dress around the neck, and both men and women wore amulets made of shells and the teeth of predatory animals.

Andronovo pottery was of clay tempered with sand and vegetal fibres and was shaped from bottom to top or applied over a mould (a cloth-lined form) and then finished. The most common shape had a flat bottom, straight walls, ribbed or rounded shoulders and a fluted neck. Decorations were applied on horizontal bands over the entire surface by stamping or drawing geometric patterns with a stick or a comb (see Figure 4 below). Triangles were used on the neck, lines on the shoulder and the bodies were adorned with wavy lines, zigzags, stepped pyramids or even swastikas. In later Andronovo stages their pottery became more rounded and the decorative patterns less dense or even completely absent.

Petroglyphs are abundant in Kazakhstan and many are aesthetically striking. The majority of the petroglyphs show clearly the transitions from the Late Bronze Age to its final stage

before the coming of the Iron Age, but the border between the Late Neolithic and Bronze periods are much harder to define. Some authorities still support the idea that the execution of petroglyph art began in the Bronze Age. However, an early layer of small images executed by stone tools has actually been detected, with small representations of animals, archers and human scenes, as well as very large (1x2-metre) single images of bulls that seem to pertain to a Neolithic stratum. It is therefore more reasonable to think that the Bronze Age peoples merged with cultures already devoted to rock art in regions where sunburned patination on rocks presented a perfect canvas for artistic expression.

These more advanced cultures brought new engraving techniques that favoured the development of new stylistic patterns: there was now an emphasis on well-defined single figures, naturalism and three-dimensional images. Some regionally specific styles emerged pointing to ethnographic niches, while others – more scattered, such as the scratched style found in the Altai, Dzungar Alatau and northern Tien Shan, which recur in proximity to mineral deposits and have a

Figure 4: Ceramics from the Late Middle to Final Bronze periods, showing varieties in shape and decoration

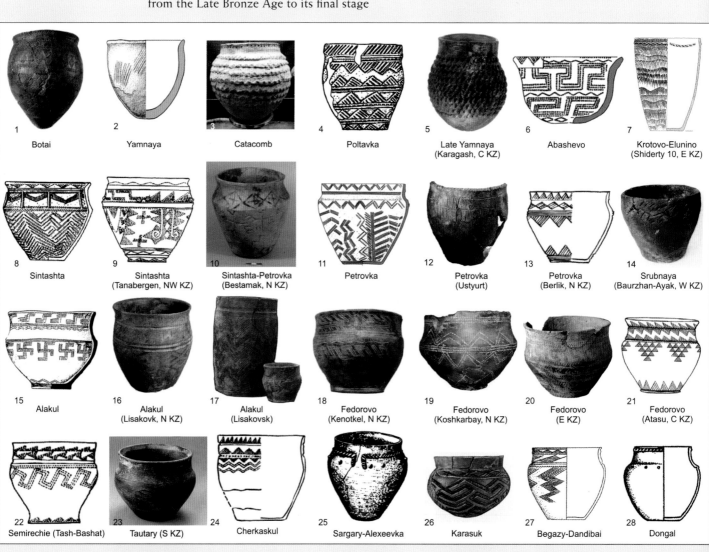

1 Botai
2 Yamnaya
3 Catacomb
4 Poltavka
5 Late Yamnaya (Karagash, C KZ)
6 Abashevo
7 Krotovo-Elunino (Shiderty 10, E KZ)

8 Sintashta
9 Sintashta (Tanabergen, NW KZ)
10 Sintashta-Petrovka (Bestamak, N KZ)
11 Petrovka
12 Petrovka (Ustyurt)
13 Petrovka (Berlik, N KZ)
14 Srubnaya (Baurzhan-Ayak, W KZ)

15 Alakul
16 Alakul (Lisakovk, N KZ)
17 Alakul (Lisakovsk)
18 Fedorovo (Kenotkel, N KZ)
19 Fedorovo (Koshkarbay, N KZ)
20 Fedorovo (E KZ)
21 Fedorovo (Atasu, C KZ)

22 Semirechie (Tash-Bashat)
23 Tautary (S KZ)
24 Cherkaskul
25 Sargary-Alexeevka
26 Karasuk
27 Begazy-Dandibai
28 Dongal

higher rate of chariot images – can be deduced to be the work of Fedorovo mining groups.

The subject matter of these petroglyphs was gradually enlarged to represent all the large animals of the era, human personages such as shamans and worshippers, humans with metaphoric heads shaped like the sun, labyrinths, mirrors, etc, and social scenes like hunting groups, friendly meetings, duels, sexual intercourse of various types and couples with children. Vehicles of transport were shown (wagons, carts, chariots, pack animals, skiers, riders on horses, camels or even goats), and abstract or mysterious forms were also carved into the rock faces.

In Kazakhstan, throughout all the petroglyph periods the most common engraved images are of small rams and goats, executed in an unattractive simple linear style. However, each period presented other figures whose importance was shown by size, centrality and activity, mainly consisting of the most typical animals of each specific landscape. During the Bronze Age the image of the wild horse was predominant in northern Kazakhstan, the wild bull was popular in the steppes of the mountain foothills, while the camel was the main subject in the arid zones. During the final centuries of the Bronze Age the images of sheep and goats started to be executed with great skill, and the image of the mounted horse acquired a central position.

As the Early Iron Age began, a radical aesthetic revolution occurred that saw style take precedence over content: the previous wide repertory of subject matter was reduced to rams, mountain goats, deer and predators, and a vivid animalistic style emerged triumphant.

### NEW PASTURES AND NEW CULTURES

Between 1900 BCE and 1500 BCE the Andronovo cultures had spread much farther than had their ancestors – in particular the Fedorovo culture, who were more mobile, with higher ratios of sheep and goats in their herds rather than cattle, and who lived in unfortified settlements. Both cultures gravitated in small groups towards mineral deposits, and within a century had reached central Kazakhstan, where they built metallurgic centres that became outposts for the colonization of the west by the Alakul (where they mingled with the Srubna culture of the Don-Volga region in the southern Urals) and the east by the Fedorovo, where in northeast Kazakhstan they interacted with the Okunevo and, later, the Karasuk culture. The Fedorovo also moved south along the mountain foothills as far as Bactria, exploiting their tin deposits.

After 1500 BCE the WAsMP metallurgical network began to contract and die away as a result of renewed ore extraction in Europe. However, in Kazakhstan mining and metallurgy still continued to supply the steppe market – if at a reduced pace in the context of the EAsMP, now under the control of Karasuk tribes. A more temperate climate encouraged population growth and enhanced pastoralist activity, and the Alakul and Fedorovo groups further colonized the steppes, semi-deserts and remote mining fields, leading to derivative cultures such as the Amangeldy (16th-13th centuries BCE) in northern Kazakhstan, Atasu (15th-13th centuries BCE) in the central steppe region, and Kozhumberdy (16th-13th centuries BCE) and Soliletsk (15th-14th centuries BCE) in western Kazakhstan. These all stemmed from the Alakul, while Fedorovo derivatives included the Nurinsky culture (1500-1100 BCE) that became dominant in central Kazakhstan, Kanay (1500-1300 BCE)

Top left and middle and bottom right: An example of "sun deities" and other petroglyphs at Tamgaly Archaeological Landscape, a gorge in the Chu-Ili mountains that was declared a UNESCO World Heritage site in 2004. Top right: A hunter on skis, located at Tekkeli in the Dzungar Alatau in Zhetisu (Semirechye)

in the Altai and Tautary (12th century BCE) in southern Kazakhstan. Mixed-type cultures also arose in Semirechye and the Tien Shan mountains of modern Kyrgyzstan starting around the 15th century BCE. But all these cultures and sub-cultures were destined to disappear by 1200-1100 BCE.

## THE FINAL BRONZE PERIOD

Although the Bronze Age for much of the ancient world is considered to have ended around 1200 BCE, iron did not spread immediately in the northern and eastern parts of Eurasia, and the success and sophistication of bronze making in Kazakhstan's territory resulted in a postponement of the introduction of iron metallurgy for around four centuries. This is known as the Final Bronze period (1200-800 BCE), which started with sudden cultural changes that saw the disappearance of the Late Bronze Andronovo cultures, and the formation of a new cultural complex comprising proto-Iranian and proto-Turkic ethno-linguistic groups.

Most of the newborn cultures were based on the Andronovo foundation, but archaeologists have detected the appearance of revolutionary elements. Mining and metallurgical activities were drastically reduced, and settlements and houses decreased in size and spread out widely across the territory. Burial rituals became simpler and poorer, and ceramics were also simplified, using more resistant shapes (rounded and more elongated) but with poorer decoration. Jewellery also decreased in size and complexity, and petroglyphs were marked by a clear drop in quality, style and subject matter. By the end of this period every cultural trait had become simpler and more homogenous, suggesting the rise of more competitive mobile groups, who easily interacted with and assimilated the other groups they came across. Territorially oriented pastoralist and political strategies now became the determinant factor in the formation of social structures.

There are several reasons for the speed at which this transformation occurred. A shortage of tin in southwest Asia combined with the emergence of iron-based warfare, in which infantry and horsemen now replaced charioteers. This provoked centuries of political turmoil and cultural disruption, an Asian "Dark Age". Bronze, inferior as weaponry compared to iron, was slowly superseded by the harder metal and began to be used mainly to make ornamental and ritual objects. This heralded the collapse of the Bronze Age and the beginning of the Iron Age. The long-

distance bronze trading network broke down, although the Karasuk tribes continued to make and trade bronze for the steppe cultures until the eighth century BCE.

A change in climate, with a sharp cool peak followed within a century by an arid phase, also contributed to instability, with the need for greater mobility resulting in conflict for water and pastures as well as adaptation to better exploit the changeable landscape; regional social cooperation and structural regrouping was another consequence of this. A particularly significant manifestation of such regionalization was the emergence in the northern Tien Shan foothills of homogenous tribes (the Semirechye culture) that made use of vertical migration between high mountain pastures in summer and piedmont steppes in winter; these relatively short seasonal displacements created the basis for the growth, during the Iron Age, of a powerful nomadic confederation: the Saka Tigraxauda.

At the same time pastoralism increased in importance compared to metallurgy, and significant improvements were made in stockbreeding techniques, with smaller, more efficient dwellings and camps, and swifter and more resistant herds comprising sheep, goats and horses, allowing for greater migration distances where necessary. The riding of horses and harnessing of Bactrian camels are well documented in petroglyphs, and the use of bridles with cheek-pieces increased control and mastery of the mounted animals. The foundations were now laid for the ascendance of mounted nomadic pastoralism – one of the most important innovations of the Old World.

The cultural reorganization that characterized the Final Bronze period meant that cultural groupings were now much more regionally concentrated. With the exception of the Karasuk and Dandybai tribes, most groups'

The fertile valleys of the northern Tien Shan (top) and the Altai Mountains (above) boasted ideal conditions for the development of nomadic pastoralism as the Bronze Age came to an end and the Iron Age began

territories were now clearly defined by pastoralist economic strategies and tribal conventions. Six important cultures of this time period have been documented – all were nomadic pastoralists while at the same time remaining good metallurgists.

The Cherkaskul-Mezhovo culture (1400-800 BCE) lived on the border between steppe and forest-steppe on both sides of the Urals, and evolved from the Fedorovo culture. The Sargary (Alekseevka) culture (1300-1000 BCE) originated in the steppe zone of the western Urals and northern Kazakhstan from the Alakul group and was influenced by the neighbouring Late Srubna culture to the west. Culturally stable and strong, it assimilated the other sparse and mobile groups and became the base for the formation of the Iranian-speaking Saka. The Dongal culture (1000-900 BCE) was centred in the Kent region of the central Kazakh Highlands, and was the direct ancestor of the Sako-Sarmatian culture.

The Karasuk culture (1500-800 BCE) was a powerful and long-lasting tribal group originally from southern Siberia, the Altai and eastern Kazakhstan. It inherited control of the EAsMP and spread across a wide area in every direction, reaching the Ordos in the east (the Yellow River in China), central Kazakhstan around 1200 BCE (where one Karasuk group founded the Dandybai culture) and west as far as the upper Volga River. DNA analysis points to the Karasuk having proto-Turkic features with some Mongoloid traits but light hair and green-blue eyes, making theirs the first of the many westward waves of Turkic tribes that, throughout millennia to come, migrated westwards from their homelands in the east. The "sun head" representations found at the Tamgaly petroglyph site in the Chu-Ili mountains (and Saimaly-Tash in the Ferghana range) were created in this historical context.

The Dandybai (or Begazy-Dandybai) culture (1100-800 BCE) had its centre in the Kent region of central Kazakhstan, and was formed after the westward migration of a Karasuk tribe. However, like the Karasuk it too was very widespread – 30 cemeteries have been discovered across a broad swathe of land from north Kazakhstan to the Syr Darya delta (Tagisken), as well as north of the Caspian Sea. Their ceramics and the ceremonial pottery made for elite tombs were particularly elegant, with round, elongated bodies, very small flattened bases and cylindrical necks. They were intricately decorated by various types of stamp and roller, as well as nail impressions and sometimes black and brown painting. Dandybai cemeteries consisted of kurgans covering majestic burial constructions which were circumscribed by a double round or square enclosure of massive granite pillars (two metres high and weighing up to three tons) that was topped by large slabs to create a roofed corridor. The central tomb hosted a buried body or cremated remains, together with a rich burial assemblage that highlighted large property inequalities and the presence of a tribal elite.

The Late Srubna culture (Late Timber-grave, 1100-800 BCE), is considered to be a manifestation of proto-Scythian peoples. Warring and expansion-minded steppe tribes, they occupied the southern Russian plains and spread through the southern Urals and then south along water courses and basins to reach the Amu Darya delta and farther to the Kopet-Dag foothills and the Murghab Delta. Its funerary constructions saw the classical timber burial houses (from which the Srubna got its name) slowly disappear, and rituals consisted of burial or cremation, the latter connected with human sacrifice.

Between the eighth and seventh centuries BCE iron reached the southern Urals, and by the fifth century BCE it had spread through all the steppes and deserts of western Central Asia. This process was carried out by powerful mounted nomadic confederations. Like the metallurgist charioteers of the Bronze Age, these equestrian warriors had their origins in the forest-steppe and steppe regions between the Urals and the Altai, resulting from a complex blending of Final Bronze cultures: the Sauromatians from the Urals, the Tasmola culture from central Kazakhstan, and the Tagar and Pazyryk cultures from the Altai. The result was a swift and broad-reaching societal change of huge significance.

*Renato Sala is an Italian researcher at the Laboratory of Geoarchaeology of the Department of History, Archaeology and Ethnology at Al-Farabi Kazakh National University.*

Burial sites of the Begazy-Dandybai culture in central Kazakhstan, dating back 3,000 years

# A GOLDEN ERA: THE SCYTHIANS, HORSE LORDS OF THE STEPPE

Relatively little is known of Central Asia and the Siberian steppe during the first millennium BCE. This is due to a lack of reliable historical information, and even those sources that are most often referred to – in particular the writings of the fifth century BCE Greek Herodotus – can be confusing and lead to unsatisfactory conclusions. Improving archaeological techniques for excavating and dating ancient artefacts, as well as greater access to a wider range of historical written source material, are now beginning to bring this fascinating period into clearer focus, but many mysteries still remain.

One point of contention is the origin of the Scythians – the horse-riding, warlike nomads who ruled the majority of northern Eurasia from around the eighth century BCE until the first migrations of the Turkic-speaking peoples from the east and the beginning of the Silk Road era. Tribes from the Carpathian Mountains of Europe to the Mongolian steppe have all become grouped under this umbrella term, but it was originally coined by the ancient Greeks to describe the nomadic tribes north of the Black Sea and Caucasus Mountains. Herodotus said that the ancient Persians called all the Scyths "Sacae", and inscriptions from the Achaemenid Empire do refer to the nomadic tribes on their northeastern frontiers as "Saka", while the Chinese knew the nomadic tribes to the northwest of their lands as "Sai".

Today, the term Scythian is used in both a cultural and archaeological context to describe a great range of ethnically and geographically unrelated peoples who nevertheless shared similarities in their lifestyle (pastoralist nomadism), language (Indo-Iranian, the eastern branch of the Indo-European language tree) and cultural practices such as complex funerary rites involving horse sacrifice and burials in *kurgans* (burial mounds) and a highly distinctive artistic tradition that became known as the Scytho-Siberian animalistic style. Thus the various Saka tribes that inhabited southern Kazakhstan and Zhetisu (Semirechye) can be called Scythian, being part of the Scythian-Siberian unity.

The spread of this cultural continuity was brought about partly by increased economic connectivity resulting from the development of iron as the superior metal of choice for tribes that were growing into formidable sociopolitical powers through mounted warfare. Where the Bronze Age tribes had used chariots as the main element of their war bands, the increased use of – and skill with – mounted horses meant the Scythian tribes were a far more mobile and deadly force. As cavalry armed with bows, lances and swords forged of steel, they spread throughout the northern Eurasian steppe belt swiftly and conclusively.

## KURGANS AND THEIR TREASURES

The Iron Age is a difficult period to date because it developed and arrived in different regions at varying times. However, in northern Eurasia it coincided with the development among the nomadic tribes of equestrian elites with great wealth in both livestock and material goods of gold and bronze, which were worked into fantastic shapes and designs expressing their close

Opposite main picture: A copper alloy tray discovered in the Zhetisu region with a mounted archer surrounded by horned animals. Inset left and right: A standing argali and double deer head both made from gold and sporting turquoise inlays, excavated from kurgan 82 at the Shilikty complex

This page top: Excavating at the Shilikty burial complex in eastern Kazakhstan. Above: A selection of the many golden artefacts discovered in Shilikty's "Golden Kurgan"

link to the natural – and supernatural – world of their steppe, forest and mountain environments.

The earliest known Iron Age kurgan showing evidence of an elite society based around mounted warfare is Arzhan 1 in the Tuvan republic of the Russian Altai, which dates to the late ninth-early eighth centuries BCE. Within Kazakhstan's territory the earliest nomadic elite burial is kurgan 82 in the Shilikty complex between the Altai and Tarbagatai mountain ranges, which has been dated to 810-750 BCE. The evidence from these and other excavations has led to the hypothesis that the Scythian cultural tradition had its roots in the Altai and central-southern Siberian region, from which – within one or two centuries – it spread out west, east and south to all areas whose environment made nomadic pastoralism the most efficient mode of life.

The elite or "royal" members of each tribe were interred in massive kurgans that represented a strong physical and spiritual link to their "homeland". The nomad's main wealth was measured by his herds of animals, which had to be moved frequently to new pastures; this constant shifting meant that no permanent power centre developed in a tribe's territory, and so the function of the kurgan complexes broadened to become an important element in genealogical associations, tribal identity and land claims – a sacred and closely protected ritualistic and spiritual focal point.

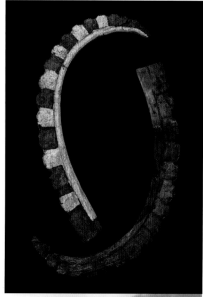

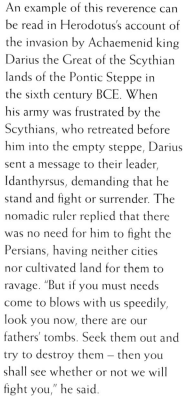

An example of this reverence can be read in Herodotus's account of the invasion by Achaemenid king Darius the Great of the Scythian lands of the Pontic Steppe in the sixth century BCE. When his army was frustrated by the Scythians, who retreated before him into the empty steppe, Darius sent a message to their leader, Idanthyrsus, demanding that he stand and fight or surrender. The nomadic ruler replied that there was no need for him to fight the Persians, having neither cities nor cultivated land for them to ravage. "But if you must needs come to blows with us speedily, look you now, there are our fathers' tombs. Seek them out and try to destroy them – then you shall see whether or not we will fight you," he said.

For the Scythians, gold, silver and precious stones did not have the same meaning as settled societies, who coveted them as material wealth and hoarded them away as temporal treasure. The nomads' most valuable possessions were their animals, so the artefacts they fashioned from precious metals took on significance as status symbols to show social standing or ritualistic meaning. When a man or woman was buried, their most prized possessions were placed alongside them – and this also included their horses, sacrificed and buried with full ceremonial trappings.

These artefacts were created in the Scytho-Siberian animalistic style that was the main aesthetic feature of Scythian artistic tradition, and the following essay by Professor Baipakov explains

From top: A reconstruction of the ceremonial horse trappings excavated from a kurgan in the Berel Valley; the actual sculpted ibex horns of a ceremonial horse headdress – made of wood and covered with gold foil – which were placed on a horse's forehead; the process of extricating frozen blocks containing burial items from a kurgan in Berel Valley

this in detail. They reflected the world-views of the military elite of the early nomadic mounted warrior societies; power and speed were essential qualities of life, underlined by a reverence for aggressive or highly dynamic animals. Conflict was an immutable law of nature, and predator-prey compositions were common, as well as animals such as deer or wild sheep with bent legs reflecting the presence of death within the circle of life.

## INTERACTION WITH THE WIDER WORLD

Nomadism was a highly sophisticated subsistence strategy for the Central Asian steppes, but many agricultural settlements and urban cultures were also present in

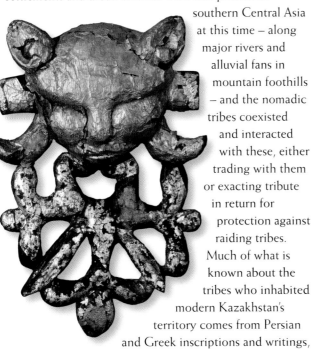

southern Central Asia at this time – along major rivers and alluvial fans in mountain foothills – and the nomadic tribes coexisted and interacted with these, either trading with them or exacting tribute in return for protection against raiding tribes. Much of what is known about the tribes who inhabited modern Kazakhstan's territory comes from Persian and Greek inscriptions and writings,

in particular from the sixth century BCE on, when the Achaemenid Empire began to expand into Central Asia, thus coming into close contact with neighbouring nomadic tribes.

Cyrus the Great (ruled 559-530 BCE), who founded the Achaemenid Empire, met his death in dramatic circumstances when he tried to conquer the warlike Massagetae in their own land – the exact geographical location of which is unknown, but assumed to be in the region around the southern Aral Sea between the Oxus (Amu Darya) and Jaxartes (Syr Darya) rivers. The Massagetae, renowned as warriors, were led by a queen named Tomyris. However, according to Herodotus, Cyrus tricked them by leaving a supposedly abandoned camp full of wineskins; the nomads, not being used to wine, became thoroughly intoxicated and were then easily defeated.

Tomyris's son Spargapises, the general of her army, was captured and taken before Cyrus, but persuading him to remove his bonds he committed suicide. Tomyris denounced Cyrus for his treachery and challenged him to a deciding battle… which the Persians lost with horrific casualties, including Cyrus himself, whose body was brought before Tomyris. She had him beheaded and his body crucified, then plunged his head into a wineskin filled with human blood, crying: "I warned you that I would quench your thirst for blood, and so I shall!"

Above left: A gold foil-covered feline face with stylized ornamentation covered in tin foil, part of the horse tack found in Berel's kurgan 11.
Above right: An Iranian carpet discovered in a Berel kurgan – part of the Pazyryk culture – and dating to the fifth century BCE. Left: "Tomyris plunges the head of the dead Cyrus into a vessel of blood", by the 19th century illustrator Alexander Zick

A later Achaemenid king, Darius I, was more successful in bringing the tribes of southern Kazakhstan under control. He conquered the Dahae, who lived between the Caspian and Aral seas, the Saka Haumavarga of the Ferghana Valley, and the Saka Tigraxauda (Tigrakhauda), who lived beyond the Syr Darya in the foothills of the Tien Shan. An image of a Saka Tigraxauda leader named Skunkha, hands bound and with typical pointed hat, is shown on the Behistun inscription in western Iran, an autobiographical rock inscription by Darius detailing his life and the peoples he conquered.

When Alexander the Great attempted his own invasion of the Central Asian steppe, he halted at the Syr Darya and built a fortress on its southern banks named Alexandria Eschate (modern-day Khujand). Despite a successful battle against the Saka, he did not press on into the steppe beyond, and it remained the domain of the Saka Tigraxauda. This period – the fourth-third century BCE – corresponds to the time the Issyk kurgan was made.

The Saka and other Scythian tribes continued to rule the steppes and mountain regions of Kazakhstan until the second century BCE brought new waves of nomadic pastoralists into Central Asia, this time from the east. First were the Wusun, who supplanted the Saka in the Tien Shan and Zhetisu, either integrating them into their own hierarchy or driving them out – a contingent of Sakas did migrate south into Bactria prior to the rise of the Kushan Empire. In the Altai the Pazyryk culture was overrun by the powerful new nomadic confederation known as the Xiongnu (Huns), while the Yuezhi moved into the southern steppe west and south of the Wusun, briefly controlling the nomadic federation of Kangju around the Aral Sea – which had grown up from the various tribes of that region, perhaps including the Massagetae – before moving south to create the Kushan Empire.

The next stage of Central Asia's history would document the rise of confederations incorporating ever larger groups of tribes, and nascent forms of centralized power that drove a desire for expansion and control of territory between the competing nomadic fraternities.

Top: The golden torc (neck ring) worn by the "Golden Man" of Issyk kurgan. Middle: The leaders of subjugated tribes are brought before Darius the Great, as detailed in the Behistun inscription carved into a rock in western Iran. At the rear, hands bound and with trademark pointed hat, is a Saka Tigraxauda leader called Skunkha. Above: The delegation of the so-called Persian Royal Hero, showing members of the Saka Tigraxauda bringing tribute to Darius the Great, part of a major relief on the Eastern Staircase of the Apadana in Persepolis

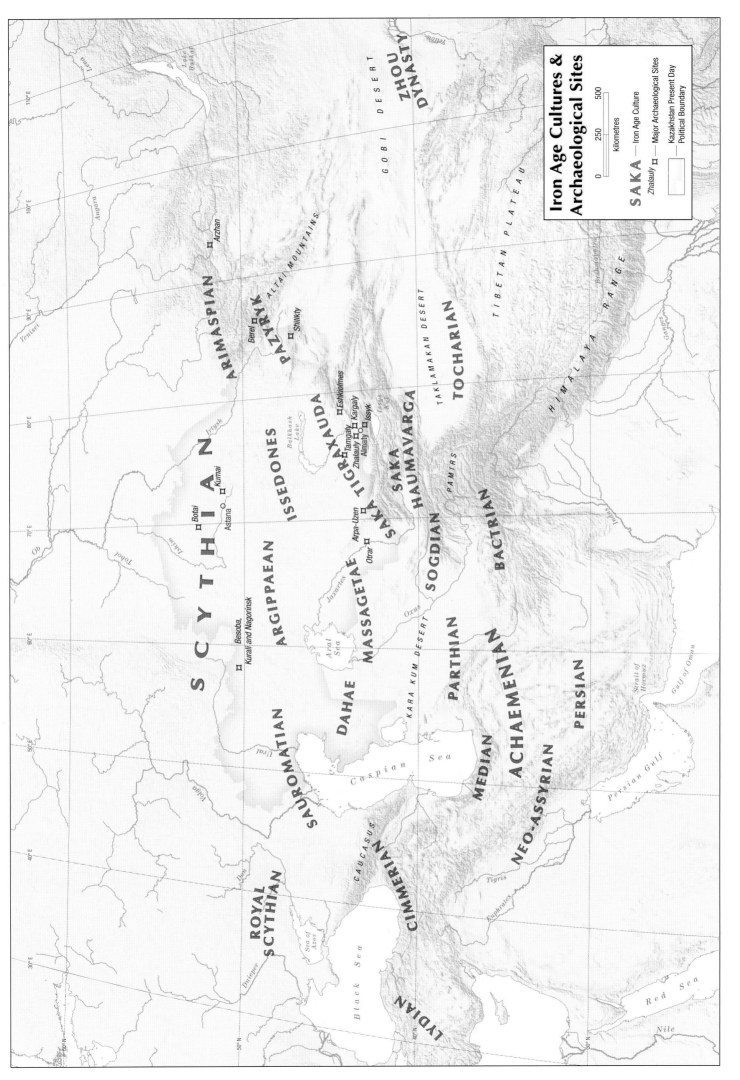

**Iron Age Cultures &
Archaeological Sites**

SAKA — Iron Age Culture
Zhalauly ⊡ Major Archaeological Sites
▭ Kazakhstan Present Day
Political Boundary

0        250        500
kilometres

ZHOU
DYNASTY

GOBI DESERT

Arzhan

ARIMASPIAN

PAZYRYK

Berel
Shilikty

ALTAI MOUNTAINS

SCYTHIAN

ISSEDONES

Eshkiolmes
Tamgaly  Kargaly
Zhalauly  Issyk
Almaty

TIGRAXAUDA

SAKA HAUMAVARGA

TOCHARIAN

TIBETAN PLATEAU

HIMALAYA RANGE

Balkhash Lake

Kumai

Botai
Astana

ARGIPPAEAN

Arpa-Uzen

SAKA

SOGDIAN

BACTRIAN

PAMIRS

TAKLAMAKAN DESERT

Issyk Kul

Besoba,
Kurali and Nagorinsk

MASSAGETAE

Otrar

Jaxartes

Aral Sea

Oxus

KARA KUM DESERT

PARTHIAN

ACHAEMENIAN

PERSIAN

DAHAE

SAUROMATIAN

Caspian Sea

MEDIAN

NEO-ASSYRIAN

Strait of Hormuz

Gulf of Oman

Persian Gulf

Sea of Azov

CAUCASUS

CIMMERIAN

ROYAL SCYTHIAN

LYDIAN

Black Sea

Tigris

Euphrates

Red Sea

Nile

Lake Baikal

Lena

Angara

Yenisei

Ob

Irtysh

Ishim

Tobol

Ural

Volga

Don

Dnieper

Ganges

Brahmaputra

Indus

Yellow

# The Saka tribes and cultural treasures of Kazakhstan

By *Karl M. Baipakov*

As the first millennium BCE began, the steppes of Central Asia were marked by a number of factors that came together to facilitate a world-changing phenomenon. First a climatic change brought more arid conditions to much of the landscape, forcing the stockbreeding inhabitants to adapt and improve their methods of livestock husbandry. This included a change in the composition of herd species – from cattle to the hardier sheep and goats – and the development of horse (and/or camel) breeding as the nomadic way of life was honed to fit each region.

A consequence of this was a new level of social relations related to increased property and social differentiation. Livestock increasingly became a form of wealth; herds grew bigger, which in turn required expansion of land as well as the possibility of greater trade. Wheel-and-draught transport became more widely spread, horse bits were introduced that gave extra control for riding, and military ability evolved accordingly. However, at this time true nomads – who were in almost constant motion – were still rare, and the great majority of Central Asia's livestock breeders remained to some extent related to settled living and agriculture.

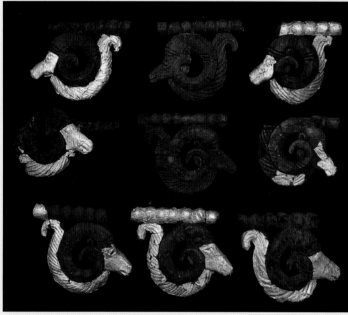

The transition to nomadic livestock breeding for a greater portion of the steppe and mountain dwellers came with the discovery of a new form of metal, iron – and its derivative, steel – and the subsequent formation of new cultures who used it. Right across the northern Eurasian steppe, from the Pontic Steppe north of the Black Sea to the Altai Mountains and the valleys and plains of the Yenisei River basin, nomadic equestrian warrior tribes grew and spread out to encompass and assimilate the resident Bronze Age groups of Central Asia. Although each culture was unique, the shared environmental conditioning and similarity in social and technological development caused them to become unified under a name by which they would be described collectively for many centuries: the Scythians.

The terms "Scythian-Siberian unity", "Scythian-Siberian society" and "Scythian world" are all used by researchers, but they often do not have exactly the same meaning. The unification of the Eurasian nomads, whose various homelands spanned a vast distance from the Danube River to Mongolia, is justified by the great similarity between their pastoralist lifestyle, the types of weapons they used, the trappings of their horses, and most importantly from an archaeological point of view, the shared artistic tradition known as the Scytho-Siberian animalistic style. Other general features common to the nomadic cultures of the Scythian-Siberian world were the use of large Scythian kettles, memorial art such as deer stones and petroglyphs, and similar forms of burial site constructions. Until recently the generally accepted date for the beginning of Scythian culture was the seventh century BCE. Today, however, many consider this period to have started between the ninth and eighth centuries BCE.

Top left: Wooden argali heads covered in gold foil were part of the horse tack found in Berel's kurgan 11. Top right: The frontispiece of the Golden Man's headdress showing two winged horses with ibex horns, the mixing of animal forms typical of Scytho-Siberian art. Above: A tripod cauldron from the fifth-third century BCE, made of copper alloy and sporting argali sheep heads on its legs

## SCYTHIAN TRIBES IN KAZAKHSTAN

In the territory of modern-day Kazakhstan a number of distinct Scythian sub-groups developed, but the most significant lived in the southern steppe and southeastern foothills of the Tien Shan: the Saka (also known as the Sak or Sacae). Nomadic warrior tribes with an elite social stratum, they interacted actively with the ancient cities of the region, whose inhabitants lived a settled agricultural life.

The Saka tribes were contemporaries of the "Royal Scythians" who lived in the Northern Black Sea and Dnieper region, and the Sauromatians who occupied the lower Volga region and southern Urals. To the southwest of their lands was the Persian Achaemenid Empire, ruled first by Cyrus and then Darius I (Darius the Great), while later they were forced to deal with the Greeks of Alexander the Great's conquering army. Achaemenid cuneiform sources state the names of three groups of Saka: the Saka Haumavarga (the Saka who cook the haoma drink), the Saka Tigraxauda (the Saka who wear pointed hats) and the Saka Paradaraya (the Saka beyond the sea), but specific information about them is rare and sketchy at best.

What little is known comes from sources such as inscriptions by the Persian kings Darius and Xerxes (composed in ancient Persian, Elamitic and Akkadian languages), as well as the "Avesta", a set of ancient Iranian books of the Zoroastrian religion. Ancient Greek and Latin sources are also very important; prominent among these are the writings of Herodotus, but valuable information on Achaemenid history was also left by Xenophon, Ctesias and later authors like Arrian, Polyaenes, Polybius, Pliny, Ptolemy and Strabo.

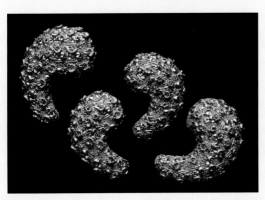

The common term "Saka" was widespread in Persian, Greek, Latin and even Chinese sources. Herodotus called the Saka Scythians, qualifying this from time to time as "Asian Scythians". But the Greeks also used other names (which cannot be found in Achaemenid cuneiform writing) to describe Central Asian tribes, including the Massagetae, Sauromatians, Argippaeans, Arimaspians, Passians and Sakarauks. Placing some of these groups on the map continues to be an almost impossible task.

In Herodotus's historical descriptions of the Central Asian campaigns of Cyrus and Darius I, he placed the lands of the Massagetae east of the Caspian Sea, "towards the sunrise across the Aras River". This is problematic, because the modern equivalent of the Aras is not known, and the Caspian might actually have been the Aral Sea (Greek knowledge of Central Asia's geography was vague at best). Some scholars think that Darius I, following the route of his predecessor, met the Saka beyond the Amu Darya near the Aral Sea; others think that Cyrus fought with the Massagetae beyond the Uzboy River (farther west, and today a dry feeder of the Amu Darya) while Darius I came to the Saka lands across the middle reaches of the Amu Darya. The best estimation is that the Massagetae occupied the arid steppe between the Amu Darya and Syr Darya rivers in the Aral Sea region.

According to Strabo the Dahae (Dai) tribe lived north of the Massagetae, and this is generally agreed to mean the land between the Aral and Caspian seas, from where interaction with the Parthians and Persians to the south was common. However, the location of the Saka Tigraxauda at least seems agreed upon, their territory being beyond the Syr Darya in the Tien Shan foothills and Zhetisu (Semirechye).

In ancient Persian texts nothing is said about the tribes who lived north of the Saka, but in the Avesta the name Sairima is mentioned, and these tribes probably correspond to the Sauromatians who were described in detail by the ancient Greeks. Herodotus named some of the tribes living to the north of the Scythians: these included the Argippaeans, with the Issedones to their east. According to stories from the Issedones, there were tribes of the Arimaspians and "vultures guarding gold" living beyond them. These tales would relate to northeastern Kazakhstan and the Altai, where the largest gold mines of that period were located, which in turn locates the Issedones within the steppes of central Kazakhstan (the location of the Tasmola culture).

The Saka had frequent interaction with state entities on their southern borders such as Khorezm (Chorasmia), Bactria, Assyria and Media during the pre-Achaemenid period, and with Persia from the mid-sixth century BCE. Cyrus the Great made an alliance with the Saka during a war with the Lydian king Croesus, but, unhappy with the union, then decided to conquer both the Saka and Massagetae. However, the Persian campaign met with fierce resistance and failed miserably, with Cyrus being killed during a battle with the Massagetae.

Darius I continued in Cyrus's footsteps but had far greater success. He managed to subdue many of the Saka tribes, including the Saka Haumavarga, Saka Tigraxauda and the Dahae, who were included in the 15th satrapy (outpost province) of the Achaemenid Empire. Saka warriors served in the Achaemenid army, and some were even included in the Persian king's personal guard.

During the later Greco-Persian wars the Saka fought as allies of the Persians, and Saka light cavalry participated in the battle of Gaugamela between Darius III (called Codomannus by the Greeks) and Alexander the Great in 331 BCE. Alexander's Greco-Macedonian army eventually defeated Darius III – the last Achaemenid king – and Alexander then began his invasion of Central Asia.

The Greek advance met stubborn resistance from all the Central Asia tribes, in particular the Massagetae. An attempt by Alexander to cross the Syr Darya with his forces failed, and he was wounded by a Saka arrow; it took almost three years of bitter struggle before the Greco-Macedonians managed to subdue the southern nations of Central Asia, but they maintained control for only a short time, and the Saka tribes who lived beyond the Syr Darya retained their independence.

## THE GOLDEN MAN

The Saka left numerous archaeological memorials, including necropolises that provide great insight into their lives. Of these sites, the most significant to be found to date is the Issyk kurgan, dated to the fourth-third century BCE and the burial place of the famed "Golden Man".

The Golden Man was discovered during archaeological excavation of a large kurgan (burial mound) in the Issyk region near Almaty

by the famous archaeologist Professor Kimal A. Akishev in 1969-1970. It was situated on the southern outskirts of an area where more than 40 kurgans were located, but this kurgan's diameter was 60 metres at its base, with a height of six metres. The construction was multilayered, with layers of pebbles interchanged with layers of even-sized rocks and clay. Below the kurgan were two burial chambers – one was central but the other had

Top: The Golden Man's ceremonial attire on display in front of an old image of Issyk kurgan. Above: An aerial view of Issyk kurgan illustrates its enormous size

Top and above: An archive image shows the initial excavation site of the Issyk kurgan burial chamber, with a detailed graphic of the layout of the body and its accoutrements. Right: The Golden Man's signature ring, which establishes him as nobility

arrowhead; above that was a whip, whose handle was covered with spiralling gold ribbon, and higher still was a silk bag holding a bronze mirror and red paint. Ceramic and ritual pots, once filled with food and beverages, lay on the chamber floor, and among them was a silver cup with an inscription – possibly in ancient runic Scythian.

On his head he wore a tall (65-70cm) tapering hat decorated with around 150 golden plates of various forms and sizes. Most of them are images of snow leopards, Siberian ibex, argali sheep, horses and birds, but the golden frontispiece of the headdress comprises two winged horses sporting ibex horns. Around his neck was a golden torque (neck band) whose ends were fashioned into the heads of tigers.

The young warrior's clothes too were richly embroidered with gold. His outerwear was comprised of a red leather shirt and trousers. The shirt was completely covered with triangular figurative plaques, those of the collar, chest line and bottom being larger images of tiger's heads. In total 3,000 golden items decorated this shirt. The trousers, meanwhile, were sewn with small rectangular gold plates along the external and internal longitudinal stitches. They were tucked into high leather boots decorated with triangular golden plaques like those of the shirt. Finally, a leather belt over the shirt was decorated with a number of massive golden plaques displaying the heads of elks and polymorphous beings with the head of an elk and tail of a horse in relief. The size of the kurgan and richness of the finery label this young man as nobility, high up in the elite social structure of his tribe, but an additional clue are the two massive golden rings he wore, one smooth, but the other a signet ring depicting a man's head in profile with elaborate headgear.

been placed laterally to the south. The central burial had been completely destroyed by robbers in ancient times, but the lateral burial had not been found and was undisturbed.

The burial chamber was a rectangular hole 3.3 metres long, 1.9 metres wide and 1.5 metres high, inside which was a log construction made from processed Schrenk's spruce – a tree native to the Tien Shan range. The body lay on wooden planks in the northern section, with kitchenware laid out in the south and west parts of the chamber. The deceased had been put on his back in a stretched position with his head to the west; he measured 165cm tall, and clothing, headgear, footwear and golden decorations were scattered over and under the skeleton. Weapons, toiletries and other utensils had been placed next to the body, which lay on a fabric mat embroidered with small golden plaques. After the funeral ritual the chamber was covered over with timber, the hole was filled with soil, and then the mound was erected.

According to anthropologists, the person buried in Issyk kurgan was a 17- or 18-year-old man. Dressed in ceremonial attire with a full array of weapons, along one of his thighs lay an iron sword in a red-painted wooden scabbard, with an iron dagger (called an *akinak*, also in a wooden scabbard) on the other, decorated with two golden plates depicting a horse and an elk. Near his left elbow was an arrow with a golden

## THE SCYTHIAN ARTISTIC TRADITION
The gold items excavated from the Issyk kurgan illustrate the high level of metalworking quality attained by the Saka/Scythian tribes of Eurasia during the first millennium BCE. They were made using various techniques, from moulding to stamping, toreutics and engraving in the form of round sculptures with high relief of silhouetted images. Other materials were skilfully worked as well, and combinations of metal with wood, leather with fabric, and different metals together have all been found.

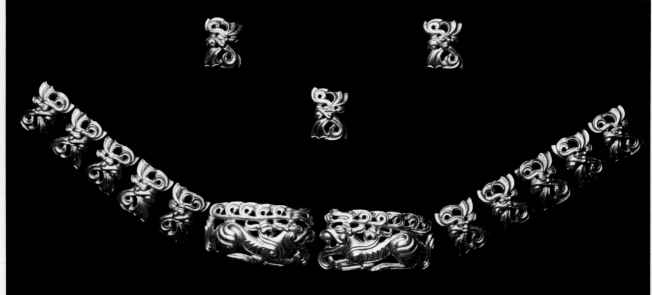

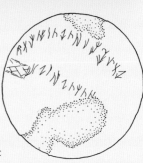

The Issyk kurgan did not reveal any items of clear Persian origin, but the influence of fine art practices from Western Asia is detectable, with motifs clearly borrowed from Indo-Iranian art, such as zoomorphic images of lions, griffins and other winged animals, as well as the tree of life. There were several artistic and stylistic schools of design within the Scytho-Siberian animalistic artistic language. The Semirechye school of jewellers was one of these; Saka craftsmen improved the different technologies (relief and intaglio designs) and perfected a superior type of realism when compared to that of the ancestral home of the animal style in the north.

The Issyk kurgan treasure has also provided insight into the social and belief systems of the Saka. The wealth contained in the gold-draped clothing of the young warrior was meant to dazzle those who saw it and elevate the "royal" wearer's rank to that of a sun deity. The religious and ideological symbolism of the zoomorphic images on the headdress corroborates this idea, epitomised in the winged and horned horses. The horse was symbolic of the sun, a solar deity in the religious beliefs of many nomadic tribes. Adding the ibex horns would symbolize a fusion of the sun deity with a patrimonial totem.

The discovery at Issyk of a silver goblet with an inscription was highly significant. The existence of writing in any society provides evidence of a high level of social and economic development.

Indeed, when taking into consideration the many valuable discoveries at the Issyk kurgan as well as numerous other sites in Kazakhstan, the presence of a well-organized Saka state during the middle and later years of the first millennium BCE is obvious. Saka society was multilayered, with a wealthy elite, military and noble classes, merchants, craftsmen and commoners. The great advancements in artistic traditions during this time gave expression to a close personal link to the natural world but also a strong spiritual belief system that was also highlighted in the many necropolises containing dozens of kurgans.

As well as Issyk, southeastern Kazakhstan (Zhetisu or Semirechye) is home to numerous other large burial sites where Saka tribes interred their dead. Their nomadic lifestyle and mobile tented homes meant that, lacking other permanent, long-lasting structures, the kurgans became a hugely important part of the landscape in the region, proving a clan or tribe's claim to its heartland. Extensive burial sites can be found in or near Almaty, Talgar, Novoalexeyevka, Kugaly, Burundai, Issyk, Turgen, Chilik, Kegen, Merke, Zhetytobe and Ushtobe. All of them have been examined and partially excavated, and show how the Saka populated and utilized the many valleys issuing from the northern Tien Shan, from high alpine pastures to the open, rolling steppe.

## BESSHATYR, ZHALAULY AND SHILIKTY
On the right bank of the Ili River at the foot of the Zhelshalgyr mountains, 170 kilometres east of Almaty and situated within the Altyn-Emel National Park, stand the Besshatyr (Five tents) kurgans, which date to the fifth-fourth centuries BCE and were created by the Saka Tigraxauda. Thirty-one burial mounds are scattered around the site seemingly at random, but two groupings can be distinguished in the north and south.

Top and left: The finely wrought gold plaques adorning the Golden Man's belt, from which hung his *akinak* or dagger, also worked with the highest craftsmanship. Above: The enigmatic runic script found on a silver goblet in Issyk kurgan

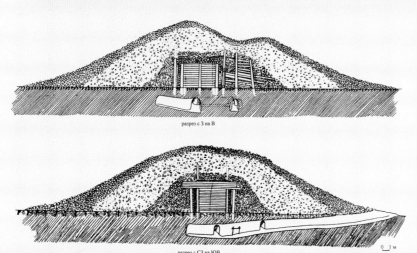

разрез с З на В

разрез с СЗ на ЮВ

0 ___ I м

is a ring of huge stone pillars (menhirs) and large boulders.

The kurgans range in size from huge – as mentioned above – to much smaller, only a metre high and six across; these were probably the tombs of common soldiers who distinguished themselves in battle. Many of the kurgans were excavated in the late 1950s, revealing the bones of men and women, horses, sheep and goats, as well as daggers and arrowheads – but no golden treasure, which would have been mercilessly targeted by robbers throughout the ages.

However, close to the village of Zhalauly, 200 kilometres east of Almaty, an amazing discovery was made in 1988 when a felt sack was found washed downstream by meltwater. Inside were more than 200 golden items from the ceremonial attire of a Saka aristocrat, including intricate belt plates, decorative pieces for clothes and headwear, and a horseshoe-shaped chest plate embellished with a border of twisted golden wire and decorated with miniature figures of argali mountain sheep in a pose typical of Saka art with their legs "pulled up". The same figures were fixed onto the almond-shaped belt plaques, whose surfaces were granulated by soldering on myriad tiny golden balls. Also worth noting were beautifully wrought

The first Besshatyr kurgan to be investigated was situated north of the others; it was 52 metres wide and more than seven metres high. Within the mound a large wooden building was discovered, made of treated timber from the Schrenk's spruce. It consisted of a corridor (dromos), ante room and burial chamber, most likely the tomb of a "king" or tribal leader. The corridor was 5.75 metres long, 1.5 metres wide and over five metres high but was uncovered; the ante room adjoined the eastern wall of the burial chamber, which was in the form of an irregular square oriented to the cardinal points and constructed from 16 rows of Schrenk's spruce wood. Cane mats tied with rope lay over the chamber's roof.

Sadly the burial chamber had been robbed, probably within a short time after its creation, and only the bones of men, women and animals were found on the floor after the debris had been removed. This is also true of the largest of the Besshatyr kurgans, which has a diameter of 104 metres and an average height of 15 metres. The mound is in the form of a flattened cone and an embankment surrounds it. Around that

pieces in the form of paired deer mirroring each other with branching tree-like horns gracefully entwined. This precious hoard has been dated to the seventh-sixth centuries BCE.

To the north, near Zaysan Lake between the Tarbagatai Mountains and the foothills of the Altai, the "Golden Kurgan" at Shiliky (Chilikty) was partially excavated, revealing a burial chamber of larch logs covered by a layer of crushed stones, another of heavy clay, then soil and finally small pebbles topping the mound. Inside were a 40-50 year-old man and a 50-60 year-old woman with their belongings, laid along the western wall of the chamber.

Although the kurgan had been robbed in ancient times, many items remained, including 13 bronze socketed arrowheads and 524 outstanding examples of Scytho-Siberian animalistic art wrought in gold. Among these were deer plaques, their legs pulled up in classic style; figures of eagles in high relief with their heads turned to the right; panthers curled into a ring; a fish encrusted with turquoise and decorated with small granulated golden balls, as well as a lot of other smaller jewellery. This kurgan was dated to the seventh century BCE, and is one of the earliest "royal" kurgans in the northern steppe region of Kazakhstan.

However, in 2003 another kurgan in the Shilikty complex was excavated and dated to between the ninth and seventh centuries BCE. Despite it also having been robbed, quite a lot of its minor treasures were lost by the robbers as they dug their trench into the central chamber. These included the decorative clothing and headgear of the kurgan's high-ranking internee, as well as cast figurines of deer, paired deer with interlocked antlers and turquoise inlays (similar to the one found in the Zhalauly

treasure), argalis, eagles and fascinating "snow leopard masks" that have two facing ibex heads and a flying bird ingeniously worked into them.

These are some of the oldest kurgans in Eurasia, and the exquisite quality of their treasures show not only the high level of metalworking and applied arts of the pastoralist tribes of the Eurasian steppes, but also the cultural, technological and spiritual links between the tribes populating the Tien Shan region and those to the north in the Altai, Siberia and west all the way to the Black Sea.

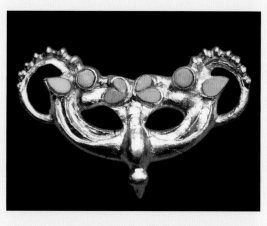

## BEREL AND THE PAZYRYK

Perhaps the most striking instances of burial as memorials to the dead can be found in the Altai Mountains, where the permafrost-sealed ground preserved ancient burials to an incredible degree at sites such as Russia's Pazyryk, Bashadyr and Ukok. A Scythian burial complex of equal importance lies in the beautiful Berel Valley in far northeastern Kazakhstan, close to the

Above: A superb snow leopard mask, incorporating two ibex heads facing inwards and a flying bird, excavated from a kurgan at Shilikty. Below left: The elaborate construction of a sepulchre at Shilikty. Below right: An aerial view of the Berel Valley shows the locations of some of its kurgans

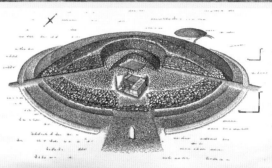

Clockwise from above left: Kurgan 10 from the floor of Berel Valley; an aerial perspective of kurgan 11; a diagram of its construction; and its wooden burial chamber containing a larchwood sarcophagus

Russian and Mongolian borders. More than 30 kurgans lie on the valley floor in a chain, and the picturesque natural scenery of the surrounding landscape probably resulted in this location being considered sacred to the ancient nomadic groups living in the region.

The people here belonged to the Pazyryk culture, who lived throughout the Altai region between the sixth and third centuries BCE. A warlike tribal group, they buried their leaders in highly complex underground structures that are similar to Scythian funerary sites across all northern Eurasia's taiga belt as far as the steppes of modern Ukraine.

The severe climate of the taiga forests meant that for much of the year the soil was frozen as permafrost, and the nomads made ingenious use of this climatic factor to ensure those they buried would remain, along with their clothes, belongings and prized horses, in an unaltered state for millennia, frozen solid in the ground. For archaeologists this was a great boon, as it provided unique evidence of the lives of Iron Age nomads in the Altai. The first archaeological excavations were carried out in 1865 by V. Radlov, who excavated a kurgan on Katanda River prior to Berel, and found perfectly preserved items made from wood, felt and wool, clothes made from fur, sable and silk, as well as the bodies of humans and horses.

The first Berel kurgan to be examined, in 1998-99, had a diameter of more than 30 metres and was more than two metres high. It was a complex architectural structure: the mound was not just a simple heap of stones; it consisted of several layers of carefully selected slabs, boulders and pebbles of differing size, with massive slabs covering the base platform and surrounded by a fence of vertical stone slabs. This very specific

construction probably kept the temperature consistently low, never allowing the contents of the tomb to thaw.

The burial chamber itself was a larch log construction covered with massive blocks, sheets of birchbark and a layer of twigs. The floor of the tomb was paved with stone tiles – again a good way to keep everything frozen – on which was laid a single larchwood trunk, polished smooth and probably treated against decay. The cover of the chamber had four gilded griffin figures at each corner.

Within the tomb were the remains of a 35-40 year-old man and a slightly older woman, their heads resting on wooden blocks. The man had a beard, moustache and braided hair, and both had been embalmed using herbs and other aromatic substances – part of the preservation process in the complex burial traditions of these people. Obviously of noble status, the bodies had been dressed in clothes adorned with the finest gold foil and embroidered bronze beads.

Emphasizing their high social status were the 13 horses buried alongside the tomb chamber. They had been killed by a single blow to the forehead from a type of pickaxe and placed in two layers, seven below and six above, separated by a layer of birchbark and bushes. They faced towards the east and were amazingly well preserved; as well as their ceremonial attire, their skin and even soft tissue were still present – testament to the efficacy of the process of mummification by freezing perfected by the Pazyryk nomads.

The Berel kurgan dates from the fourth to early third centuries BCE, and provided superb examples of the Scytho-Siberian animalistic style in a variety of different mediums. The oldest saddles in Kazakhstan were exhumed here, one of which had felt appliqué on the saddle cover showing a scene of a predator tearing a hoofed animal to pieces. The horse trappings and weapons reflected the military lifestyle and a reverence for nature with numerous fascinating sculpted wooden pieces covered with gold or tin foil (the use of wood covered by foil created an illusion of great wealth in gold and silver).

Images of deer, elk, ibex, argali, birds and felines were all present, representing all the major fauna of the region. But special place was given to images of fantastic griffins, whose features exhibited a blend of various animals, from the body of a feline predator (with its long tail curling over its back) to a bird of prey's head and beak, curled crest and helical horns. Scenes of animals fighting were a common feature of the animalistic style of the period; plaques and pendants showed great cats (tigers or leopards) attacking deer or mountain goats, or griffins biting their own tails.

## THE ARAL SEA AND SOUTHERN DESERT

Southern Kazakhstan also harbours interesting memorials of Saka culture in South Tegisken and Uygarak. The former is host to around 50 kurgans, of which 38 have been excavated, while 80 or so kurgans lie in the Uygarak complex, 70 of which have been studied thus far, showing a mix of burials and cremations within kurgans ranging from 10 to 40 metres wide.

In this more arid desert region the bodies were placed on cane mats inside light wooden-framed chambers interwoven with twigs and canes. Inevitably the majority of the tombs had been robbed, with the upper body parts scattered around the chambers implying that the most valuable treasures were on clothing and headwear or placed around the head. Of the items that have been recovered, plaques covered in golden foil, appliqué clothing, and strings of carnelian, turquoise and chalcedony beads illustrate how the deceased were buried. In Uygarak the men wore earrings and the women bracelets, and bronze and iron daggers were placed at the feet of both sexes, as well as horse trappings to imitate actual horse burial.

The many household items that were dug up provide a fascinating glimpse into the everyday lives of the Iron Age tribes who lived in the region of the Aral Sea between the seventh and fifth centuries BCE – to which these kurgans date. There are oval bronze mirrors, small stone altars, stone grinders, pieces of realgar and cinnabar (colouring agents), graters and spindle whorls, and ceramics such as cups, bowls, jugs both with handles and without, and flat-bottomed pots with tubular spouts.

Above: A horned sphinx partially covered in gold foil from kurgan 11's coffin shroud. Bottom left: An early excavation photo of kurgan 9 in Berel shows the burial chamber on the right and horse remains beside it. Left: A reconstruction of kurgan 10's burial site showing the arrangement of 10 horses and birch bark covering the burial chamber

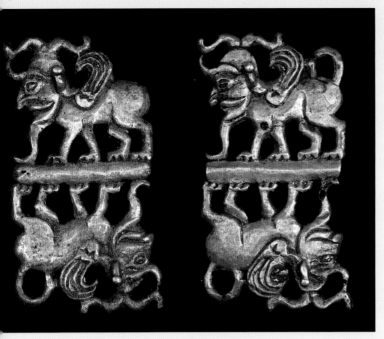

saiga antelopes – inhabitants of the deserts and arid steppes – were present, and representations of a lion were frequent in the art of the Aral Saka (lions being creatures of the southern lands towards the subcontinent and Middle East).

In the latter stages of the first millennium BCE the populations of the lower Syr Darya and Aral Sea region often lived in fortified settlements for protection from frequent attack by aggressive neighbouring states and tribes. The site of Chirik-Rabat, located by the banks of the Zhana Darya, covered an entire hilltop in an oval plan (850 metres x 600 metres), with a 40-hectare fortress surrounded by a double cordon of fortifications.

Left: These silver plaques
of double-headed winged
sphinxes were unearthed at
the Issyk kurgan. Below left:
A bronze plaque from the
Besoba site in the Aktobe
region depicts two Bactrian
camels fighting

The most common type of weapon for these semi-desert dwellers was a bow and arrows. The arrows were usually kept in a quiver – a leather quiver found in a fifth century BCE Tegisken kurgan held 50 arrows (all 70cm long) and was richly decorated with golden plaques. The quiver was worn on the left side, and as a rule the arrows were placed with the arrowheads down. Both bone and bronze arrowheads were used, and daggers also were made of both bronze and iron – in the centuries after the arrival of iron, bronze weapons were still made to augment a tribe's arsenal.

Locally made jewellery and ritual objects clearly show that the Saka of the lower Syr Darya and Aral Sea region were a part of the Scytho-Siberian animalistic cultural sphere: deer, horses, ibex, wild boars, leopards and birds of prey were all depicted on their horse trappings, golden plaques and ornamental dress. But within this cultural unity a certain amount of local peculiarities are revealed, indicative of the difference in their environment and geographical location relative to other states to the south and west. Images of camels and

The settlement was further protected by a 40-metre-wide and four-metre-deep trench. The ancient fortress wall was 4.5 metres thick, reinforced by protruding rectangular towers, and was topped by a 1.8-metre-wide rampart for archers. Excavation of the residential areas of the settlement show that although it was first built as early as the fourth century BCE, it was still being used as late as the 12th-13th centuries CE, prior to the invasion of the Mongols.

As a fortified shelter for local tribes, Chirik-Rabat was also used as a burial site for tribal leaders – kurgans and mausoleums have been discovered there too. Imported jars with inscriptions, one Khorezmian and another Greek, show that trade and inter-state contact was an intrinsic part of the culture of the horse lords of the mountain valleys, steppes and semi-deserts of Iron Age Kazakhstan. Through a variety of ancient written sources and rich archaeological discoveries, today we have a far better understanding of the complex lives of the Saka and the fast-changing world within which they lived.

*Professor Karl M. Baipakov is Director of the Institute of Archaeology of the Academy of Sciences of Kazakhstan, having previously been Director of the A. Kh. Margulan Institute of Archaeology from 1991 until 2010. A graduate of Leningrad State University's Department of Archaeology, he is an associate member of the German Archaeological Institute, an international expert of UNESCO, and a specialist in the ancient and medieval urbanization of Kazakhstan and Central Asia. He is the author of several monographs and many scientific articles.*

# THE SILK ROAD: THE WUSUN AND THE LINKING OF EAST AND WEST

The history of Central Asia during the final few centuries BCE and the first half of the following millennium (referred to as CE, or Common Era, a more neutral term than the Christian-biased AD) is both obscure and somewhat confusing, but the haziness of the period is thrown into relief by the evolution of what became known as the Silk Road. In 138 BCE, the Han Chinese Emperor Wudi, threatened by the Xiongnu, a powerful nomadic tribal confederation of Inner Asia to the north of his kingdom, sent an emissary called Zhang Qian to see if there were any powers in the "Western regions" with whom the Chinese could ally.

Zhang Qian's 13-year journey took him from the ancient Chinese capital of Chang'an (modern-day Xian) around the rim of the Taklamakan Desert and into the depths of Central Asia. His main aim was to seek an alliance with the Yuezhi, a tribe who had previously been driven west by the Xiongnu, but although he was unable to do this, he brought back to Chang'an a wealth of information about these previously unknown areas. His report (documented in the Chinese *Shiji* or "Records of the Grand Historian" by Sima Qian around 100 BCE) described 36 kingdoms of the Western Regions, including Dayuan (in the Ferghana Valley), the Yuezhi (in Transoxiana), the Kangju (in the Syr Darya, Chu and Talas river region) and Yancai (in the steppes north of the Aral Sea); a later diplomatic and trade mission in 119 BCE took him to the Wusun, who were based around Issyk-Kul, the Ili Valley and Semirechye (Zhetisu).

It is from these ancient historical documents, and more recently from extensive archaeological exploration in the territory of Kazakhstan and elsewhere in Central Asia, that a picture emerges of a changing world, where previous inhabitants like the Saka and Scythians were either overrun by or merged with migrating tribes from the east, who created their own new territories of control, absorbing existing cultures and developing on many levels as communication and trade with the wider world – from Rome to Han China, from eastern Europe to northern India – blossomed, bringing new ideas, products and technologies to the nomadic pastoralists and agricultural settlers of the mountain, desert and steppe regions.

A close-up view of a section of the Kargaly diadem (a crown-like headband) shows the high level of skill attained by the Wusun craftsmen more than 2,000 years ago, who worked gold and semiprecious stones into stunning pieces of jewellery

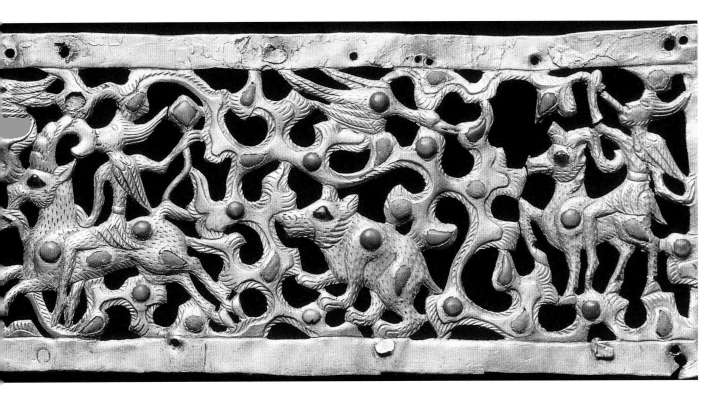

## THE WUSUN AND XIONGNU

In the second century BCE, the Saka Tigraxauda were gradually overrun by a tribe known as the Wusun (Usun). This confederation of pastoral nomads had originally lived in the east Gansu region of China but were forced west under pressure from the neighbouring Yuezhi tribe. Opinion is split as to their ethnicity, but they are generally considered to have been Turkic-speaking, perhaps of Mongol descent – although some claim they were Indo-European like the Tocharians of the Tarim Basin.

The Wusun took up residence in the Ili River region and around Issyk-Kul, where their capital, Chigu ("Red Valley"), was situated. Their sphere of influence grew to encompass all of Semirechye and they became a powerful force in Central Asia, developing a state system with a leader called a *gunmo*, or "Lord of Lords", tribal nobility, priests and ordinary herdsmen and farmers. When Zhang Qian arrived at Chigu on his diplomatic mission from the Han emperor, he estimated their number at 630,000 people, of whom 188,000 could be called to arms. The gunmo himself had 30,000 cavalry and 10,000 archers at his disposal.

When a Chinese princess was sent to the Wusun leader in a political marriage to seal their alliance against the Xiongnu, she described them as nomads who lived in felt tents, ate raw meat and drank fermented mare's milk. However, although nomadism was central to their lifestyle, with huge herds of mainly horses and sheep being moved between summer grazing pastures in the high alpine meadows and wintering grounds in the Moiynkum and Balkhash areas, the distances between summer and winter residences in Semirechye – 30-100km – was not as great as in the vast steppe regions to the north, allowing the Wusun to construct permanent buildings and farm irrigated land along the rivers. The discovery of large amounts of pottery, stone grinders and remnants of cereal crops at riverside settlements and in the mountain gorges of the northern

Tien Shan show that an agricultural culture grew alongside the traditional animal husbandry of the nomads, and its role increased throughout the 500 years or more that the Wusun state ruled in this region.

By the first century CE the Wusun state had regular relations with China, with which it traded horses for silk and other luxury goods – the Wusun nobility wore clothes of silk and fine woollen fabrics. They also mined copper, lead, tin and gold, smelting iron for weapons and other uses, and creating intricate gold jewellery embellished with precious stones.

Excavations of Wusun burial mounds have revealed much about their society. The barrows, often arranged in chains along rivers and in mountain valleys, range from huge mounds up to 80 metres in diameter and 15 metres high, down to more numerous smaller ones 10 metres in diameter and a metre high. Small barrows – the graves of the common folk – offer up clay pottery, iron knives and bronze earrings and necklaces. The largest mounds were the resting places of high-ranking Wusun leaders; those that were not plundered in years gone by have revealed large amounts of gold jewellery, weapons, bronze mirrors and high-quality pottery.

Of course even while trade increased, there was almost continuous conflict with neighbouring tribes and kingdoms over land, access to water and the best pastures, as well as simple raiding for booty. To the east and north the Xiongnu – also called the Huns – were an ever-present threat. A confederation of tribes stretching across Mongolia, the Junggarian Basin and the Altai, the Xiongnu fought the Han Chinese and their Wusun allies, at one point forming an alliance with the Kangju kingdom on the Wusun's western border. The Wusun repelled this invasion and eventually the Xiongnu were defeated by a Chinese army in 89 CE, marking the end of the Xiongnu state.

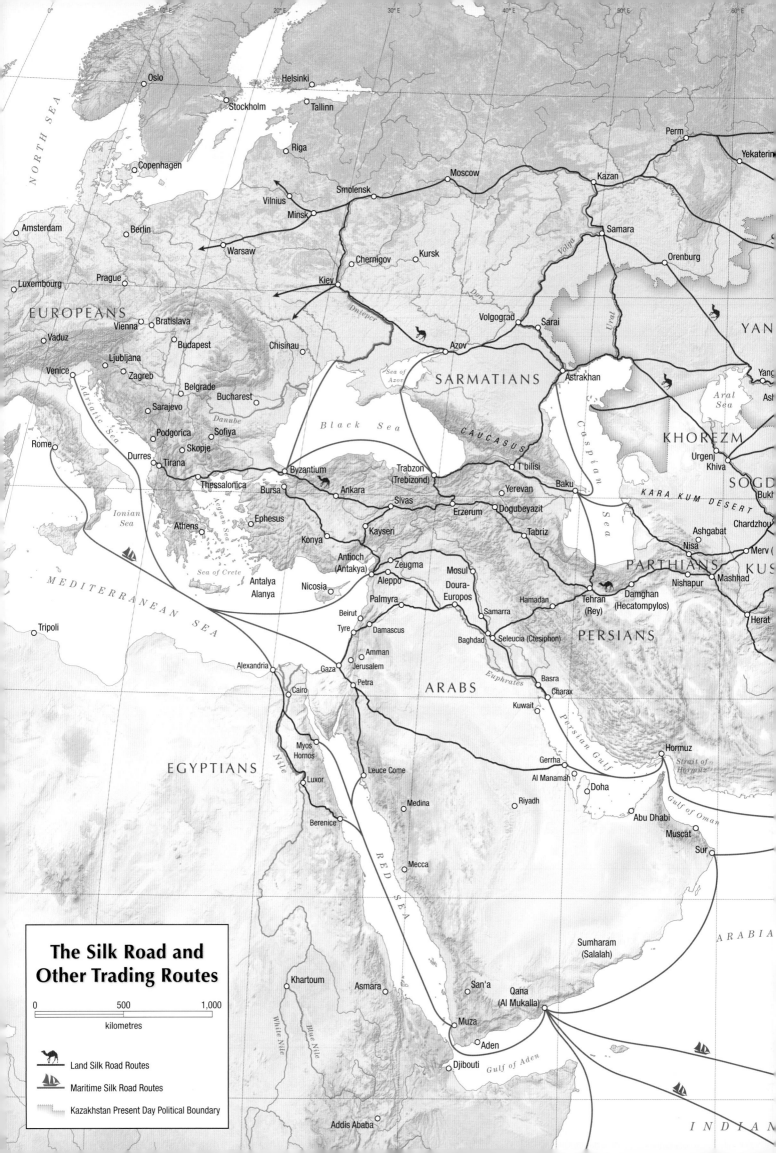

The Silk Road and Other Trading Routes

0    500    1,000
kilometres

🐫 Land Silk Road Routes

⛵ Maritime Silk Road Routes

〰️ Kazakhstan Present Day Political Boundary

EUROPEANS

SARMATIANS

ARABS

EGYPTIANS

PERSIANS

PARTHIANS

KHOREZM

SOGD

YAN

KUS

ARABIA

INDIAN

NORTH SEA

Adriatic Sea

Ionian Sea

MEDITERRANEAN SEA

Aegean Sea

Sea of Crete

Black Sea

Sea of Azov

CAUCASUS

Caspian Sea

Aral Sea

KARA KUM DESERT

RED SEA

Persian Gulf

Strait of Hormuz

Gulf of Oman

Gulf of Aden

Danube

Dnieper

Don

Volga

Ural

Euphrates

Nile

White Nile

Blue Nile

Oslo
Helsinki
Stockholm
Tallinn
Riga
Copenhagen
Amsterdam
Berlin
Vilnius
Minsk
Smolensk
Moscow
Perm
Yekaterin
Kazan
Warsaw
Chernigov
Kursk
Samara
Orenburg
Luxembourg
Prague
Kiev
Volgograd
Sarai
Astrakhan
Vaduz
Vienna
Bratislava
Budapest
Chisinau
Azov
Yang
Venice
Ljubljana
Zagreb
Belgrade
Bucharest
KHOREZM
Urgenj
Khiva
SOGD
Rome
Sarajevo
Podgorica
Sofiya
Skopje
Durres
Tirana
Byzantium
Trabzon
(Trebizond)
T'bilisi
Baku
Bukh
Thessalonica
Bursa
Ankara
Sivas
Yerevan
Ashgabat
Chardzhou
Athens
Ephesus
Erzerum
Dogubeyazit
Nisa
Merv
Konya
Kayseri
Tabriz
Nishapur
Mashhad
Antioch
(Antakya)
Zeugma
Mosul
PARTHIANS
Antalya
Alanya
Nicosia
Aleppo
Doura-Europos
Hamadan
Tehran
(Rey)
Damghan
(Hecatompylos)
Herat
Tripoli
Palmyra
Samarra
Seleucia (Ctesiphon)
Beirut
Tyre
Damascus
Baghdad
PERSIANS
Amman
Jerusalem
Basra
Alexandria
Gaza
Petra
Charax
Cairo
Kuwait
Gerrha
Hormuz
Myos
Hornos
Leuce Come
Al Manamah
Doha
Luxor
Medina
Riyadh
Abu Dhabi
Muscat
Berenice
Sur
Khartoum
Asmara
San'a
Qana
(Al Mukalla)
Sumharam
(Salalah)
Mecca
Muza
Aden
Djibouti
Addis Ababa

However, a surviving contingent fled west into the great steppe, moving first to the Syr Darya and Aral Sea, then to the northern shores of the Caspian Sea, where they were named the Hunnoi by the Roman historian Tacitus in 91 CE. By the fourth century CE the Hunnic Empire had become a major steppe power in the western Eurasian Steppe, culminating in the mid-fifth century with Attila, who terrorized Europe from his steppe homeland.

The Xiongnu/Huns, according to most researchers, spoke a proto-Turkic language, and their influence on the east-Iranian speaking tribes of the Kangju is postulated as the beginning of the "Turkicization" of the peoples of Kazakhstan. Like the Wusun and other tribal groups of the Central Asian steppe, the Xiongnu were primarily nomadic pastoralists, with a very similar lifestyle based on strong patriarchal-tribal relations. They too made use of fertile riverine soil for limited agriculture; they mined and smelted metals, and developed arts and crafts in much the same way as the Wusun. It is worth noting just how culturally homogenous the various tribes of the Central Asian steppe were at this time (Wusun, Xiongnu, Yuezhi, Kangju and Yancai), their lifestyles dictated by the environment within which they coexisted either peacefully or antagonistically.

A Hunnic-era burial mound in the Kumai archaeological complex to the east of Astana in the central Steppe. Curving away from the round stone kurgan are two lines of stones symbolizing a great moustache (inset image) or *usami*, which may have been aligned to mark a particular date in the lunar or solar calendar. Right: A bird'-eye view of the ruins of Otrar, one of the great Silk Road cities

## THE YUEZHI, KANGJU AND YANCAI

South of the Wusun lay the Ferghana Valley and the kingdom of Dayuan, which according to Zhang Qian was populated by a settled people who lived in up to 70 fortified cities and grew rice and wheat, as well as making wine from grapes.

To the west of Dayuan were the lands of the nomadic Yuezhi, the tribe who had forced the Wusun out of their Gansu homeland, only to be driven west themselves by the ascendant Xiongnu. The Yuezhi – arguably an Indo-European Tocharian tribe – first settled in the Transoxiana region north of the Oxus River (Amu Darya), then expanded south into Bactria and formed the Kushan Empire in the first century CE. Before that, however, they controlled part of the kingdom of Kangju, which included Tashkent and the Chu and Talas river systems and bordered with the Wusun to the east.

Zhang Qian described Kangju thus: "[It] is situated some 2,000 li [832 kilometres] northwest of Dayuan. Its people are nomads and resemble the Yuezhi in their customs. They have 80,000 or 90,000 skilled archers. The country is small, and... acknowledges sovereignty to the Yuezhi in the south and the Xiongnu in the East." Kangju subservience to the Yuezhi did not last long; by the 1st century CE it was no longer a vassal state and had expanded down the Syr Darya to the shores of the Aral Sea, and taken control of Dayuan and Sogdiana.

The Kangju controlled the Silk Road trading routes northwest from Ferghana and the Tien Shan along the Syr Darya, north of the Aral Sea towards the Caspian Sea and Urals. Excavations of ancient settlements and necropolises in this region have revealed Chinese coins and mirrors, coral beads from India, bronze broaches from Europe and precious stones with intaglio carving from Persia. The ethnicity of the Kangju is open to much debate, some ethnologists believing they were Turkic-speaking, others considering them to be the descendants of the Saka and therefore Indo-Iranian speaking nomads. Whatever their origins, the population was engaged in agriculture and livestock breeding, handicrafts and trade. Settlements such as in the Otrar region near the Syr Darya were relatively sophisticated and complex, the surrounding areas were irrigated, and archaeological discoveries show finely crafted pottery, copper utensils, and bronze and gold jewellery.

In the first few centuries of the first millennium CE, the Kangju formed a powerful state force in the southern regions of Kazakhstan, and played an influential role in the development of the Silk Road and regional culture, being politically, economically and culturally connected with the empires of China, Parthia, Rome and Kushan.

North of the Aral Sea lay the endless expanses of the Central Steppe. This was the kingdom of Yancai (literally "Vast Steppe), which was a vassal state of the Kangju. Chinese sources report that the Yancai lifestyle was similar to that of the Kangju and Yuezhi – they were nomadic pastoralists of Iranian stock, and part of the extensive tribal union collectively known as Sarmatians. The Sarmatian tribes spoke an Indo-Iranian language like the Scythians, who they systematically displaced on the steppe starting around the third century BCE.

According to the first-century BCE Greek historian Diodorus, the Sarmatians "devastated" a significant part of Scythia, resisting the mounted Scythian archers' attacks by using lamellar armour of bronze or iron plates sewn on leather garments and retaliating with four-metre-long lances. By the second century CE the Yancai had spread west to the Caspian Sea and changed their name to Alanliao. By the third century CE it is recorded that they were no longer vassals of the Kangju. The Alans eventually became the dominant Sarmatian tribe and moved west to the region between the Caspian Sea and Black Sea, presenting a serious threat to the Roman Empire. The fourth-century CE Roman historian Marcellinus considered the Alans to be the descendants of the Massagetae tribe from the region between the Aral Sea and Caspian, but there is little evidence to support this.

## TRADE ROUTES AND URBAN DEVELOPMENT

By the fourth century CE the Silk Road had become a vast, multi-branched network of caravan and trade routes, branches of which crisscrossed the territory of modern-day Kazakhstan. Along these routes, especially in south Kazakhstan along the Chu, Talas and Syr Darya rivers, and in Semirechye in the Ili River Valley and the northern foothills of the Tien Shan, fortified towns and cities had sprung up, often run by Sogdian merchants, who became the dominant figures in commerce along much of the Silk Road.

Names like Shasha (Tashkent), Ispidzhab (Sayram), Taraz, Jamukat, Kulan (Lugovoye), Suyab (Ak-Beshim, near modern-day Tokmak), Balasagun and Navaket (Red River city) were all well documented. In the Ili River region merchants passed through towns in the locations of modern Kastek, Kastelen and Almaty, before reaching Talkhiz (Talgar), then on to Issyk, Turgen, Chilik and Khorgos to arrive in Almalyk. Another trail crossed the Altyn-Emel Pass to the Koksu Valley and on to Iki-Oguz and Kayalyk, from where it led to Alakol Lake and the Junggar Gate into the eastern realms.

Northwest routes left Ispidzab for Arsubaniket on the Arys River, then down to Farab (Otrar) and the towns of the Otrar oasis. Along the Syr Darya were Yassi (Turkistan), Shavgar, Sauran, Sygnak, the towns of the Dzhetyasar oasis, Dzhent, Dzhankent (Yangikent) and Khuvara. But there were many more routes, such as those that led north to the Ertis (Irtysh) and Esil (Ishim) rivers, to the Ulytau Mountains and west to the Mangyshlak region. Thus the many tribes of the Central Steppe, who were rich in livestock, wool, leather and metals, were brought into the Silk Road sphere.

But as the following essay by Professor Karl Baipakov discusses, the Silk Road carried far more than merchandise of all varieties. Religions, cultures and customs were also exchanged along this network – for example, Greek art and religious motifs were taken up and echoed in nomadic artefacts of the steppe. The nomads themselves played a significant part in the trade, conducting caravans of merchandise between major centres, as well as trading their own produce from the steppe in the growing number of urban mercantile centres. In this way, despite the appearance of these more formalized routes of international trade, the pattern of life and coexistence between nomads and the settled population remained in essence unchanged.

Inevitably though, change was on the horizon once again. The collapse of the Xiongnu Empire left a political void which another tribal confederation filled in the early fourth century CE. These were the Rouran, led by the Xianbei people, and for just over 200 years they ruled much of the Xiongnu's territory, making incursions into Central Asia as their predecessors had. The Rouran were thought to be ethnically Mongol – they were the first people to use the title *khagan* or *khan* for their supreme leader.

In the early fifth century yet another powerful nomadic confederation emerged in southern Central Asia, taking over the territory of the recently crumbled Kushan Empire. These were the Hephthalites, who from their base in modern Afghanistan expanded south into northern India,

east into the Tarim Basin and north into Transoxiana and southern Kazakhstan, where they absorbed the Kangju kingdom.

Under pressure from east and west the Wusun state began to collapse, but it was a new nomadic confederation that would succeed them in Semirechye and eventually control the majority of modern Kazakhstan's territory: the Gokturks or Kok Turks. This confederation of nomadic Turkic tribes defeated the Rouran (in alliance with the Chinese Wei Dynasty) and took control of Mongolia in 551, then rapidly expanded west into Central Asia, forming the Turkic Khaganate. This extensive empire was split into two wings, and the Western Turkic Khaganate became the ruling state in the Kazakhstan region, reaching as far as the Caspian Sea.

This was a pivotal moment in Central Asian history, as it marked the coming to dominance of Turkic-speaking peoples in the entire region. The Kok Turks had close relations with China in the east and Byzantium in the west, leading to even greater trading and interaction along the Silk Road.

*An artist's drawing of Taraz during the Silk Road's heyday, when it was one of the wealthiest cities in Central Asia. Excavations of Kazakhstan's ancient city ruins have revealed goods from far afield, such as this beautiful glass vessel from Syria and an intricately worked Persian mirror*

# The Great Silk Way – a dialogue of cultures

By *Karl M. Baipakov*

To most people the ancient trade between East and West through Central Asia is encapsulated in the term "The Silk Road", generally considered to be represented by the trade routes passing from China through modern-day Xinjiang, over the high passes of the Tien Shan and Pamir mountains to the fabled cities of Samarkand, Bukhara and Balkh, etc, before continuing across Persian territory to the Middle East and the civilisations of the Mediterranean. The generally accepted starting date for the Silk Road is 138 BCE, corresponding to the western journey of Zhang Qian from Han China, but the idea that it was his information about the "Western Regions" that opened the way for intercontinental trade is inaccurate and requires revision.

"Kirghiz on a camel", an oil on canvas painting by Richard Karlovich Zommer (1866-1939). Although labelled Kirghiz, this picture actually depicts a Kazakh from the south – during the artist's time the term "Kirghiz" referred to both Kirghiz and Kazakh tribes

Certainly from the mid-second century BCE there was a leap in diplomatic and commercial communication, and more concerted and organised trading began to take place in both directions, but there is a huge amount of evidence proving that considerable traffic along the routes between China, the Mediterranean, the Indian subcontinent and northern Europe, had begun even earlier.

According to the Russian archaeologist Elena Kuzmina, the prehistory of the Great Silk Road can be traced back to the late second to early third millennia BCE, when the expansion of the Bronze Age Sintashta-Petrovka and Andronovo cultures in the Eurasian Steppe spanning the Ural Mountains saw agricultural products, livestock (including domesticated horses) and metallurgical technology (chariots, etc) spread throughout the region, from southern Central Asia to Mycenaean Greece.

Routes can be traced connecting Siberia with Central Asia and Semirechye with Xinjiang – Andronovo ceramics and bronze products such as axes, sickles, adzes, spearheads and arrowheads, as well as golden earrings and mirrors, have been found to substantiate this. Trade of two valuable minerals had also developed at this time; mining of lapis lazuli in the mountains of Badakhshan and jade in the upper Yarkand River near Khotan resulted in lapis being exported to Iran, Mesopotamia, Anatolia, Egypt and Syria, and the "Jade Road" connecting the Tarim Basin with China.

During the early Iron Age these routes continued to develop; the exchange and range of goods increased, and a dialogue of cultures developed, with innovations in technologies, types of metal products, military strategy and skill with the horse and chariot all being shared. The sixth-third centuries BCE saw a period when large empires were formed and military campaigns between the Persians and the Saka, as well as conquests by Alexander the Great, characterized a new stage in the trading routes which may be called the "Proto-Silk Road".

This time corresponds to the formation of states such as Bactria, Khorezm, and the tribal groupings of the Saka and Scythians in the Zhetisu (Semirechye) and Aral Sea regions

Creatively worked silver earrings, bracelets and other ornamental finery were discovered in excavations of ancient Otrar

respectively, which had close ties with Han China and Achaemenid Iran. Both Chinese silk and Iranian goods have been discovered in the excavations of "royal" kurgans within Semirechye (Issyk) and the Altai (Pazyryk, Bashadyr, Tuekty, Shibe, Ulandryk, Ak-Allah and Berel – a silk blanket with phoenixes on it was excavated from a Pazyryk kurgan dating to the fifth century BCE); within burial sites in Xinjiang (Subashi, Kyzylgok and Zaghunluk); even as far north as the Arzhan sites in Tuva (modern-day Russian Siberia).

In all likelihood Central Asian cities and settlements belonging to tribal groups including the Saka, Pazyryk and Scythians, and later the Wusun, Xiongnu, Kangju, Savromats and Sarmatians, formed links in a far-reaching road that began at the big bend of the Yellow (Huang He) River in northern China, crossed the Altai Mountains to the Irtysh River, spanned the endless steppes of Kazakhstan and the Black Sea region, before finally reaching the lands of the Greeks and Etruscans. Descriptions

by the Greek "father of history" Herodotus show that this was a regular route for the transfer of goods and cultural ideas, with the nomadic steppe tribes of the Saka and Scythians playing an active part in their distribution between East and West.

## TRADE AND CULTURAL INTERACTION

From the second century BCE on, new tribes and kingdoms took over Central Asia. The Wusun migrated from the Gansu region of China and overran the Saka Tigraxauda of the Semirechye region, the Kangju created a kingdom on the middle and lower Syr Darya, and the Yuezhi – also migrants from China's Gansu area – passed through the Tien Shan and created the Kushan Empire in former Bactria and Ferghana.

The consequences of Zhang Qian's journeying and greater communication with China were game-changing. The system of caravan routes that connected China, Korea and Japan with Europe, the Middle East and India now grew more extensive and organized, evolving until it represented a phenomenal achievement of human civilization. It was to this period that the German scholar Ferdinand von Richthofen was referring when in 1877 he named it "the Great Silk Road". Along this road – or more accurately this multitude of tracks and trails – there was constant two-way movement of goods, scientific innovations, cultural values and religions. It was a conduit for merchants, missionaries and diplomats, a channel of important information – in fact it was the Internet of its day.

The huge distances and cultural diversity between the far reaches of Eurasia gave rise to exaggeration and fanciful tales by those who journeyed along the Silk Road – the reports of such notables as Zhang Qian, the seventh-century Chinese monk Xuan Zang and William of Rubruck during the later Mongol period, can seem fantastic at first glance. Their travel descriptions abounded with miracles and were

often coloured by fairy tale: legends of blood-sweating "heavenly" horses, of fearsome warrior women called Amazons, of amazing creatures called centaurs that were half human, half horse, all had their roots in fact. The horses of the Ferghana Valley were of superior stock and famed for their endurance, the women of the steppe tribes were known to don armour and fight alongside their men, and the remarkable horsemanship of the nomadic warriors caused some to imagine that beast and man were in fact one. Other tales of people with dog heads, of hairy Cyclops and "griffins guarding gold" in the remote northern mountains are harder to explain but all contributed to the mythical nature of the Silk Road in Central Asia.

The migration of the Wusun tribe from the east into the Ili Valley, Semirechye and the Tien Shan around Issyk-Kul coincided roughly with the "beginning" of the Silk Road as many perceive it. From the first century BCE through to the fall of the Han Dynasty in 220 CE the export of Chinese silk and other Chinese products to Western kingdoms blossomed. In turn, goods from Rome, India and Iran came back east. The list of exotic goods that passed through Central Asia, crossing desert, steppe and mountain pass, is almost endless. There was myrrh and frankincense oil, jasmine water and amber, cardamom and nutmeg, ginseng and python bile, carpets and canvas, pigments and minerals, diamonds and jasper, jade and corals, ivory and furs, silver and gold ingots, weapons such as bows and arrows, swords and spears, and many other items.

Animals of all shapes and sizes were transported: Ferghana and Arabian horses, camels and elephants; rhinoceroses and lions; cheetahs and gazelles; hawks and falcons; peacocks, parrots and ostriches were all brought for sale along the Silk Road. Cultivated plants such as grapes, peaches and melons were also transported and introduced far from their origins, along with spices and sugar, vegetables, fruits and herbs.

But material goods aside, there were other equally significant benefits for all the peoples living along the trading routes and at their terminuses. Cultural developments spread down the Silk Road with the merchandise; travelling with the cargo-laden camels of the great caravans were artists, musicians, early scientists and craftsmen. Although there is little evidence left from this early period of Silk Road history, later ruins from the eighth-ninth century site of Kostobe in the Talas Valley, which have been identified with Jamukat city, show a thick layer

of plaster sculpted into panels of grapevines, tulips and rosettes with intricate borders, similar in artistic style to the Baghdad caliphate and Egyptian culture of the time.

The art of music and dance was also shared along the Silk Road. Spectacular shows, a kind of medieval "show business", became popular in countries of both the East and West. Performances of musicians and dancers, wild animal acts, acrobats and magicians could be seen in cities and encampments from China to Rome. Translations were not needed for most of these acts; language barriers were not an issue, so the same performances were shown to Greek socialites, Kievan princes, nomadic lords, Turkic khagans and Chinese emperors.

It is well documented that the Chinese courts of the early centuries CE, and in particular of the Tang Dynasty during the later Turkic period, were besotted with the "Music of the West". Music, dance, even hairstyles and clothing from the Central Asian cities of Bukhara and Samarkand – and those of East Turkestan like Khotan and Kucha, which in turn had been influenced from India – merged with Chinese musical tradition. The idea of foreign exoticism became all the rage in Tang China's imperial court, and from there spread to wider society; people followed the nomadic fashion of clothing, wearing Turkic hats and long coats, while noble ladies preferred to ride horses than travel in carriages.

At a Tang Dynasty show in Xian, China, a musician performs dressed in period costume. China was heavily influenced by Central Asian cultures from the early years of the Silk Road, incorporating music, dance, hairstyles and clothing trends from the kingdoms of the Western Regions

## RELIGIONS ALONG THE SILK ROAD

One of the Silk Road's most important contributions to world history is its role in the dissemination of religious ideas across Eurasia. Buddhism came from India, Nestorian Christianity and later Islam came from the Middle East, and eastern Persia was the

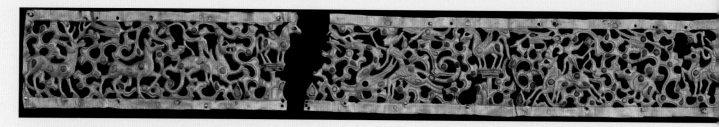

birthplace of Zoroastrianism and Manichaeism. Through the movement of their adherents, over the centuries all these faiths came to the towns, countries and regions of the Silk Road, taking root in the thriving cities of Transoxiana and the nascent urban centres of the middle and lower Syr Darya, or influencing the tribal confederations that occupied Kazakhstan and who practised polytheistic and shamanistic beliefs.

Archaeological discoveries provide evidence of the expansion of ancient beliefs, a prime example being the Kargaly diadem (a golden bejewelled headband) found near Almaty. Alexander Bernshtam dated the diadem to the Wusun of the first-second centuries CE and interpreted its figures as winged horses on mountain peaks, winged females riding dragons, a panther, wild goat and sheep, a bear and deer with geese or swans flying over them – all surrounded by floral ornamentation. He associated the symbols on the diadem with shamanism and noted a Chinese influence.

However, Elena Kuzmina dates the diadem from the second century BCE to first century CE and thinks that the diadem originates from Saka art (like that of Issyk, Tillya Tepe and Khokhlach). She considers the diadem to be a model of the world, with the birds above it being mediators between the three worlds: sky, earth and water. The winged horse is the sun, while the deer is a symbol of the renewal of spring. The diadem is therefore related to the cult of Dionysus, the god of dying and revival of nature, and Nowruz, the Persian New Year.

Whatever its provenance and symbology, the diadem shows the importance and huge influence that new beliefs had on the inhabitants of Central Asia. Theologians and missionaries, in particular Sogdians, Parthians and Kangju, played an important role as they ranged up and down the Silk Road, proselytizing their dogmas. Zoroastrianism, which originated in the seventh-sixth centuries BCE in ancient Iran, made early inroads into Central Asia – there is evidence that elements of the faith took hold in the Saka and Massagetae tribes of southern Kazakhstan.

The Zoroastrianism that spread through the later Kangju and Wusun territories courtesy of the Sogdians was a variant form of the canonical faith; it was closely interwoven with local shamanistic beliefs, particularly with the cult of fire, ancestor worship and animism as related to sheep, horses and camels. Archaeological discoveries of burial sites containing ossuaries of human bones, and corpses laid in above-ground sepulchres, indicate that these were worshippers of Zoroastrianism.

In the Otrar oasis a palace complex was excavated at the site of Kuiryktobe citadel that shed new light on the level of religious artistry to be found in this region during the early years of the first millennium CE. In the centre of the complex a 157.5-square-metre main hall was uncovered, damaged by fire but with part of its ceiling fresco preserved. This showed a divine couple, the male sporting a classical jagged crown, holding a rod with three curved spears at the end and seated on a zoomorphic throne in the form of two winged camels, the female wearing a ribbon with a bow around her forehead and seated on two argali sheep with curving horns. Also displayed is a siege of a fortified city, two warriors shown with bent bows standing on the city wall, which has castellated towers. In front stands the four-armed god Nana-Anahita wearing a winged crown, with both hands raised holding the sun in one hand and the moon in the other.

Collections of carved wood from Kuiryktobe can tell us much about the religious views of those who lived in the cities along the Syr Darya, where Sogdian influence was widespread. Initially bringing Buddhism, the Sogdians were also responsible for introducing Manichaeism, which originated in Iran in the third century CE and combined elements of Christianity and Zoroastrianism. Manichaeism quickly gained in popularity, establishing footholds from the Mediterranean through to China. The ruins of Manichaean monasteries can still be found in Semirechye, and an ancient Uighur manuscript using Manichaean script called *The Sacred Book of Two Foundations*, found in Xinjiang's Turpan oasis, states that it was written in the city of Argu-Talas "to awake [faith] in the country of ten arrows" – a reference to the city of Taraz. During excavation of a site in Taraz, a bronze medallion was discovered displaying the image of a female with the crescent moon, a symbol of the Manichaean astral deity.

Nestorian Christianity came from the eastern Roman Empire (Syria) in the fifth century CE, brought by followers of the priest Nestorius, whose doctrine had been condemned as heresy at the Council of Ephesus in 431. Cruel persecution of the Nestorians forced them to escape to Persia, from where they looked to the East to find converts and new commercial markets. Nestorianism eventually became widespread throughout the cities of south Kazakhstan and Semirechye, and by the seventh-eighth centuries had reached Tang China.

Between the second century BCE and the sixth century CE these waves of new religious beliefs swept through Central Asia, finding favour among the citizens of the burgeoning Silk Road cities in Transoxiana, the Syr Darya Valley, Semirechye, the Tien Shan foothills and on into the Tarim Basin and its city-states around the edge of the Taklamakan Desert. While without doubt this was still a violent time, with frequent wars and conflicts between kingdoms, it was also a period of immense gain – materially, spiritually and culturally – for the many diverse peoples to be found along the Silk Road in its heyday.

*Professor Karl M. Baipakov is Director of the Institute of Archaeology of the Academy of Sciences of Kazakhstan, having previously been Director of the A. Kh. Margulan Institute of Archaeology from 1991 until 2010. A graduate of Leningrad State University's Department of Archaeology, he is an associate member of the German Archaeological Institute, an international expert of UNESCO, and a specialist in the ancient and medieval urbanization of Kazakhstan and Central Asia. He is the author of several monographs and many scientific articles.*

Above: A Nestorian mortar from the *tortkul* (square fortress) of Balykchi showing a dove and cross. Below left: A Buddha figurine from the Talgar region

# TURKIC EXPANSION: KHAGANATES AND THE GREAT STEPPE CITIES

The period known as the "Turkic expansion" lasted from the sixth century CE through to the 12th century, and represents a seminal change in Central Asian history, as Turkic-speaking tribes took control in the region and spread farther west, leaving a lasting legacy of diverse ethnic groups connected through a common language root.

It began in 551 CE when, according to the Chinese chronicles *History of the Northern Dynasties* and *Zizhi Tongjian*, a leader of the Turkic Ashina (wolf) clan named Bumin thwarted a potential revolt by the Uighur and Tiele tribes against the ruling Rouran Khaganate in the region of central Mongolia. Expecting to be rewarded with a Rouran princess, he was infuriated by the Rouran Anagui Khagan's reply, which rejected his claim and called him a "blacksmith slave". (This quote cannot be taken literally, and most likely referred to the Turkic tribes' major role in iron mining and metallurgy, and the fact that at that time they were vassals to the Rouran.)

Bumin retaliated by gathering the Turkic tribes, making an alliance with the Western Wei Dynasty of China, and defeating Anagui to end the rule of the Rouran. Bumin named himself Khagan of a new Turkic state (the Kok Turks), and set about building a steppe empire that would eclipse any that had come before. (You will see the term "Khagan" also spelt as "Kaghan" and "Qaghan"in historical texts; first used by the Rouran for their leaders, the "kh" or "q" is pronounced softly from the back of the throat, while the central "g" or "gh" is almost silent – thus the pronunciation is virtually the same as the word "khan", which succeeded it and was used by the Mongols.)

Although Bumin died within a matter of months of his victory, his sons and his brother Istemi Khagan, the former in the empire's central and eastern sections, the latter in its western reaches, took over the mandate and quickly conquered the

## SYMBIOSIS BETWEEN CITY AND STEPPE

Throughout the seventh and eighth century the nomadic Turkic tribes of the western Turkic Khaganate were the overlords of the Central Asian section of the Silk Road trade routes. From their capital Suyab, they maintained generally good relations with the Sogdian merchants and inhabitants of the many cities and trading centres along the ancient trade routes between East and West, and exchanged diplomatic missions with the Tang Dynasty in China and the Byzantine court by the Mediterranean. As the previous chapter explained, contrary to popular belief the steppe regions of southern Kazakhstan during the first millennium CE were not empty lands populated only by constantly moving tribes of nomadic barbarians – rather they were filled with towns, fortresses and cities thriving on inter-regional trade, and agricultural settlements that provided for their needs as well as those of the nomadic Turks who interacted with them to a high degree.

Rouran territory, then began to expand their sphere of control. Istemi Khagan in particular encouraged expansion, driving west across the steppes all the way to Crimea and eastern Europe in 576 CE.

Conventional history books tell of a civil war breaking out around 582 after the death of the fourth ruler, Tatpar Khagan, when various competing leaders struggled for power and in the process caused the Turkic Khaganate to split into two: the "Eastern Turkic Khaganate" and "Western Turkic Khaganate". The historical sources for this come from the Sui and Tang dynasties, who purportedly played the factions off against each other for strategic advantage, but as Napil Bazylkhan states in the following essay, nothing regarding this supposed rift has been found in any ancient Turkic sources, so it is possible that the Chinese expediently made more of it than the reality, and rather than becoming two distinct states, the two "wings" of the Turkic Khaganate remained closely tied, though acting autonomously due to the great distances between their respective power centres.

A symbiotic relationship developed, the Sogdians located in the cities and overseeing the trade, the nomadic Turks exacting tribute but ensuring peace and security in the region. Ancient Silk Road cities such as Farab (Otrar), Ispidzhab (Sayram), Sauran, Yangikent and Taraz all benefited, growing rich on the caravans loaded with goods that passed through the territory of southern Kazakhstan, and dozens of new urban centres developed at this time as well. However, the various tribes of the Turkic confederation became embroiled in internecine struggle,

Top left: Three anthropomorphic stone figures, or *balbals*, stand near funerary barrows in the Merke region of the Tien Shan. Above: Although this painting was made by Alexei Vladimirovich Issupoff in the early 20th century, the scene of a wealthy Kazakh in a Samarkand market illustrates the important link between the nomads and city dwellers, which was highly productive during the Turkic era

and the increasingly powerful Tang Dynasty now invaded and conquered the Turks' vassal states in the Tarim Basin, its army commanded by General Su Dingfang.

The western Turkic Khaganate crumbled before the Tang invaders and was replaced at the end of the seventh century by the Turgesh, a branch of the Dulu tribe who themselves had been part of the *Onoq* (Ten Arrows) of the western Turks, a system of division whereby each major tribe was known as an *oquz* ("arrow"). The Turgesh created their own brief Khaganate, allying with the Tang against the new "Second Turkic Khaganate" arising in Mongolia, and for a brief time wresting parts of Transoxiana from the Arab caliphate. They did not last long, however and disappear from Chinese and Arab annals in 766, crushed by a new Turkic tribal force led by the Karluks.

The Karluks came from the region of the upper Irtysh and Tarbagatai Mountains, and had been a distinct ethnic group of the Kok Turk empire, then a vassal tribe of Tang China until a fateful event in 751. This was the Battle of Talas, which pitted the forces of the advancing Arab Abbasid Caliphate against those of the Tang Dynasty near the Talas River. The majority of the Chinese forces were Karluk mercenaries, and when during the battle they suddenly switched sides and attacked the Chinese troops, the Arab army was able to inflict a major defeat on the Chinese, who retreated and then were called back to the Tang capital Chang'an to help with the An Lushan rebellion.

This was a momentous event, because it signalled the end of Chinese influence in western Central Asia, and allowed Arabic influence, in particular Islam, to spread throughout the Turkic tribes (although this was a slow process). The Karluks now established their own Khanate, headed by a ruler with the title Yabghu; their capital was also in Suyab, and they allied themselves with the new Uighur Khaganate that had arisen in central Mongolia, between them controlling all the trade routes previously held by the Turkic Khaganate and extending the power and wealth of cities like Farab and Taraz.

During the ninth century the Karluks' neighbours in the central steppes north of the Syr Darya and across to the Caspian Sea were the Turkic Pechenegs and Oghuz tribes, and north of the Irtysh into Siberia another confederation known as the Kimaks (Kimeks) created their own khanate from the eighth to 11th centuries (the Kipchaks were members of this union). The Ural-Volga region was under the control of the Khazars, whose khanate stretched across the Pontic Steppe and thrived on the commerce between Central Asia and northern Europe.

## RELIGIOUS DISSEMINATION ALONG THE TRADE ROUTES

An important side note to any historical discussion of Central Asia during the first millennium CE is the prevalence and diversity of religions that took hold and prospered among its human populations. The Turkic nomads traditionally worshipped the sky god Tengri, and the shamanistic beliefs of Tengrism comprised the state religion of the Turkic Khaganate (the following essay explains this in more detail). However, the Turkic tribes were surprisingly open to and tolerant of different religions within the territory that they ruled.

Since the latter half of the previous millennium Zoroastrianism had spread into Central Asia from Persia, and during the Turkic period many cults associated with it continued to prevail in the region's cities – fireplace-altars have been discovered embedded in the floor of houses in the Otrar ruins, dating to as late as the 12th century.

Buddhism too had a lasting effect. The great seventh-century Chinese traveller and Buddhist monk Xuan Zang, during his "Journey to the West" and sojourn with the

Above: The ruined city walls of Sauran, which was a major trading city during the Turkic period, boasting underground water canals. Opposite top: A very detailed *balbal* in the Zhaysan memorial complex within the Chu River Valley. Opposite bottom and inset: Two balbals stand guard in front of burial sites in the Kumai complex of central Kazakhstan. The figure on the right (and inset) has a different shape with an enlarged head, thought to symbolize a shaman

Khagan of the western Turkic Khaganate, wrote that Buddhism had had a strong influence on the Turks, who had a favourable attitude to the religion. In the early seventh century some Turkic rulers may have been patrons of Buddhism or even converted – the ruins of many temples, monasteries and chapels have been discovered in Zhetisu and the Chu Valley, including at Ak-Beshim, Navaket, Novopokrovsky and Novopavlovsky. Numerous discoveries of ancient Buddhist items include Indian-made bronze and silver statuettes of Buddha and bodhisattvas encrusted with gems, bronze plaques, stelae with scenes of Buddhist temples and monasteries, and even an ivory Buddha figure excavated from the ruins of the old medieval city of Talkhiz (Talhiza) near modern-day Talgar.

Nestorian Christianity also made inroads among the Turks. It is said that a Karluk Yabghu converted to Christianity in the eighth century; Christian churches were opened in both Taraz and Merke, and by the 12th century both Navaket and Kashgar had been established as archdiocese. Excavations of necropolises in Navaket and Jamukat have unearthed Christian burials containing silver and bronze crosses, and a ceramic mug found in Taraz and dating to the 6th-8th centuries had an inscription in Syrian saying "Peter and Gabriel". Also noteworthy are two 9th-10th century silver dishes engraved with scenes from early Christian iconography, created by Nestorian master craftsmen and known as the Anikovskoye and Grigorovskoye.

But when Islam arrived with the Arabs, it gradually replaced Zoroastrianism, Buddhism, Nestorian Christianity and other local cults across Central Asia. This was a slow process, initiated by Muslim merchants and becoming established in many cities along the Silk Road during the rule of the Karluks. Conversion by "fire and sword" was not seen until the late ninth and early 10th century – in 893 Ismail ibn-Akhmad captured Taraz and "turned the main church of this city into the mosque". Islam was declared the state religion by the Karakhanids in 960, although mass conversion only occurred in cities such as Balasagun, whose 11th-century Burana Minaret still stands today. The new religion took time to spread among the nomadic tribes, but eventually became the dominant belief system (albeit with elements of Tengri's animistic and shamanistic ideas woven in).

## THE KARAKHANIDS

Southern Central Asia was now ruled by the Persian Samanid Empire (819-999), and conflict between them and the Turkic confederations was fierce. In 840 the Karluks joined forces with Chigils, Yagmas and a number of other Turkic tribes (of Turgesh and other heritage) to form the Karakhanid Khanate, which incorporated Zhetisu (Semirechye), the western Tien Shan (including modern Kyrgyzstan) and Kashgaria (western Xinjiang). Its capital was Balasagun and it lasted for almost 400 years until just before the arrival of the Mongols.

The 10th-12th centuries saw a blossoming of Turkic culture under the Karakhanids, and was a golden age for the many agricultural oases and city-states that lined the foothills of the Tien Shan and sat alongside major rivers such as the Chu, Talas, Syr Darya and Amu Darya. The city of Taraz was one of the largest and most important, boasting an underground water system of terracotta pipes, sewage collection and well-paved streets.

One of the very few existing pieces of architecture from that period is the Aisha Bibi Mausoleum, and the story that surrounds it is a timeless tale of tragic love. In 1050 the ruler of Taraz, Karakhan, was on a political mission to Samarkand. Amongst the crowd that had gathered to watch him and his warriors pass by, he noticed a young maiden of extraordinary beauty and fell instantly in love. She was the daughter of Samarkand's ruler, but Karakhan began

Left: The Burana Minaret – near the ruins of Balasagun in modern-day Kyrgyzstan – is all that remains intact of the architecture of the Karakhanids' capital city. Above: A statue of Al-Farabi, a renowned philosopher-scientist named after his hometown Farab, which later became known as Otrar

arranging secret meetings with her until he was called back to Taraz to defend it against invaders from the east. Deciding to ask for her hand in marriage he requested an audience with her father, but was rebuked and insulted as an unworthy match.

Karakhan and Aisha met before he departed and sealed a secret bond, but when, after not hearing from him for some time Aisha told her father and asked for his blessing, he was furious and cursed her, saying he would never give consent to the union. Aisha dressed in men's clothing and fled Samarkand with her faithful nurse on their fastest horses, intent on being with her love. When they finally came within sight of Taraz, they stopped by the River Tsaryk so Aisha could bathe and put on her wedding gown. As she reached for her *saukele* headdress and put it on her head, a venomous snake that had found its way inside shot out and bit her on the cheek.

Aisha collapsed and urged her nurse to ride as fast as possible to the city and tell Karakhan that she had come. The nurse did her best, but on returning with Karakhan, his

guards and a hastily mobilized clergyman, there was hardly any life left in the poor girl. Understanding that he could not save his beloved, Karakhan told the clergyman to marry them on the spot, and with the last of her strength Aisha Bibi – the wedded Aisha – nodded to seal the marriage. In despair Karakhan swore never to marry again nor love another, and he kept his vow, living to 100 years old and ruling in a wise and just manner.

The Karakhanid Khanate, like other nomadic Turkic states, split its realm into appanages or provinces, each based around an urban centre. Balasagun was one, the others being Kashgar, Uzgen in Fergana, and Samarkand. While retaining Turkic laws and cultural traditions, the

Karakhanids slowly assimilated elements of Persian and Arabic culture, and in the mid-10th century many of them converted to Islam.

The 11th century saw internal conflict divide the khanate, and the arrival of the Seljuk Turks marked the beginning of the end for the Karakhanids as rulers. They remained as vassals of the Seljuks until the 12th century, when the Buddhist Karakitai (Kara-Khitan) moved into Karakhanid territory, fleeing from the destruction of the Liao Dynasty in northern China. The Karakitai defeated the Seljuks – thereby allowing the Khorezmids (Khwarezmids) to expand and increase their power – and made their headquarters at Balasagun, acting as overlords of the Karakhanids.

Meanwhile, since the beginning of the 10th century the Kipchak tribe had become the dominant force in the central and northern steppes, and together with the Cumans, who are thought to have been related to the Pechenegs and with whom the Kipchaks formed a united confederation, they created a vast khanate stretching from the Irtysh River to the Hungarian steppe, interacting – sometimes peacefully, sometimes aggressively – with all their many neighbouring states throughout the 11th and 12th centuries.

As the 12th century came to a close, the territory of Kazakhstan was home to a plethora of tribes, tribal unions and warring states, many in a state of flux. The Kipchaks resided in the north and west, the Kangly (Kangar) tribe occupied the central steppe between the Aral Sea and Irtysh River, the Naimans now lived in the Altai and northern Zhetisu (having been pushed west by Mongol tribes), and the Karluks, once dominant in the south and east, had moved west. The Karakitai, with their Karakhanid and Khorezm vassals, ruled in the south, but their time was soon to run out, first at the hands of the rebel Naiman chief Kuchlug, then as one of myriad victims of the all-conquering Mongol ruler Genghis Khan.

*Above: The carefully restored Aisha Bibi Mausoleum is located a short distance west of Taraz – behind it is another tomb dedicated to her faithful nurse Babadzha Khatun*

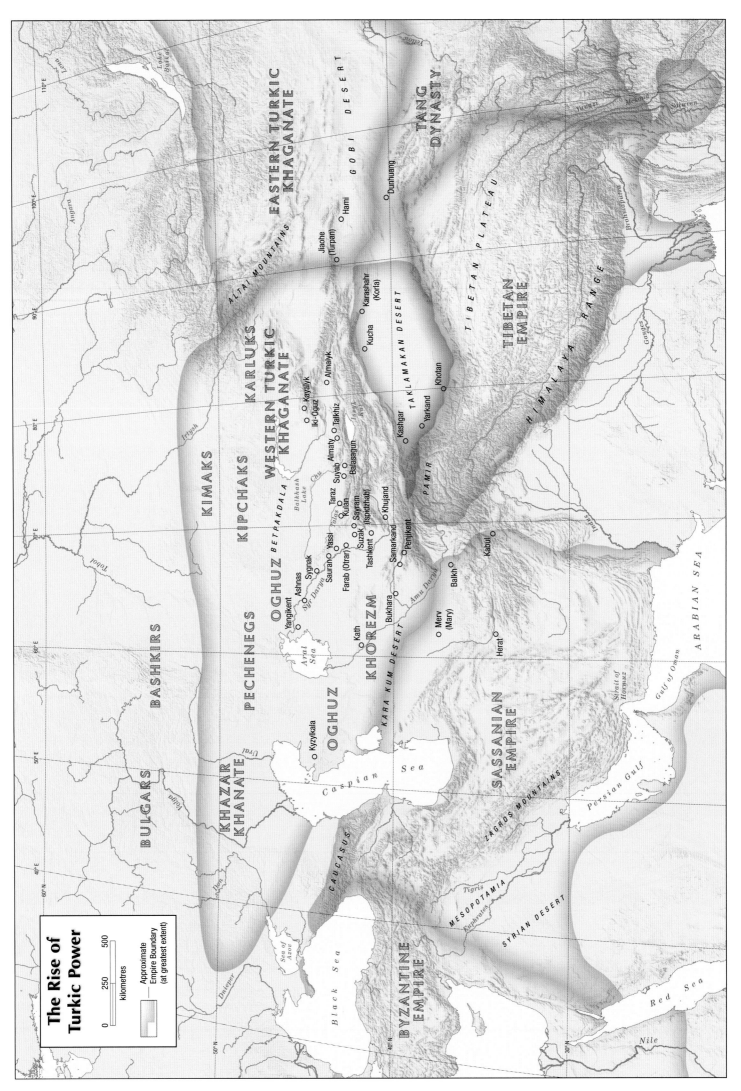

## The Rise of Turkic Power

0  250  500
kilometres

Approximate
Empire Boundary
(at greatest extent)

BULGARS

BASHKIRS

KHAZAR
KHANATE

PECHENEGS

KIMAKS

KIPCHAKS

OGHUZ

KARLUKS

WESTERN TURKIC
KHAGANATE

EASTERN TURKIC
KHAGANATE

TANG
DYNASTY

BETPAKDALA

OGHUZ

KHOREZM

Kyzylkala

Yangikent

Ashnas
Sygnak
Saurano
Farab (Otrar)
Suzak
Yassi
Kath
Bukhara

Taraz
Kulan
Sayram
Khujand
Tashkent
Samarkand
Penjikent

Suyab
Balasagun
Almaty
Talkhiz
Kayalyk
Iki-Oguz

Merv
(Mary)
Herat

Balkh
Kabul

Kashgar
Yarkand
Khotan

Kucha

Karashahr
(Korla)

Almalyk

Jiaohe
(Turpan)

Hami

Dunhuang

PAMIR

KARA KUM DESERT

TAKLAMAKAN DESERT

GOBI  DESERT

ALTAI MOUNTAINS

TIBETAN PLATEAU

TIBETAN
EMPIRE

HIMALAYA RANGE

SASSANIAN
EMPIRE

ZAGROS MOUNTAINS

BYZANTINE
EMPIRE

CAUCASUS

MESOPOTAMIA

SYRIAN DESERT

Aral
Sea

Caspian      Sea

Balkhash
Lake

Issyk
Kul

Lake Baikal

Black  Sea

Sea of
Azov

Persian Gulf

Gulf of Oman

Strait of
Hormuz

ARABIAN
SEA

Red  Sea

Nile

Tigris
Euphrates

Don

Volga

Ural

Tobol

Irtysh

Syr Darya

Amu Darya

Chu

Talas

Indus

Ganges

Brahmaputra

Yangzi
Mekong
Salween

Yellow

Ura

Dnieper

Angara

60° N

50° N

40° N

30° N

40° E

50° E

60° E

70° E

80° E

90° E

100° E

110° E

# The Turkic Khaganate: A brief history and unique cultural features

By *Napil Bazylkhan*

The ancient Turkic steppe civilization of Central Asia plays a special part in the history of Kazakhstan and the Kazakh people, but its significance ranges much farther afield than that. The formation of many other modern Turkic-speaking nations and ethnic groups (including Azerbaijan, Kyrgyzstan, Uzbekistan, Turkmenistan and Turkey, as well as the Tatars, Uighurs, Nogais, Bashkirs, Gagauz, Karaites, Karakalpaks, Karachay-Balkars, Kumyks, Tuvans, Khakas, Chuvashes, Chulyms, Shors and Yakuts) and both the origin of their languages and their ethno-genesis, are closely connected with the Turkic nomads whose ethnic roots began as far back as the fifth century BCE and who created one of Eurasia's greatest steppe empires.

The vast empire of the Xiongnu/Huns that lasted from the third century BCE to the fourth century CE united all the nomads and semi-nomads of Central Asia under its rule at various times, and was comprised of 24 significant ethnic tribes. The Xiongnu actively waged war on the Han Dynasty for centuries, at the same time fighting the Yuezhi, Wusun and Kangju for control over Central Asian trade routes. After the collapse of the Xiongnu Empire some of its northwestern tribes migrated to Europe and established the Hunnic Empire that was most famous under the rule of Attila.

From that time on, ethno-political associations and tribal unions of Turkic-speaking peoples slowly prevailed in central Eurasia, while tribes speaking Mongolian and Tungusic languages took control in northeastern Asia. The military, political and administrative structure of the nomadic Xiongnu federation established a base from which the state formations of the Turkic steppe nomads developed, their culture and economy being essentially the same.

The epicentre of the first Turkic Khaganate (Empire), however, was in the central region of modern-day Mongolia, located in the valleys of the Orhon, Tuul and Selenge rivers and in the Khangai (Hangai) mountain range. The Turks called their empire *Türük Eli* or "State of the Turks", but as well as uniting all the Turkic ethnic groups under its flag as Kok Turks (or Gokturks), it also encompassed some Mongolian and Tungusic speaking tribes.

As such, the Turkic Khaganate (and its Turgesh and Karakhanid successors) became a major superpower in Central Asia that lasted until the 12th century. At its greatest extent, it stretched as far as the Korean Peninsula in the east,

A panel from the sixth century sarcophagus of a Sogdian official (*sartbau* or *sabao*) named An Jia – who served the Chinese Northern Zhou Dynasty – shows the Sogdian sharing food and wine with a Turkic *khagan* inside a yurt, surrounded by various Turks, Sogdians and pack animals

to the "Iron Gate" (Black Sea) in the west, and was bordered in the north by the Siberian taiga forests and in the south by the Tibetan Plateau. It was the most powerful steppe empire of the period.

The politonym Türük Eli derives from *törü* + k, meaning "people having the law", and this is the etymological root of the word "Turk" (*törü* specifically means "powerful" or "legal"). It came to serve as a common name for all Turkic-speaking ethno-political unions (including the Oghuz, Uch Oguz, Baiyrku, Turgesh, Basmyly, Karluk, Uch Karluk, Uch Khurykhan, On-Okh, Kyrgyz, On-Uighurs and Uighurs) as referred to in ancient Turkic written monuments. These monuments also contain written references to foreign states with whom the Turks had political and economic ties, such as Bokli Chollig (Korea), Tabgach (China), Tibet, Apar (the Avars), Purum (Rome) Otuz Tatar, Khitan (Kidan), Tatab, Sogdak, Tajik, Bukarak and others.

## THE RISE OF TURKIC POWER

The Turkic Khaganate was established in 551 by Bumin Khagan (also spelt Qaghan or Kaghan), who subdued many other Turkic-speaking tribes and conquered the ruling Rouran (Juan-Juan) Khaganate, a confederation of mainly Mongolian and Tungus-speaking tribes. Bumin Khagan made his headquarters in the Orhon River valley at Otüken, but he died under a year later and was succeeded by his brother, Istemi Khagan (Estemi Qaghan, ruled 552-575). Istemi ruled the western wing of the empire and

Above: This *balbal* at the Zhaysan site in the Chu Valley is particularly lifelike – a representation of the buried man, you can clearly see the dagger hanging from his belt, a cup held in his right hand, and an impressive moustache.
Left: Remarkably similar balbals in the Kumai region, around 1,000km to the north, indicate the cultural continuity of the Turkic nomads during the second half of the first millennium CE

The etymology of nomadic Turkic groups from this era is fascinating but has not yet been fully explored. For example, the words *oquz* or *oghuz* come from *oq* ("arrow") + *uz* (a plural form) and were used with semantic value to mean a "tribe". In Turkic society many tribes' names related to "numbers", such as the Toguz, Sekiz, Uch, Kyryk-Uz, Kyrkyz, On-Okh, On Uighur and Otuz Tatar. Chinese sources speak of the *"Tele"* (or *Tiele*, meaning wainwrights or high carts), *"Tujiue"* and *"Ashina"* clans (*Ashide* as plural), who were all called Turks. However, the Mongolian-speaking tribes' name for the Ashina was *"chino"* (wolf) – the legend about a female wolf who nursed a boy and produced half-wolf, half-human offspring arose during the Xiongnu period and remained in Turkic-Mongolian folklore, and the Ashina claimed descent from them.

within a short period of time achieved military and political power there, subduing much of Central Asia and in the process destroying the Hephthalite state and conquering Sogdiana. He then rode northwest with his army, defeating the Alans of the northern Caucasus and the Utigurs in Bosporus (Kerch) on the Crimean Peninsula.

Istemi Khagan made a military alliance with the Persian Sassanids in 561-563 in his war against the Hephthalites, who had been allies of the Rouran, but later in 567-569 he then formed an alliance with Byzantium against the Sassanids. This astute military and political campaigning allowed the Turks to gain control of the silk trade across a broad swathe of Eurasia. They became the principal players in a major portion of the Silk Road between China and the Mediterranean states, exacting huge trade

revenues for both themselves as rulers and the Sogdian merchants who administered the trade itself.

After Bumin Khagan's death, his son Kara Khagan (Qara Qaghan, ruled 551-552) headed the central section of the empire for only a year, and he was followed by Mukan Khagan (Muqan Qaghan, ruled 553-572). Under Mukan's rule the Turks crushed the Rouran completely, then subdued the Khitan and Kyrgyz tribes as well as the northern Chinese states, all of whom became their vassals. The Turkic Khaganate consolidated its strength during the reign of Tatpar Khagan (Tatbar Qaghan, ruled 572-582), and although some researchers believe that Türük Eli split into eastern and western parts between 582 and 603, there is no reference to this in any ancient Turkic sources. In fact they were simply the western and central/eastern units of a single powerful empire.

From their central base in Mongolia, the Turkic rulers Shibi Khagan (609-619) and El Khagan (620-630) continued to wage war on their southern border, which was the main arena in the war with the Chinese Sui Dynasty (581-618) and the Tang Dynasty (618-907) that followed. The west wing of the empire became very powerful and controlled Silk Road trade during the reign of Sheguy Khagan (Seku Qaghan, ruled 611-618) and Tong-yabgu Khagan (Tun yabghu Qaghan, ruled 618-630). They expanded their western border, creating many vassal states, but the west wing lost power in 630-634 because of feuding between its two main tribal unions, the Dulu (Dulo) and Nushibi.

The Turgesh state, headed by Uch Elig Khagan, was established in the empire's western wing at the end of the seventh century. The Turgesh Khaganate developed fast because of its location on the Silk Road, and during the eighth century trade, crafts and urban culture were developed at a rapid pace in the region of the Tien Shan

mountains and Syr Darya river basin. Meanwhile, Turkic-speaking tribes, including some major tribes that had been under Tang Chinese control for a few decades, were unified once again in 679-689 in the central part of the empire under the rule of Kutlug Khagan (Elteriš Qaghan).

During the reign of Kapagan Khagan (Qapaghan Qaghan, ruled 691-716) the central part of the empire achieved the peak of its military and political power. Kapagan subdued the western Turgesh state, which at the time was ruled by Suluk Khagan. A famous adviser named Tonyukuk who served three Khagans – Kutlug and his sons Bilge (Türük Bilge Qaghan) and Kultegin – participated in that western campaign. Bilge became Khagan in 716 and ruled until 734 thanks to the courageous deeds of his younger brother Kultegin. As a result the Turkic Khaganate was revived as a powerful steppe empire.

But internal war once again weakened the Turkic Khaganate and in 744 a "Uighur" confederation of Toguz Oguz, Uighur, Basmyly and Karluk tribes appeared in central Mongolia, signalling the end of Kok Turk rule in the east. However, the Uighur Khaganate continued the military and political traditions of the Turkic Khaganate, especially during the reign of El Etmish Bilge Khagan (ruled 747-759), when they actively waged war against the Tang Dynasty.

Top left and right: The photo shows a Turkic era petroglyph of mounted and armoured warriors with lances (situated in Hovd province, Mongolia); the drawing depicts a similar petroglyph found in the Koshkor region of Kyrgyzstan. Below: "A Desert Fort", by Aleksandr Yakovlev, gives a good idea of how formidable the walled fortifications were when built on raised ground in the desert steppes of the Aral Sea region

Left: The golden crown of Bilge Khagan (ruled 716-734), discovered at his memorial complex in Mongolia's Arkhangai province near the Orhon River. Below x2: Both sides of a Karakhanid coin from the 10th century. Bottom: A Sogdian coin of Chinese style but minted in the Zhetisu region in the eighth century

Back in the western Turkic Khaganate significant ethno-political changes were taking place. The Karluk tribe (of the Black Irtysh River and Tarbagatai Mountains region) played an important role in political processes after the collapse of the Turgesh Khaganate. In league with an Arab army of the Abbasid Caliphate they crushed the Tang army in the Talas Valley in 751, finally ending Chinese political and military influence in the western wing of the Turkic Khaganate.

But before long more invasions occurred; in 756 the Uighur Khaganate conquered the Turkic tribes of East Turkestan (the Tarim Basin) and Zhetisu (Semirechye). The Karluks then captured Taraz and Suyab (the old western Turkic Khaganate capital) in 766, but lost Turfan (Turpan in modern Xinjiang) to the Uighurs in 803.

A new tribal power now came on the scene – the Kyrgyz, whose homeland was the Yenisei River region in Siberia. In 840 the Kyrgyz swept south into the Orhon Valley and conquered Orda Balyk, the capital of the Uighur Khaganate, which had been one of the Silk Road's most important trade centres. Some of the defeated tribes fled south to Beshbalik (Beiting) and farther into the Tarim Basin to city-states such as Kucha (Kuche).

Some may also have headed west to the Karluks, who were closely related to the Uighurs and occupied Semirechye and the northern Tien Shan. A new state emerged here in 840 known as the Karakhanid Khanate, a confederation headed by the Chigil and Yagma tribes with its centre in Kashgar and Balasagun (in modern-day Kyrgyzstan). The Karakhanids waged many cruel wars against the Persian Samanids for power in southern Central Asia, and in the 10th century converted to Islam.

In the central and northern steppes another tribal group had come to dominance during the mid-eighth century. These were the Kimaks, who were based on the Irtysh River and known by the Chinese as Chuban or "weak Huns". Originally part of the western wing of the Turkic Khaganate, they emerged as a dominant influence in the central steppe and north into Siberia. The Kimak Khaganate was succeeded by the Kipchaks, who spread across the northern Central Asian steppe at the start of the 10th century to encompass the states of the Bulgar and Khazar tribes in Eastern Europe by the 11th century. This huge region was called *Dasht-i Kipchak* by the Persians.

## SOCIAL STRUCTURE AMONG THE TURKS

The Turkic Khaganate marked a period of prosperity in Central Asia. According to the writing on one monument of the time, "*Beks* [beys or tribal leaders] did not allow their sons to be taken into slavery, nor beautiful ladies to become slaves, the *dastarkhan* was always full, there was no lack of clothing, poor people became rich, and from small numbers the people became numerous".

Tribute and taxes were received regularly from China, Byzantium and Sassanid Persia (coins were minted and currency exchanged between states). Political administration was carried out by the Khagan, Yabghu and Shad. The Khagan was the unifier of the Turkic state, the supreme ruler. A Khagan was considered to be an ambassador of the "Eternal Blue Sky (Tengri)", the wielder of its power. This status was inherited; the sons of a Khagan were called *tegin*, his wife was called *qatun* (katun) and his daughters *qïz* (kyz). The Khagan's heavenly mandate was to subdue all other tribal rulers, control alliances, and prove his incomparable power. When a tegin was elected to be Khagan, it took place at a great *kurultai* (a gathering of tribal nobility).

The ancient Turkic world-view followed a triadic system of "Tengri (Heaven), Humans and Earth", and this was

The Khagan, as befitted his supreme power and connection to Tengri, was given an exclusive "heavenly" name, wore a golden crown sewn onto five-sided headwear (*borik*), and sat on a golden throne holding a golden state seal bearing ancient Turkic inscriptions. His armour was encrusted with gold and silver, from his war helmet and iron coat of mail to his sword, bow and arrows, and his yurt was richly adorned with golden items. Ambassadors representing the Khagan –known as *korug* – wore special gold, silver and bronze insignia on their chests sporting ancient Turkic inscriptions.

Mythical birds like the phoenix and birds of prey such as golden eagles and falcons were considered to be emissaries of Tengri, and as such they were frequently used to decorate officials' headgear. The rank of a commander could be told from the images of birds of prey on his helmet, and feathers adorned both hats and war helmets, as well as children's dresses and musical instruments.

manifest in its military and political structure. Administrative division was comprised of *tarduš* (tardush), *ic* (ich) and *töles* (toles), while military and political titles also fit into this concept, with nine titles in descending order split into three groups reflecting "state -military-tribal" status: *qaghan/tegin*, *yabghu* (yabgu) and *šad* (shad) – *apït* (apyt), *tarqan* (tarkhan) and *buyruq* (buyuruk) – *cur* (chur), tudun and *tutuq* (tutuk). This principle of an inter-related triad extended beyond the elite level of the Khagan and his government to infuse all aspects of life among the Turks.

A threefold division comprised the military structure of Khaganate armies, which were composed of central, eastern and western wings. Heavily armed warriors with long spears made up units of 10,000 known as *Tumens*, headed by beks, each split into thousands, then hundreds and tens. The Khagan took control of the central wing with his tegins, while generals holding the rank of shad or tardush ran the east and west wings. This unified system was strictly followed and very efficient, ensuring unwavering military discipline from Turkic nobility and common people (known as "*turk kara budun*") alike.

This rigid political and military administration was what guaranteed the peace and integrity of Turkic lands. It protected the people and their cities and settlements from invasion by external forces, as well as internal conflict. Everyone was subordinate to the military-political centre of the Turkic Khaganate, and those who opposed it or agitated for autonomy were quickly subjugated by force. Thus was the classic concept of nomadic steppe civilization engendered by the ancient Turks.

## UNIQUE ETHNOCULTURAL FEATURES

The Kok Turks' economy was based on traditional extensive nomadic pastoralism but they were also partially engaged in agriculture. They formulated international agreements with other states according to their own agendas (switching sides was a common and acceptable strategy), and constructed cities and fortresses in strategic locations to further the development of trade. The Turkic Khaganate formed a common ethnocultural lifestyle among the various ethnic groups within its boundaries, to such an extent that its succession can still be seen today, with certain elements preserved in the everyday lives of modern Turkic-speaking nations (especially the Kazakhs, Kyrgyz, Khakas, Tuvans and Altai-Kizhi).

The nomadic Turkic lifestyle differed fundamentally from that of settled agricultural and urban states. The "sacred land" or *Yer su* was of extrinsic value and the ancient Turkic tradition of *"Yduk Yer"* (*Zher Uyik*), meaning herding, played a leading role in life; fertile pastures along migration routes that could stretch thousands of kilometres were therefore of vital importance. But contact and communication with agricultural settlements was also a noteworthy feature of the nomadic Turks, who traded in animal products with the cities and settlements along the Silk Road. Among the five traditional species of livestock, preference was given to breeding horses and sheep – meat and fermented mare's milk (*kumis*) were abundant in the Turkic environment.

Below: An unusual *balbal* from the Chu Valley includes crossed legs and feet. Bottom: The Kumai archaeological complex of central Kazakhstan lies in classic steppe bordered by low forested hills and a river – the large number of Turkic, Hunnic and Bronze Age sites here mark it as a sacred place for nomads through the ages

The Turks wore clothes of silk, chiffon, wool and leather. During the summer they moved between *zhaylau* or "summer pastures", dwelling in four-, six-, eight- or 12-rope yurts, but when winter came they resided in fortresses named *balyks*. Hunting was a favourite pastime, and the Turks smelted and refined iron/steel to a higher quality than their neighbours, which made their weapons and tools highly prized. Crafts were passed from generation to generation and were constantly improved upon; famous masters created arrows, saddles and swords, and blacksmiths, writers, stonecutters, weavers and many other artisans attained great renown.

The steppe army of the various Turkic khaganates in the second half of the first millennium CE were well-equipped and mighty forces. Both warrior and horse were covered with steel armour, and each man was heavily armed with lance, bow, sword and dagger. An enemy was swiftly surrounded and attacked simultaneously on three fronts by the three wings. The concept of "running with fear" from the battlefield was alien to the Turks, who often sought out face-to-face duels on the field which could be very important to the outcome of a battle. Treason and betrayal were punishable by death.

Each ruler petitioned for success and prosperity from Tengri and implicitly obeyed Him according to shamanistic interpretation. Ancestor worship was an intrinsic part of the Turks' religious beliefs – they revered the spirits of the dead and idolized Earth relics. As with the Wusun and Saka before them, the Turks enacted complex burial ceremonies for the departure of their dead. The *"Yogu"* rite was widespread and included the placement around a kurgan of tombstones, stelae bearing inscriptions, animalistic sculptures and figurative stone statues called *balbals*, symbolizing the path to the upper world. Both small and large kurgans have been discovered in Kazakhstan and Mongolia, including major memorial complexes in honour of Bilge Khagan, Kultegin, Tonyukuk, Moyin chura (El Etmish Qaghan), El Etmish Yabghu and others.

## EURASIA'S ANCIENT TURKIC SCRIPT

The main sources of information on ancient Turkic history and culture are written monuments installed in the form of "arrows" in burial complexes, and also inscriptions cut into rocks and other archaic items. They contain not only historical facts, but also numerous ethnographic, ethnolinguistic and other data.

A few thousand such monuments have been discovered across the Eurasian Steppe stretching from Mongolia to Europe. They are dedicated both to great Turkic leaders but also to ordinary "turk kara budun". They are most frequently found in the valleys of the rivers Orhon, Lena and Yenisei in Mongolia and Russian Siberia, in Kazakhstan's Zhetisu region and along the Syr Darya River, in the Volga region and in the northern Caucasus and eastern Europe.

The original ancient Turkic script is called *Türük bitik*, which fixed phonological consistencies within the entire linguistic range of ancient Turkic ethnic groups. This written language had its roots in ideograms and tamga symbols arranged in an alphabet system, and its structure allowed clear and easy understanding by all Turkic ethnic groups of that period, enabling it to spread across the entire empire. All official documentation was kept in bitik, which was probably created by order of one of the Turkic khagans around the beginning of the seventh century in the Orhon River Valley in Mongolia. Although most researchers and Turkologists consider the Altai Mountains to be the "ancestral home" of the Turks, the Turkic Khaganate was actually created in the valleys of the Orhon, Tuul and Selenge rivers and the Khangai mountains. This region was also the epicentre of the Xiongnu and Rouran empires, the predecessors of the Turkic- and Mongolian-speaking ethnic groups, and the data from archaeological and written sources there is of vital importance to our understanding of the Turkic peoples.

Since they are scattered over such a vast geographical distance, researchers today generally call the ancient Turkic monuments by the name of the river, lake or region in which they are located. Monuments containing Turkic bitik have been found in Mongolia, Khakassia, Tuva, Altai, Buryatia, Sakha-Yakutia, Xinjiang, Kazakhstan, Kyrgyzstan, Uzbekistan, the northern Caucasus and eastern Europe. In their bitik writing the ancient Turks detailed their highest spiritual and cultural achievements, and these relate to the various stages in evolution of the khaganates and other Turkic states between the sixth and 11th centuries, which include the Turkic Khaganate, the ancient "Kyrgyz" state, the "Khazar-Pecheneg" alliance, the Turgesh state, etc.

The Orhon monuments of Mongolia (Turkic bitik is often referred to as "Orkhon script") include many memorial complexes dedicated to famous khagans and leaders such as Bilge Khagan, Kultegin, Tonyukuk, Kyulichura, El Etmish Yabghu, Altyn Tamgan Tarkhan and El Etmish Khagan. Hundreds of inscriptions were cut into cliffs and onto ceramic bricks, copper coins and stamps, and some monuments boasted bilingual or even trilingual inscriptions – affirming the Turks' close relationship with the Sogdians and Chinese due to Silk Road trade.

Trade and cultural relations between the Sogdians and nomadic Turks (and other steppe nomads) led to the use of Sogdian script in the western part of the Turkic Khaganate. After the collapse of Türük Eli (the Second

Turkic Khaganate) in 744 both Turkic bitik and Sogdian writing continued to exist concurrently. Uighur script developed only in the ninth century – this was the first attempt at phonetic transformation of the ancient Turkic language based on a foreign alphabet, and it can be seen in numerous written monuments (most of them of a religious or didactic nature). However, ancient Turkic bitik did not lose its imperial significance until the 12th century, a period of great geopolitical change when new writing systems linked to Manichaeism, Buddhism, Christianity and Islam were taking hold in nomadic Eurasia.

*Napil Bazylkhan is a Leading Researcher at the RB Suleimenov Institute of Oriental Studies of the Committee of Science at the Ministry of Education and Science of the Republic of Kazakhstan.*

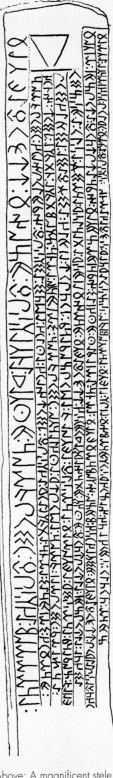

Above: A magnificent stele covered in Turkic script or *Türük bitik* (meticulously copied in the graphic at right), at the memorial complex of Tonyukuk (646-732) in central Mongolia

# THE MONGOL ERA:
# GREAT KHANS AND THE GOLDEN HORDE

Central Asia in the early 13th century was a far more sophisticated place than is commonly thought – it was not the wilderness filled with wild, horse-mounted savages that many imagine. The nomadic culture was well ordered, and more than a thousand years of commerce had resulted in the development of scores of cities along the numerous caravan routes crisscrossing mountain, steppe and desert; urban centres such as Otrar were very advanced in arts, crafts and science.

When world histories discuss the greatest land empire in human history and its creator, the "Unbending Lord" Chinggis Khaan (commonly called Genghis Khan), there is a tendency to omit or gloss over his movement through the territory of modern Kazakhstan, and instead focus on the sacking of the great cities of southern Central Asia, painting a picture of rampaging demons without mercy.

In his book *Foreign Devils on the Silk Road*, Peter Hopkirk writes: "You could smell them coming, it was said, even before you heard the thunder of their hooves. But by then it was too late. Within seconds came the first murderous torrent of arrows, blotting out the sun and turning day into night. Then they were upon you – slaughtering, raping, pillaging and burning. Like molten lava, they destroyed everything in their path. Behind them they left a trail of smoking cities and bleached bones, leading all the way back to their homeland in Central Asia. 'Soldiers of Anti-christ come to reap the last dreadful harvest' one 13th-century scholar called the Mongol hordes."

However, although the Mongols did undoubtedly commit horrific massacres and devastate entire cities and their environs, this was certainly not always the case – there was a method to their madness and Genghis Khan, in his all-conquering attempt to create a world order, knew that simply slaughtering everyone was not a viable strategy. When in 1218 Genghis entered Semirechye, he discovered a populace who were sick of the oppression of the Naiman leader Kuchlug (see essay on page 102). Their submission to the Mongol army was rewarded by a minimum of looting and no massacres, by order of the Great Khan.

Above: This Ming dynasty ink on silk painting is a 15th century copy of an earlier composition by Chen Juzhong (late 12th/early 13th century) titled "Tartars on Horseback" – Mongols were often collectively (though erroneously) called Tartars. Right: "Mongol Warriors" by Pavel Petrovich Ivanov (1891-1967) offers a highly stylized view of the fearsome nature of the Mongol hordes

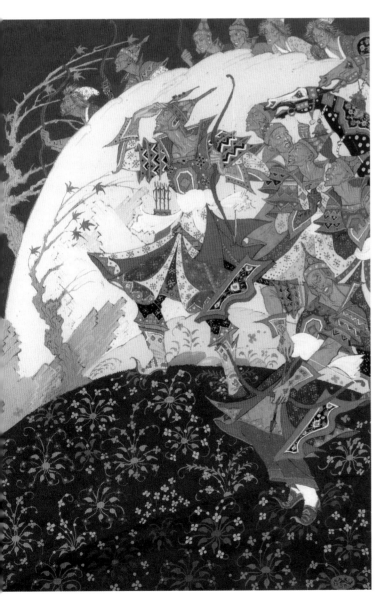

This was often the case when the Mongols entered a new territory or approached a town or city: if the populace and their ruler submitted without a fight, they were generally left unharmed, and their leaders often allowed to remain in power as long as they recognized Mongol authority and paid any tribute demanded of them. If, however, a city or state resisted the Mongol advance, then their ferocity and mercilessness quickly came to the fore.

The story of Otrar is a case in point: Genghis Khan began his move into southern Central Asia from Semirechye by sending a trade caravan of 500 camels loaded with merchandise to Khorezm, accompanied by 450 tradesmen. Having traded in the markets of Bukhara, Samarkand and Urgench (Urgenj) – in the meantime gathering information on the territory, it should be noted – they headed back east, only to be arrested for spying by the governor of Otrar, Gayir Khan. All but one of the Mongol merchants were executed; the sole survivor – whether he was released on purpose or escaped is subject to debate – returned to Genghis Khan and reported what had taken place.

Genghis immediately sent two envoys to the Shah of Khorezm, the overlord of Otrar, demanding the head of the city's governor. When these emissaries were themselves executed, the Mongol response was swift and terrible. Genghis Khan himself led a punitive expedition with 150,000 warriors and by September 1219 stood at the gates of Otrar. The city was prepared for a long siege, so Genghis left his sons Chagatai and Ogedei there with 35,000 soldiers, sent his son Juchi down the Syr Darya with another force, while he himself led the main army to Bukhara, from whence he conquered all of Transoxiana, then known as Mawarannahr.

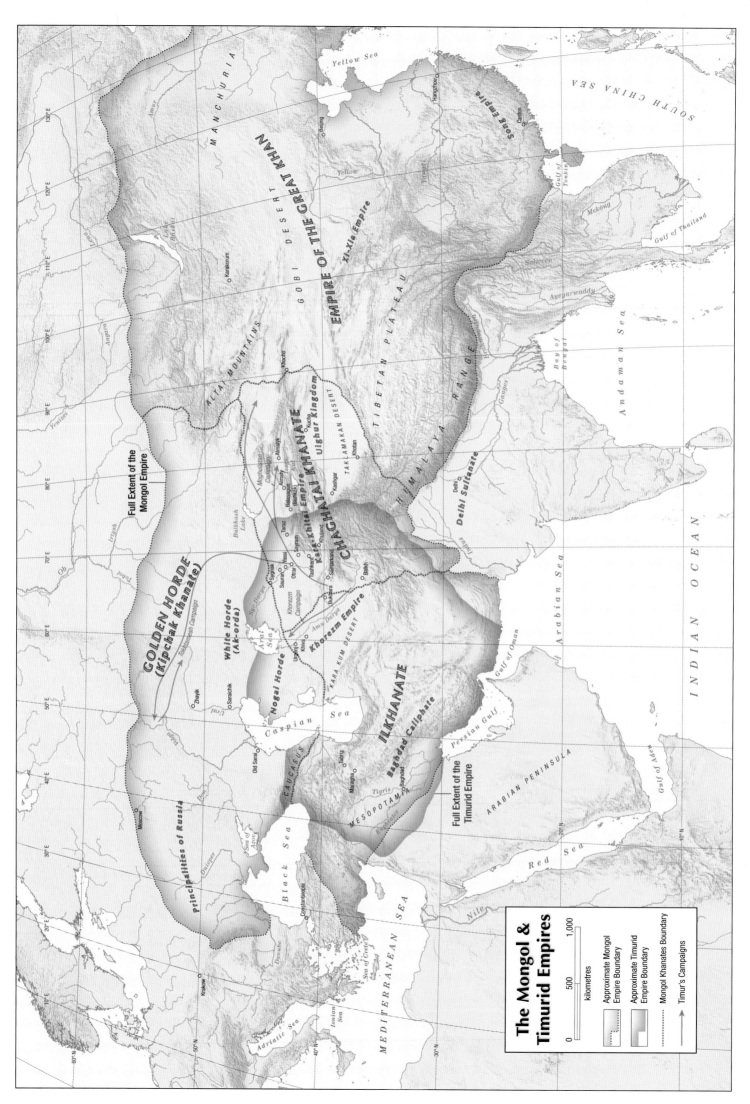

## The Mongol & Timurid Empires

Yellow Sea

SOUTH CHINA SEA

Hangzhou
Canton

Gulf of Tonkin

Mekong

Gulf of Thailand

Andaman Sea

Bay of Bengal

INDIAN OCEAN

Arabian Sea

Gulf of Oman

Persian Gulf

Gulf of Aden

Red Sea

ARABIAN PENINSULA

MEDITERRANEAN SEA

Ionian Sea

Adriatic Sea

Sea of Crete

Black Sea

Constantinople

Krakow

Sea of Azov

Dnieper

Danube

Don

Volga

Moscow

Principalities of Russia

Saraichik
Chayik

Old Sarai

Maraqha
Tabriz

Caspian Sea

CAUCASUS

ILKHANATE

Baghdad Caliphate
Baghdad

MESOPOTAMIA

Tigris
Euphrates

Nile

Full Extent of the Timurid Empire

Delhi Sultanate
Delhi

HIMALAYA RANGE

Indus
Ganges

Brahmaputra

TIBETAN PLATEAU

Salween

Ayeyarwaddy

GOLDEN HORDE
(Kipchak Khanate)

Tokhtamesh Campaign

White Horde
(Ak-orda)

Nogai Horde

Aral Sea

Syr Darya

Khorezm Campaign

Urgench
Khiva

Amu Darya
KARA KUM DESERT

Khorezm Empire

Balkh

Bukhara
Samarkand

Tashkent
Khujand

Otrar
Sayram
Yassu
Saurau
Sygnak

CHAGHATAI KHANATE

Moghulistan Campaign

Karakhita Empire

Kashgar

Taraz
Balasagun
Almaty
Issyk

Khotan

TAKLAMAKAN DESERT

Kucha

Uighur Kingdom

Xi-Xia Empire

Yellow

Beijing

GOBI DESERT

EMPIRE OF THE GREAT KHAN

ALTAI MOUNTAINS

Karakorum

MANCHURIA

Amur

Angara

Yenisey

Ob
Irtysh
Tobol
Ural

Balkhash Lake

Full Extent of the Mongol Empire

### The Mongol & Timurid Empires

kilometres
0   500   1,000

— · · — Approximate Mongol Empire Boundary

———— Approximate Timurid Empire Boundary

· · · · · · Mongol Khanates Boundary

———→ Timur's Campaigns

Otrar held out for five months before the defence forces sent by the Shah surrendered. The hapless governor was able to hold the citadel with his followers for another month, but in February 1220 the city fell, the Mongol hordes bursting into its alleys, murdering, ransacking and setting everything ablaze. Otrar, once so rich and beautiful, was left in utter ruin – such was the fate of many Central Asian cities before Genghis Khan was done.

## MOMENTOUS DECISIONS AND MAJOR CONSEQUENCES

Although the agriculture and infrastructure of sedentary society in the Kazakhstan region was devastated by Genghis Khan's invasion, with the establishment of the *Pax mongolica* or "Mongol Peace" and the political and economic stability it engendered, the trade routes across Central Asia were restored, and caravans could once more travel without fear of tribal feuds and attacks. From the notes of travellers such as Marco Polo and others who ventured into the region at the time, it seems that tolerance prevailed. Certainly, the Great Khan was in frequent communication with Christendom, and Christian and other religious beliefs spread among Asian courts. The Mongol world empire at this stage was a true amalgam of cultures.

With the death of Ghengis and the dividing of his empire between his sons, however, it was not long before internal conflict began to tear it apart. Soon borders were being fought over by Genghis's grandsons and other claimants to the right to rule. One telling division occurred when Mongke, the son of Genghis's son Tolui, who was at the time Great Khan, came to an agreement with Batu, the son of Juchi (Genghis's eldest child) and Khan of the Golden Horde in the Kazakh steppe. They settled any dispute by dividing the Great Steppe following a line from the Altai through the Tarbagatai mountains to the Ili Valley, foreshadowing future border lines between the lands of Russia (and subsequently Kazakhstan) and China many centuries later.

Batu's Golden Horde ruled a massive swathe of the Eurasian Steppe, but with the permission of Ogedei, the second Great Khan who had succeeded Genghis, they invaded Europe, conquering Russia, Poland and Hungary. They might well have conquered every kingdom to the Atlantic Ocean – which would have been a world-changing moment in history with staggering consequences – if Ogedei had not died in 1241 as the Mongol army approached Vienna, causing Batu to turn back for the long journey to Mongolia and the *kurultai* (a grand council of chiefs and khans) that would decide Ogedei's successor.

It is important to remember that although Batu and the ruling elite of the various *uluses* and khanates were Genghisid Mongols, the vast majority of the Golden Horde were Kipchaks and other tribes, who continued their lifestyle in much the same way as they had done before the arrival of this latest conquering army. This was true throughout Central Asia; the Mongol overlords were numerically tiny in comparison to local populations, and the inevitable consequence was that each ruler slowly became naturalized, absorbed into the local culture.

Batu's brother Berke was the first Mongol ruler to convert to Islam, and when Ghazan Khan, the seventh ruler of the Hulaguid Ilkhanate state to the southwest of the Chagatai Khanate, became a Muslim at the turn of the 14th century, a process of expansion began that was to see Islam become the dominant religion throughout Central Asia. Uzbeg Khan, leader of the Golden Horde at the height of its power, was a convert and declared Islam the state religion, exhorting his subjects to become Muslim. He allowed missionaries to travel through the steppe converting the tribes, but at the same time he was tolerant of other

Top: The funeral of Ghazan Khan in 1304. The Genghisid Ghazan was leader of the Ilkhanate and his conversion to Islam and reformist ideas on monetary and fiscal policies signalled the beginning of sweeping religious and administrative changes in Central Asia.
Above: Here Ghazan is seen studying the Koran in an open tent

religions so long as their adherents submitted to Islamic rule. In Semirechye, Kebek Khan's conversion (and that of Tarmashirin Khan after him) split the tribes of the Chagatai Khanate and arguably caused its downfall.

Uzbeg's son Janibeg, who succeeded him as Khan of the Golden Horde, was the instigator – if the stories are true – of one of Europe's greatest catastrophes. Janibeg was in frequent conflict with the Russian princes, and in 1343 he besieged the Crimean port of Kaffa. He was driven back by a relief force from Italy, but in 1345 he returned and laid siege to the city again. However, he was destined to fail once more because his army was stricken by an outbreak of the Black Plague. In an attempt to weaken the city's defence he ordered the dead bodies of infected soldiers to be catapulted over the walls. It is thought that infected Genoese sailors returning home to Genoa subsequently introduced the "Black Death" to Europe.

## Timur's campaigns and the Uzbek horde

A period of unrest and ever-changing rulers in the second half of the 14th century was curtailed by the rise of perhaps Central Asia's most infamous leader: Tamerlane, the "Scourge of God". A warlord and military genius of Turkic-Mongol descent, Timur (Tamerlane was a nickname) built up a second Mongolian Empire with Samarkand as its capital. In swift military campaigns he conquered Central Asia, Persia, India down to the mouth of the Ganges, the southern Caucasus and Russia to the outskirts of Moscow, but because he was not a direct descendant of Genghis Khan, by Mongol custom he could not be declared "Khan", so he took the title Emir (Amir) and ruled through a puppet Khan of the Chagatayid bloodline.

Timur was a brilliant and ruthless tactician and few could stand against him in open battle. He led a number of campaigns against his Moghulistan neighbours in Semirechye, but perhaps his most dangerous foe was a member of the Juchid dynasty from the Golden Horde in the central steppe, who came to him as a refugee in 1376. This was Tokhtamysh, who had just failed in an attempt to overthrow his uncle Urus Khan of the Ak-Orda or White Horde (see essay on page 102).

It made sense to foment trouble in the region of one of his enemies, so Timur welcomed Tokhtamysh and supported him in his ambition to gain control of the Ak-Orda, granting him lands on the northern border and an army with which to depose Urus Khan. Tokhtamysh was beaten back several times by the Kipchak warriors of the Golden Horde, but each time Timur gave him new troops and eventually went to war alongside his protégé, helping him to finally take control of the Ak-Orda and become khan.

Tokhtamysh had learnt a lot from his mentor, and went on to conquer all the lands of Juchi's Ulus, reuniting the Golden Horde during the 1380s and masterminding his own campaigns of expansion. But eventually his ambitions – equal to Timur's – led to his ruin, when he invaded Mawarannahr and besieged Bukhara while Timur was campaigning in the west.

Timur was outraged that Tokhtamysh should betray him after all the help he had given, but he was also aware that the Golden Horde's leader was potentially his most serious competitor, so he made careful plans and in 1391, along with an army of 200,000 warriors, he drove across the Syr Darya and into enemy territory in midwinter, hoping to catch Tokhtamysh unawares. For four months the army moved north through the "Hunger Steppe" of central Kazakhstan, crossing the Sarysu River and arcing northwest to the Ural River. It was an astonishing feat, and only Timur could have held his men together in conditions of such mental and physical deprivation. At one point, when his soldiers had been reduced to eating grass and thin broth, Timur ordered a great hunt, sending the left and right wings of his army in huge, arcing lines across the steppe while his central ranks stood still. It took each wing two days to curl around to meet the other and then drive back in towards their leader, driving before them a host of wildlife – including saiga antelope, elk, wolves, wild boar and hares – to be slaughtered and consumed ravenously.

Tokhtamysh's forces, meanwhile, had vanished into the steppe, retreating and waiting for their enemy to weaken and lose morale. This was a classic strategy of the steppe nomads, but in summer 1391 the two armies finally met at the Battle of Kunduzcha, to the east of the Volga River. It was a brutal and bloody confrontation; the Damascan writer and traveller Muhammad ibn Arabshah described it thus: "Then both armies… became hot with the fire of war, and they joined battle and necks were extended for sword blows and throats outstretched for spear thrusts, and faces were drawn with sternness and fouled with dust… men's skin bristled, clad with the feathers of arrows, and the brows of the leaders drooped... and the dust was thickened and stood black and the leaders and common soldiers alike plunged into seas of blood…"

*Above: Janibeg Khan looks on as Alexis, Metroplitan of Russia, heals his wife Taidula of blindness, thereby saving Moscow from attack by the Golden Horde (painting by Yakov Kapkov). Right: A dynamic miniature in the Indian style by Sharaf ad-Din Ali Yiazdi of Samarkand (1628) shows the fierce battle between Timur and Tokhtamysh's armies*

Although the Kipchaks were numerically greater, the advantage ebbed and flowed between the two sides until Timur's forces triumphed, with Tokhtamysh fleeing the battlefield. He was allowed to go, but Timur was to rue the decision not to hunt him down, because four years later in 1395 the Khan of the Golden Horde, having recovered and raised another army, attacked Timur's lands through Georgia. This time no mercy was shown – the emperor's punitive forces pushed north through the Caucasus Mountains into Tokhtamysh's heartland and laid waste to everything. At the Battle of Terek River Tokhtamysh was routed once and for all, and although he escaped again, he was never able to recover power or prestige, and eventually was killed in Russian Siberia near modern-day Tyumen.

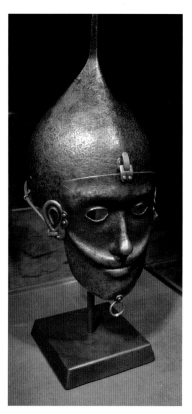

Timur, determined to crush the Kipchaks and destroy the Golden Horde once and for all, systematically devastated its cities and lands – thereby dismantling the valuable trade routes of the northern Silk Road and diverting the majority of the flow of trade to the south through his own empire.

Although clearly capable of immense cruelty and indifference to the suffering of multitudes, Timur was also a devout Muslim and a student of architecture. Among the many superlative Islamic buildings he caused to be built, one of the greatest is Kazakhstan's Mausoleum of Khoja Ahmed Yasawi (Hoddzha Ahmed Yassaoui), situated near the ruins of the ancient city of Yassi (modern-day Turkistan) near the Syr Darya.

Ahmed Yasawi was born in 1094 in Sayram and studied Islam under the famous teacher Aristan Bab (Arslan Bab), before spending time in Bukhara then moving to preach in Yassi. A prophet, poet and mystic who founded the Sufi Tariqah order, he gained many followers and was credited with making the teachings of Mohammed more understandable to the common people of Central Asia by preaching and writing in the Turkic language instead of Farsi. When he died in 1166, he was buried in great honour and splendour within a *mazar*, or domed tomb.

Yasawi's tomb was plundered a number of times by Tokhtamysh and others, and when Emir Timur, on his way to collect a new bride in 1389, stopped to say a prayer at the mazar, he was dismayed by its poor, rundown condition. He immediately ordered the construction of a grand mausoleum that would do justice to Khoja Ahmed Yasawi's memory – it is said that Timur himself drew up the

detailed designs for the new building. The mausoleum was never finished entirely, but with its two monumental domes, one exquisitely ribbed and the other smooth, gleaming and enormous (22 metres in diameter – the largest preserved unsupported dome in Central Asia), it still stands today as a magnificent example of Timurid architecture.

When Timur died of a fever in the city of Otrar in 1405, he was preparing a massive campaign for the conquest of China. How that would have impacted on world history will never be known, but with his death the plan evaporated. His descendants swiftly fell into civil conflict, leaving many regions virtually independent, and this opened the door for the Shaybanid tribes north of the Aral Sea to expand south. Their leaders were descended from Shiban, the fifth son of Juchi, and as the lines of Batu and Orda Khan faltered, the Shaybanids seized control of the eastern *Dasht-i-Kipchak*.

Although a confederation of many different tribes, collectively they gradually assumed the name "Uzbeks",

which may have its origins in the Oghuz tribe, or be a reference to Uzbeg Khan, or even the Turkic words "Oz" (self) and *"bek/bey"* (a tribal leader), thus meaning one's own leader, or independent. The Uzbeks became very powerful in the early 15th century, and under Abulkhair Khan they forged south into the Syr Darya region, wresting control from the Timurids and forming the Abulkhair Khanate.

But Abulkhair and his closest followers began to love the cities more than the steppe, and their "Persianization" did not sit well with many of the Uzbek sultans and their tribes, for whom the nomadic ways of the steppe were paramount to their sense of self. From this division emerged a new khanate, and over the course of time a new ethnic group with their own identity and nationhood: the Kazakhs.

Above and right: The superlative Mausoleum of Khoja Ahmed Yasawi, said to have been commissioned and designed by Timur (Tamerlane) to honour the Sufi prophet, is located by the ruins of the ancient city of Yassi near modern-day Turkistan in South Kazakhstan.
Left: A Kipchak helmet and war mask of the 13th century

# The Mongol epoch and its consequences for Kazakhstan

By *Zhanat Kundakbayeva*

I n the 12th century, before the conquering Mongol armies swept into Central Asia, much of the huge territory that today comprises modern Kazakhstan was inhabited by Turkic-speaking tribes – the Kipchaks, Kangly, Karluks and Naimans – and the Khorezm (Khwarezm or Chorasmia) and Karakitai (Kara-Khitan) empires. Indeed, their areas of control extended much farther: the Kipchaks ranged north into the Russian steppes, occupied the steppes of the North Caucasus and eastern Europe, and even lived in Khorezm territory south of the Aral Sea; the Kangly lived by the Aral Sea and as far east as the Irtysh, as well as in Semirechye; and the Karluks could be found in the east. The Naimans occupied areas of northwestern Mongolia but straddled the Altai Mountains into the steppes of today's East Kazakhstan. The domain of the Karakitais, meanwhile, encompassed southeast Kazakhstan and the adjoining lands of southern Central Asia and East Turkestan, while the land of the Khorezm-shahs was centred on the Amu Darya from the Aral Sea to Balkh.

Being predominantly nomadic cultures, there were few linear demarcations between areas of control, and tribes shifted and moved in a state of constant flux. However, at this time the Kipchaks were the dominant tribe, their reach extending from the Altai Mountains across the Great Steppe to the shores of the Danube River. Records from the Chinese dynastic history *Yuan Shih* (History of Yuan), as well as works by Persian authors, confirm this. The Kipchaks were known as Polovians by the Russians and Cumans in Byzantine and European chronicles, but it was the Arab writers al-Omari, Ibn Khaldun and Ibn Arabshah who determined the overall size of the territory occupied by this confederation of Turkic tribes, and called it *Dasht-i Kipchak* (Kipchak country).

## THE GREAT STEPPE ON THE EVE OF THE MONGOL ERA

In the steppe region of modern-day Kazakhstan the Kipchaks formed unions with and ultimately absorbed the ethnic groups and tribes inhabiting the land. Of note among these tribes were the Kimaks, who originally lived by the Irtysh River but moved to western Kazakhstan during the 12th century, and the Kangly. The lifestyle and economy of the Kipchak confederation followed that of its predecessors – the Saka, Huns, Turks, Turgesh, Pechenegs and Oghuz – which is to say nomadic pastoralism.

Oriental writers noted that they migrated along strictly defined routes, and archaeologists have confirmed that sheep prevailed in their herds, and horses were of course highly valued. As with previous nomadic groups, these tribal

Temujin is pronounced Unbending Lord (Chinggis Khaan or Genghis Khan) while his sons look on, in this illustration by Rashid al-Din in the 14th century "Compendium of Chronicles" (aka History of the World)

groups lived in the felt tents known as yurts – described in 1246 by the Italian traveller John of Plano Carpini in the earliest Western account of Central Asia's inhabitants. In 1253 the Flemish missionary William of Rubruck also passed through the steppe regions and documented the nomads' lives, from their food to craftsmanship and the making of *kumis* (fermented mare's milk). However, what was not mentioned, but recent archaeological studies suggest, is that a certain amount of farming was also developed among the Kipchak tribes. Archaeological data indicate that crops were cultivated in the river basins of the Syr Darya, Sarysu and Esil (Ishim).

Records show that from the 11th century onwards the Kipchaks had extensive contact with foreign states both in the East and West; Chinese sources showed regular contact, and the Kipchaks were important external and internal factors in the policies of such states as Byzantium, Bulgaria, Russia, Georgia and the Seljuk Sultanate. Many Kipchak groups also lived within the boundaries of other states, for example the Khorezm-shahs, where they provided a large proportion of its fighting force; for this reason Genghis Khan (Chinggis Khaan) and his sons did everything they could to destroy the collective power of the Kipchaks.

In the mid-12th century the region centred around southeastern and southern Kazakhstan and the Tien Shan mountains was taken over by the Karakitai, a tribe of Tungusic-Manchurian origin who had created the Liao Dynasty in northern China but moved west when that collapsed under attack from the Song Dynasty and its Jurchen allies. The Karakitai Khanate was an empire of unstable borders depending on fluctuating political situations, but from its heartland in the Tien Shan it extended north into the central steppe, south into the Ferghana Valley and Transoxiana, east into the Tarim Basin and west to the borders of Khorezm.

As with earlier invasions and those to follow, the Karakitais conquered the local tribes but then integrated with them and formed an ethno-political power base with their capital in Balasagun (in modern-day Kyrgyzstan).

An illustration from Wang Qi's "San Cai Tu Hui" (1607) shows a Karakitai man and his horse

They did not destroy the towns and settled areas but rather allowed them to continue as vassal states, and generally speaking their rule was of a peaceful nature. Nor did they try to change the political system – although some of their traditions caused concern among the local Muslim population, such as allowing supreme power to be inherited by a woman.

Later in the 12th century, however, the Karakitais changed their policy and turned to more aggressive tactics, robbing and raiding peaceful settlements and borderlands. This destabilized the region, and in the first decade of the 13th century a leader of the Naiman tribe named Kuchlug captured the northern part of Semirechye, while the territory between the Talas and Chu rivers and Issyk-Kul lake was occupied by the Kangly tribe. The Syr Darya river basin meanwhile, with its many cities and fortresses, as well as the region of Mawarannahr (also called Maverannahr or Transoxiana) between the Syr Darya (Jaxartes) and Amu Darya (Oxus), had come under the control of the Khorezm-shah Ala ad-Din Muhammad II.

## STEPPE CITIES AND NOMADS

On the eve of the arrival of the Mongols, Central Asia was home to two distinct lifestyles: nomadic pastoralism and sedentary agricultural settlement. The centre of the settled civilization was in the south, especially along the Amu Darya, Syr Darya and in Semirechye. The period from the 10th to 12th centuries can be said to have been the heyday of the steppe cities. Throughout the region old cities such as Otrar, Sauran, Taraz, Ispidzhab (Sayram), Kulan and Yangikent were resurgent while new urban centres like Kayalyk and Ashnas were appearing. The Ili Valley also saw towns multiplying in the 11th-12th centuries.

The cities of this period were relatively advanced and sophisticated; they boasted sewer systems, fresh-water supply and bath-houses. Monetary trade flourished, with gold, silver and copper mined in the Alatau Mountains to the south – two mints are known from that time, one in Taraz and the other in Ispidzhab.

By the second decade of the 13th century, the southern cities were under the authority of the Khorezm-shahs while those of Semirechye remained in the hands of the Karakitais or their vassals. But regardless of who they paid tribute to, all these cities were power centres in their own right, as well as the focus of great craftsmanship. Their success was built on trade between oasis and steppe, East and West, and they flourished. Economic relations in medieval

Under the Mongol Empire's new world order, the minting of coins began to facilitate commercial transactions across the vast reaches of Eurasia. The top images show the two sides of a coin minted during Ghazan Khan's rule in Persia in the late 13th century. The coin at lower left was minted in Balkh, Afghanistan in 1221, as was the gold coin at lower right, inscribed with Genghis Khan's full name, the place of minting and the date (618 in the Islamic calendar)

Central Asia developed around a symbiosis of nomadic and settled life. Both city dwellers and nomadic steppe tribes were part of a single economic and political organism, providing for each other's needs.

The Turkic tribes worshiped the sky (Tengri) and earth-water (*Yer-su*) – a religion called Tengrism. The third element in their triad of deities was Umai – a patroness of the hearth and children. But alongside these beliefs many other religions grew and took hold among the Turkic-speaking populations of Central Asia, particularly in the cities; these included Buddhism, Manichaeism, Christianity and Islam. The Islamicization of Central Asia's Turkic-speaking population began in the late ninth century, but for a long time the diversity and freedom of religious beliefs was notable.

Also of note in the period before the Mongol conquest of Central Asia was the development of great cultural, scientific and artistic traditions. Local cultural tradition fused with the highest achievements of the Arab, Persian and Indian cultures brought to the region along the lucrative trade routes. The world-renowned scientist and philosopher Al-Farabi (c. 852-950) was born in Farab, whose name had changed to Otrar by the 12th century and which boasted a library that attracted scholars from across the Islamic world. The world of Turkic literature also excelled, with such outstanding works as the poem *"Kudadgu Bilik"* by Yusuf Balasagun, *"Divan Lugat-at-Turk"* by Mahmud Kashgar, and the poetry of Suleiman Bakyrgali.

This then was the appearance of medieval Kazakhstan at the turn of the 13th century. Highly developed agricultural oases and city states in the south lived in a symbiotic relationship with the nomadic pastoralist tribes of the seemingly endless steppe to the north. It was the crossroads of Asia, where great civilizations from distant continents met; a vast melting pot of tribes and cultures where a process of ethnic integration was taking place. But their world was about to change, for in 1218 Genghis Khan's invading army flooded into Semirechye.

## THE COMING OF GENGHIS KHAN

For more than 200 years, from the early 13th to mid-15th centuries, Central Asia was firmly under the control of Genghis Khan and his descendants. This was a significant period in the history of medieval Kazakhstan; on the one hand the Mongols brought disaster and destruction to many of the conquered states and tribal confederations, but on the other hand they also brought to the steppe the idea of a centralized state, which lasted until the 19th century, when the Russian Empire changed the political system to meet its own vision.

By the end of the 12th century Mongol-speaking tribes had steadily moved into the Altai region, defeating or pushing tribes like the Naimans west into the steppe lands beyond. The Mongols assimilated many Turkic-speaking groups, incorporating elements of their material culture, economy and lifestyle. There now emerged from the inter-tribal conflict a single

Left: A huge statue of
Genghis Khan (properly
called Chinggis Khaan or
Unbending Lord) looks out
over Suhbaatar Square
in Mongolia's capital
Ulaanbaatar, where he is
revered as the country's
greatest historical figure.
Below: A mounted Mongol
warrior – one of two –
stands guard on either side
of the seated khan

powerful leader called Temujin, who unified and organized the warring tribes into a powerful and supremely mobile army, ready to sweep out and conquer the world. In 1207 he was given the title Chinggis Khaan or "Unbending Lord" – in the West he is most commonly known as Genghis Khan, creator of the largest land empire the world has ever known.

By 1218 the Mongols had invaded and conquered all its neighbouring tribes or states, seizing control of the lands of the Kyrgyz and Buryats in the Yenisei River area in the north, the Xi-Xia Empire (Tanguts) to the south and much of northern China. Wisely the eastern Uighur kingdoms of the Tarim Basin submitted to the Mongols and swore allegiance to Genghis Khan. The way was now open to the riches of southern Central Asia and Iran, the Middle East and Eastern Europe. But first the territory of the Great Steppe had to be traversed.

Semirechye was occupied by the Mongols without resistance. The local population had endured eight years of destruction by the Naiman leader Kuchlug, who forbad public worship and persecuted Muslims. The Turkic-speaking tribes therefore met the Mongols as liberators, and Genghis Khan, wanting to win over the people, forbad looting or massacres and followed a policy of religious tolerance.

South Kazakhstan was now open to the Mongols, but Genghis Khan's first move was diplomatic. He sent a large merchant caravan to Khorezm to trade and gather information, but the governor of Otrar arrested the entire caravan as they were returning, accused them of spying and killed all but one, who returned to

the Great Khan and told his story. This was all the excuse Genghis Khan needed, and in 1219 Mongol armies marched from the banks of the Irtysh through Semirechye into the populous and economically developed towns of the middle and lower Syr Darya floodplain.

The urban populations of what is today's South Kazakhstan region offered stubborn resistance, but the Mongols used techniques of mass terror and violence, devastation of whole areas and complete destruction of cities. Nothing could stop them; Arab and Persian sources give the names of more than three dozen cities whose

Above: This detail from Rashid al-Din's "Jami`al-Tavarikh" (Compendium of Chronicles, 1309) shows Mongol troops and engineers with catapults besieging a walled city. Mongols, at first unfamiliar with siege tactics against fortified targets, recruited Chinese and Iranian experts and utilized their technology, including ceramic bombs and catapults, to devastating effect. Right: An illustration by Rashid al-Din in the 14th century shows the coronation of Ogedei as Genghis Khan's successor in 1229

populations were completely slaughtered, including Otrar, Sygnak and Ashnas.

By the spring of 1221 the conquest of Central Asia had been completed. The great cities of Bukhara, Samarkand, Urgench, Balkh and Herat, among many others, had fallen to the Mongol military machine, and the Mongols could pass freely into Iran and Afghanistan. By 1224 all the territory that Kazakhstan covers today had become part of Genghis Khan's empire.

## THE GOLDEN HORDE

Having created a gigantic empire by sword and fire, Genghis Khan now allocated an appanage –in this case a designated area of land known as an *Ulus* – to each of his sons. The vast territory of Kazakhstan was divided between his three eldest sons: Juchi (Zhuchi or Jochi), the eldest, was given the northern part of Semirechye, and the vast territories of the central and northern Great Steppe, stretching west to the Caspian Sea and including the Yaik (Zhayik or Ural) and lower Volga rivers. South and southeastern Kazakhstan came within the boundaries of Chagatai's Ulus, which included much of the western Tien Shan, the Ili Valley and the Tarim Basin. The third son Ogedei was given rule

over central Siberia, the Junggarian Basin, the Altai and Tarbagatai mountains and the lush grasslands of the upper Irtysh River (in modern Kazakhstan's northeastern region).

The bulk of Kazakhstan's territory was incorporated into Juchi's Ulus, but in 1227 Juchi died prematurely and his son Batu became khan. Batu undertook aggressive campaigns to the west; over the course of a seven-year campaign (1236-1242) he conquered lands from the Volga to the lower reaches of the Danube, including the Crimea, the northern Caucasus, and the western steppe lands ruled by the Kipchaks. In 1242 Batu returned to the lower reaches of the Volga, where from his new capital of Sarai-Batu, near modern-day Astrakhan, he ruled a new Mongolian state that came to be known as the Golden Horde. It covered an enormous portion of Eurasia, ranging from the middle reaches of the Irtysh River in the east to the Danube River in the west, and from the Ob River and western Siberia in the north to the Amu Darya and sections of the former territory of the Khorezm-shahs in the south.

Batu and his brother Berke now created a basis for political control over this huge state. The state was considered to be the property of the Juchid clan (descendants of Juchi). All important decisions were made at a *kurultai* – a general assembly of nobility, headed by high-ranking members of the ruling clans. The army and diplomatic relations with other states were the responsibility of a *beklyaribek*, while executive power belonged to a vizier and officials called *darughas* and *baskaks* were in charge of tax collection and administration. The most important positions were held by members of the khan's family.

Following Genghis Khan's lead, the Golden Horde used an appanage system of ulus to govern, with each ulus headed by one of Juchi's sons. Originally the Golden Horde was subordinate to the Mongol Empire, but by 1260 the empire had disintegrated into separate states. After Batu's death in 1255, the

Golden Horde became an independent state under his brother Berke (ruled 1256-1266), and Berke's successor Mengu Khan (ruled 1266-1280) began minting coins with his own name. But the history of the Golden Horde is full of internal strife; there were continuous wars with Russian princes, the Hulaguids (descendants of Hulagu, a grandson of Genghis Khan) of Iran in the trans-Caucasus region, and the Ak-Orda and Khorezm-shahs.

The Golden Horde reached the height of its power in the first half of the 14th century, under Uzbeg Khan (ruled 1312-1342) and his son Janibeg Khan (ruled 1342-1357). They strengthened their own influence by ceasing the gathering of kurultais and centralizing power. Uzbeg Khan converted to Islam and in 1312 declared Islam as the state religion of the Golden Horde; from then on all its rulers were Muslim.

This page from top: A romanticized painting by Vasiliy Smirnov in 1883 shows the prince of Kiev, Michael of Chernigov, about to be stabbed by Batu Khan for refusing to bow to Genghis Khan's shrine and the Mongol idols; the flag of the Golden Horde during the reign of Uzbeg Khan; a medieval Chinese drawing of a young Batu Khan; and Mikhail, Prince of Tver stands before Uzbeg Khan in an illustration by Vasiliy Vereshchagin – initially on good terms with the khan, he was accused of killing the khan's sister and executed in 1318

The second half of the 14th century saw a gradual weakening of the Golden Horde. Two decades of civil strife resulted in more than 25 governors sitting on the khan's throne, and as a result the western part of the Golden Horde broke up into smaller states in the Crimea, the Volga region, Astrakhan and Saraichik, eventually becoming the independent khanates of Kazan, Astrakhan, Crimea and the Great Horde. The eastern part of the Golden Horde saw a brief unification by Tokhtamysh, a descendant of Orda Khan, Juchi's eldest son, and khan of the Ak-Orda. However, his ambition to re-create Juchi's Ulus was snuffed out by the all-conquering Timur (Tamerlane) at the end of the century, and after that, to all intents and purposes the Golden Horde ceased to exist.

## THE CHAGATAI ULUS AND MOGHULISTAN

Southeastern Kazakhstan, meanwhile, endured its own chaotic series of events. This was where the borders of the three largest Mongol uluses met. The Semirechye territory was politically torn between them: to Juchi's Ulus belonged the land adjacent to Lake Balkhash; the southern section was under the sway of the Chagatai Ulus, and the northern reaches were an important part of Ogedei's Ulus.

A relatively fertile region, Semirechye saw endless wars between the different minor Chagatai uluses after the death of Chagatai in 1241 – there were many claimants for the throne

of the khan among both Chagatayids and Ogedei's descendants. Constant war and feuding completely destroyed the ability of local towns and agricultural oases to prosper, and Semirechye began a process of economic ruin. Many of the region's famous cities, renowned for their high level of development in the pre-Mongol period, were left to rot. Urban hubs such as Balasagun, Taraz, Almalyk, Almatau, Kayalyk and Iki-Oguz virtually disappeared from the map.

It should be noted, however, that among the Mongol khans there were some supporters of centralized authority, with a return to the old traditions of settled-agricultural and urban cultures. The most prominent of these was the Chagatayid Kebek Khan (1318-1326). He broke with the nomadic traditions, moved from Semirechye to Mawarannahr and carried out monetary and administrative reform, promoting the construction and restoration of the cities. Such a "betrayal" of the nomadic ways, along with Kebek Khan's conversion to Islam (and Tarmashirin Khan's after him), provoked anger and resistance from the Buddhist-Shamanistic Mongolian nomadic elite in Semirechye's eastern steppe lands. This rift was the catalyst for the break-up of the Chagatai Ulus and the disintegration of the Chagatayid state by the mid-14th century, when Semirechye and the Ili Valley became part of a new state: Moghulistan ("Moghul" being the Persian word for "Mongol").

An excerpt from the famous Catalan Atlas of 1375 shows Marco Polo journeying across Central Asia by camel caravan

For 70 years of the 14th century a procession of more than 20 khans wrestled for control in the region. A struggle for power ensued in the western part of the Chagatayid state between leaders of the large Turkic-Mongol tribes, and the descendants of Chagatai and Ogedei were unable to maintain control over what had become a multi-ethnic region, populated by tribes of Turkic, Mongol and Persian descent.

In the east the nomadic elite, headed by the leader of the Turkic-Mongol Duglat tribe, made a Chagatayid named Tughluk Timur the new Khan in the Ili Valley in 1347. The borders of Moghulistan – so named by medieval writers because of its preservation of nomadic traditions and the large number of Mongols who moved there – were in constant flux for the next century and a half, as first Tughluk Timur periodically drove both west into Transoxiana and east into the Tarim Basin, in an attempt to rebuild a Chagatayid empire, and then later leaders such as Yunus Khan (ruled 1462-1487) either invaded neighbouring regions or defended their own against incursions from Uzbek, Oirat and Kyrgyz tribes. This played out around almost constant internal strife and slow fragmentation of the country into fiefdoms, further undermining its unity.

Despite its name, the composition of Moghulistan included a variety of Turkic-speaking and Turkicized Mongol tribes: Duglats, Kangly, Kireis, Uysuns, Arkenuts, Baarinys, Barlas, etc. Together they constituted a Turkic-speaking ethnic and political community that was collectively called Moghuls, but in the years to come they would split and integrate, according to their geographic location, into the new nations of the Kazakhs, Kyrgyz and Uighurs. For the clans and tribes in Semirechye, this happened when the last Moghulistan ruler, Sultan Said Khan (Yunus Khan's grandson), conquered Kashgar in 1514 and founded the new Yarkand Khanate in East Turkestan. At that time the Semirechye clans finally recognized the growing power of the Kazakhs and entered the Kazakh Khanate.

## TIMUR, THE AK-ORDA AND THE SHAYBANIDS

Before this, however, Central Asia was to feel the relatively short-lasting but extremely fierce and uncompromising hand of Timur (nicknamed Tamerlane or Timur the Lame), a military genius and hugely ambitious tribal leader from the Kesh region in today's Uzbekistan. Timur was a minor noble of the Turkicized Mongol Barlas clan, but such was his talent for war that he defeated all before him and gathered together a huge following, swiftly consolidating his power and building an empire centred around the capital of Samarkand. Although Timur's empire extended mostly south and west, through Afghanistan into northern India and across Persia, he controlled and demanded tribute from the cities and tribes of the Syr Darya and most of today's southern and western Kazakhstan regions, and led lengthy military campaigns into Moghulstan and north against Tokhtamysh and the Golden Horde.

From the mid-13th century through to the early 15th century, the eastern expanses of Dasht-i Kipchak – from Lake Balkhash and the Irtysh River across to the Volga – had come under the control of the Ak-Orda. According to the 14th-century Persian historian Rashid al-Din, the eastern part of Juchi's Ulus was inherited by his eldest son Orda-Edzhen, along with three other brothers (while Batu ruled the western steppes and Juchi's Ulus overall). The successors of this so-called "White Horde" were virtually independent rulers, who only nominally recognized Batu Khan's descendants' power. The territory of Ak-Orda gradually spread as the Golden Horde weakened, encompassing

A 16th century Safavid illustration shows a court scene of Timur and a maiden from Khwarezm

northeastern Semirechye – according to John of Plano Carpini the Horde's headquarters were by the Irtysh and Lake Alakol – and there was a constant struggle to establish independence from the Golden Horde.

The land between the rivers Yaik (Zhayik or Ural), Irgiz, Tobol and Sarysu in the Aral steppes and lower reaches of the Syr Darya belonged to another of Juchi's sons – Shayban. As the 14th century progressed the ruling power of the Ak-Orda horde shifted to Shayban's clan, and eventually almost the entire territory of modern Kazakhstan – except for Semirechye, which was still part of the Chagatayid state, and later Moghulistan – came under their control.

But conflict with external forces and internal strife were never far away. Tokhtamysh took control of the Ak-Orda after his uncle Urus Khan's death in 1378, with the backing of the powerful Emir Timur in Samarkand. Briefly reuniting the Golden Horde, he led successful campaigns against Moscow and Azerbaijan, but then fell foul of Timur and reaped the consequences as his army was twice defeated in the 1390s. The Ak-Orda was weakened as a result of Timur's attacks, and although the power of the Orda-Edzhen dynasty was restored under Urus Khan's grandson Barak for a short time, after his death rule over the main portion of the Ak-Orda passed to Abulkhair Khan – a member of the Shaybanid dynasty.

By the turn of the 15th century the political centre of the Ak-Orda had moved to Sygnak in the south of Kazakhstan. The Ak-Orda is considered to be the first state on the territory of Kazakhstan based on ethnicity; it was populated by Turkic-speaking tribes that had long inhabited the central and southern steppes of Kazakhstan, shifting during the campaigns of the Mongols. Among them there were Turkic clans and tribes from eastern areas, as well as Turkicized Mongol tribes, but all with a common language and culture.

Abulkhair Khan was a leader of the nomadic Uzbeks, and from 1428 to 1468 the Kazakhstan steppe was part of an independent Uzbek state known as Abulkhair's Khanate. Its territory stretched from the Yaik River to Lake Balkhash, and from the lower reaches of the Syr Darya and the Aral Sea to the middle reaches of the Tobol and Irtysh rivers. Although ethnically diverse, in the literature of the late 14th and early 15th centuries the many tribes were grouped under the common name "Uzbeks". These were Turkic tribes mainly of Kipchak and Karluk origin, descendants of the population of

Dasht-i Kipchak and southeastern Kazakhstan before the Mongol period, as well as Turkicized Mongol tribes. Somewhat later, many of these ethnic groups became known as the tribes of the Kazakh Middle Zhuz (Juz or Horde).

Abulkhair's rule followed the well-worn paths of invasion and conflict. In the 1430s he invaded Khorezm twice, as well as the Astrakhan Khanate; in 1446 he conquered the Syr Darya; was defeated by the Kalmyks in 1457; but most significantly suffered the loss of a part of his Uzbek ulus when the sultans Janibek and Kerei led them on a migration in the late 1450s to West Moghulistan. In 1468 Abulkhair undertook a campaign to Semirechye but died on the way, and his state fell apart soon after. After the formation and consolidation of the Kazakh Khanate the power of the Shaybanids waned. A group of nomadic Uzbeks left the central steppe at the beginning of the 16th century for Mawarannahr, but the rest came under the authority of the Kazakh khans.

The region between the Aral Sea and the Caspian Sea had its own discrete history at this time. This was the territory of the Nogai

From the same Safavid book, this illustration depicts Timur defeating the Kipchaks in the northern steppes

Horde, formed as a result of the Golden Horde's collapse. From the end of the 14th century a unification of tribes between the Ural and Volga rivers was called the Mangytsky Yurt, and by the middle of the 15th century the Nogai Horde finally stood apart. The ethnic composition of its tribes was similar to that of the Ak-Orda and Abulkhair's Khanate, but after the annexing of the Kazan and Astrakhan khanates by Imperial Russia in the middle of the 16th century the Nogai Horde disintegrated. The part of its population in modern Kazakhstan's western region joined the Kazakhs' Junior Zhuz.

## Conclusion

Although we argue that the development of statehood on the territory of Kazakhstan has deep roots, actually the first Kazakh State – the Kazakh Khanate – only came into existence at the end of the Mongol epoch, when the Ghenghisid uluses in Dasht-i-Kipchak and Central Asia collapsed, leaving various offshoot states like the Ak-Orda, Moghulistan, the Nogai Horde and Abulkhair's Khanate.

These states began to manifest more favourable conditions for exchange and interaction than during Mongol control; they were politically united ethnic tribal areas, which made them stronger and allowed the development of economies, cultures, and peaceful contact between tribes and clans. The Ak-Orda, Abulkhair's Khanate, the Nogai Horde and Moghulistan paved the way for the building of ethnically homogeneous states and the forming of large nations with their own political structures. New ethno-political communities emerged from the realms of the Golden Horde and Chagatai Ulus: Nogais, Bashkirs, Uzbeks, Kazakhs and Kyrgyz .

The territory of Kazakhstan, which had been divided by the Mongols into virtually independent states, now gave birth to the first Kazakh State in the middle of the 15th century, which at its height would absorb all the modern territory of Kazakhstan. So what did Mongol domination bring to the conquered people of this region? How significant was the Mongol period in the history of Kazakhstan?

Genghis Khan's invasion certainly had a negative impact on the economic, social, ethnic and cultural development of many nations. The Mongol conquest was accompanied by the mass extermination of innumerable people, the destruction of countless cities, the demolition of cultural values, and the loss of tens of thousands of skilled craftsmen. In particular southeastern

Kazakhstan suffered greatly. From a prosperous region of agricultural settlements and ancient cities, Semirechye was turned into a land of nomadic warrior tribes. This was an important strategic location for the Mongol conquerors and the huge influx of nomads caused a sharp reduction in sown, cultivated areas, destruction of villages and irrigation systems, crop damage by grazing cattle and the ruining of orchards. As a result the economic foundation of Semirechye's cities was undermined, and the sedentary population all but disappeared.

However, the formation of the Mongol Empire, then the Golden Horde and Chagatayid states, created a process of integration across territorial borders, allowing communication and interaction between the bearers of Eurasian steppe culture and the sedentary and agriculture-based countries they conquered. Through a well-developed postal system called the *Yam*, the Mongol authorities encouraged the development of trade and international relations. Thanks to the Mongols trade and cultural ties between many far-flung peoples and countries were established or re-energized. Across the territory of the uluses moved trade caravans, diplomatic missions and European travellers who set out to distant lands and brought information back to Europe about the peoples of previously unknown Asia. The Mongols brought the idea of centralized power to the steppe, enacting legislation specific to the steppe lifestyle; many forms of social organization and state systems were subsequently used by Central Asian states after the Mongols were gone.

The Mongols brought to the steppe their own social and political system, but it is important to note that they themselves were ethnically assimilated by the resident Turks, and eventually they all converted to Islam. As the Arabic author Al-Omari says: "In ancient times it was a Kipchak country, but when the Tatars [Mongols] seized it, the Kipchaks became their subjects. Then they (the Tatars) mixed and intermarried with the Kipchaks and the land prevailed over their natural and racial characteristics, and they all became like the Kipchaks as if of the same clan…"

*Zhanat Kundakbayeva is a Professor of History at the Al-Farabi Kazakh National University in Almaty. Among her publications are books discussing the policy of the Russian Empire to the northern Caspian region's nomadic peoples in the 18th century. Kundakbayeva was a fellow of the Slavic Research Centre in Hokkaido, Japan in 2010, and of the UC Berkeley Institute of Slavic, East European and Eurasian Studies in 2012-2013.*

# RISE OF THE KAZAKH KHANATE: THE ZHUZES UNITE

The Kazakh Khanate as a distinct state, recognized by surrounding khanates and dynastic powers, was not created overnight but rather developed over a period of 300 years between the 15th and 17th centuries, passing through several stages of growth and decline. Its initial creation as an independent state under khans Kerei and Janibek was followed by a period of expansion under Kasym Khan, then a period of weakness which was turned around by the strong ruler Haq Nazar Khan (reigned 1538-1580), a phase known as the Kazakh Renaissance. Through the 17th century the Kazakh state went through a series of peaks and troughs, and in the 18th century its fortunes were tied to those of the constantly invading Dzungars (Zhungars or Junggars), which eventually led to the historically significant pacts with the Russian Empire and ultimately its full annexation of Kazakhstan.

As Professor Abusseitova discusses in greater detail in the following essay, a seminal moment in Kazakhstan's history occurred in 1459 when two scions of Genghis Khan, Janibek and Kerei, disassociated themselves from the Abulkhair Khanate, centred in present-day Uzbekistan, and moved east to find lands of their own, accompanied by a significant number of ally tribes. The exact circumstances that led to their refusal to show allegiance to Abulkhair (also spelt Abul-Khayr, and not to be mistaken for the later Kazakh leader of the early 18th century) are unclear, but it is thought that they were less than enamoured with his increasing preference for sedentary life in opulent city surroundings, wanting to maintain their nomadic lifestyle and steppe custom, and had angered him by failing to support him in one of his military campaigns.

Whatever the reasons, in neighbouring Moghulistan (in Semirechye) they were well received by its ruler Esen Buga Khan, and were granted fertile places to dwell in the Chu and Talas plains. In 1465-66, following Esen Buga Khan's death, they proclaimed the Kazakh Khanate, and thereby, according to tradition, laid the foundation for the first formation of a Kazakh state. At a great *kurultai* (gathering of leaders) in the Ulytau Mountains of the Central Steppe, the leaders of the multifarious tribes and tribal unions congregated to seal their unification, each inscribing their tribe's coat of arms (*tanba*) on the memorial stone of Tanbalytas. Numerous followers of the Uzbek *ulus* (tribe) adhered to this new state, resulting in the Khanate's expansion towards the north and west with the inclusion of Kipchak, Naiman, Kangly and Kerei tribes, among others.

At this point it is necessary to address the thorny issue of the three *zhuzes* – often translated as "hordes" but more accurately "unions" between tribes that were culturally the same but of various ethnic composition (Turkic or Mongol; Nogai, Kipchak or Kangly, etc). The origin and formation of these tribal confederations are one of the greatest mysteries of Kazakh history. There are many theories and opinions: oral folk stories tell imaginative tales of three brothers, or of three *dzhigits* (knights) chasing a runaway horse; another theory links them to the disintegration of the tribes during the early 16th century and the renewal of tribal bonds under Haq Nazar Khan when he came to power.

Some historians link the zhuzes' origin to the presence of three major landscape forms – Semire-chye's fertile region centred on the Ili and Chu river valleys, the vast steppe region of east *Dasht-i-Kipchak*, and the arid semi-desert of western Kazakhstan between the Aral Sea and the Caspian – whereas others trace them back to political factors such as the division of the territory under the heirs of Genghis Khan.

"The Battle between Shah Ismail and Abulkhair Khan" (the 15th century leader of the Uzbeks), from the "Tarikhi-i alam-aray-i Shah Ismail" (Mu'in Musavvir, c. 1688). A Safavid book, this painting obviously shows Ismail in the ascendancy

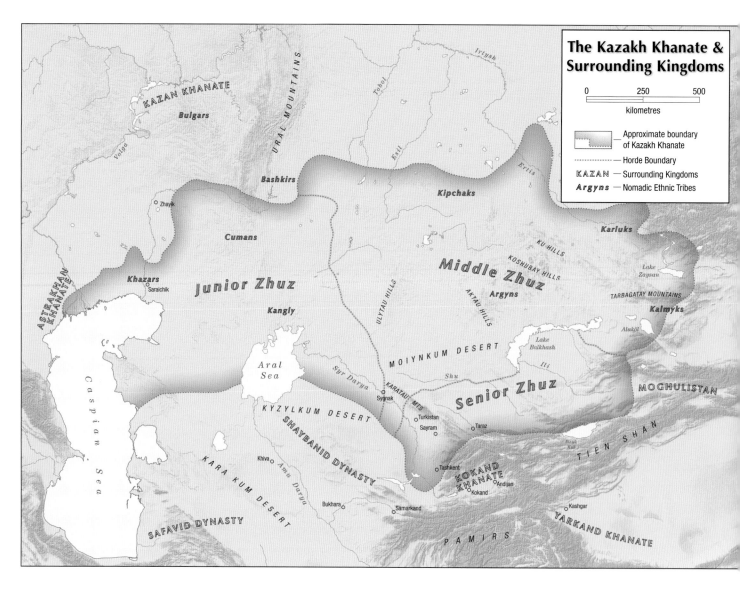

The Kazakh Khanate &
Surrounding Kingdoms

0    250    500
kilometres

Approximate boundary
of Kazakh Khanate

---- Horde Boundary

KAZAN — Surrounding Kingdoms

*Argyns* — Nomadic Ethnic Tribes

## KHANS OF THE KAZAKH KHANATE

| | |
|---|---|
| Kerei (Girei) Khan and Janibek (Zhanibek) Khan | 1465–1480 |
| Baranduk (Burunduk) Khan | 1480–1511 |
| Kasym Khan | 1511–1518 |
| Mamash Khan | 1518–1522 |
| Tahir Khan | 1522–1531 |
| Buidash Khan | 1531–1534 |
| Togym Khan | 1534–1538 |
| Haq Nazar (Khak-Nazar) Khan | 1538–1580 |
| Shigay Khan | 1580–1582 |
| Tauekel Khan | 1582–1598 |
| Ishim (Esim) Khan | 1598–1628 |
| Jahangir (Salqam-Jangir) Khan | 1629–1680 |
| Tauke Khan | 1680–1718 |
| Ablai Khan | 1771–1781 |
| Kenesary Khan | 1841–1847 |

The earliest written reference to the zhuzes is found in historical documents related to Russian-Mongol relations in 1616. The most realistic theory, it seems, is that there must have been groupings of clans and tribes throughout the steppe on many occasions in centuries past – simply as a matter of survival in a harsh environment – and when during the 17th century the entire region was under threat from the

Dzungars, the collective tribes of the Kazakh Khanate, the Nogai Horde and the former tribes of Moghulistan found themselves forming a united front against the invaders. It is from these groupings that the zhuzes most likely emerged.

The *Uli* (Senior) Zhuz united the tribes of the Alban, Uysun, Dulat, Zhalair, Kangly, Suan, Sergely, Oshakht, Ysty and Shaprashty, and their 32 clans (*ordy*), and occupied the area around the middle and upper Syr Darya and Semirechye. The *Orta* (Middle) Zhuz inhabited central and northern Kazakhstan and included the major tribes of Kipchak, Argyn, Kerei, Kongrat, Naiman and Ouak with their 40 clans. The *Kishi* (Junior) Zhuz was settled along the lower Syr Darya, on the shores of the Aral Sea and in the Caspian Depression; to it belonged the tribes of the Alimuly, Bayuly and Zhetiru with 25 clans.

The name "Kazakh" also presents some problems of origin, with its own raft of etymological and historical theories. It is most likely that the name comes from the Turkic word *qazaq*, used to describe someone who had freed themselves from a figure of authority. In fact the original spelling was indeed Qazaqs, designating them as "free" or "independent" people. What is certain is that by the end of the 15th century the "Kazakh people" were being referred to as a distinct group, set apart from the "Uzbek" confederation in which their leaders had previously been included.

The details of the Kazakh Khanate's ups and downs over the course of the 16th and 17th centuries are explained in the following essay, but it is worth emphasizing that at times the Kazakh realm included virtually all of modern Kazakhstan's territory and beyond – Samarkand, Bukhara and Ferghana were part of the Kazakh Khanate for a short time, and Russian territory in the north and west was heavily influenced, mostly by raiding for slaves.

But wherever there is prosperity, envy tends to follow – and it was inevitable that various sultans' claims to power were to increase within the Khanate. The struggle for influence within the zhuzes also increased, with the power of the tribal aristocracy (*beys*) and warlords (*batyrs*) becoming stronger and stronger. The small hereditary segment at the top of Kazakh Khanate society considered themselves successors of Genghis Khan, and dubbed themselves *Aq Suyek* ("White Bones"), while the non-hereditary masses were the *Kara Suyek* ("Black Bones") – "bone" denoting lineage. They were required to follow codes of law compiled and enacted by the strongest of the khans: Kasym, Haq Nazar, Ishim and finally Tauke, whose *Zhety Zhargy* ("Seven Rules") were developed in the beginning of the 18th century by the "three sages" Ayteke Bi, Tole Bi and Kazybek Bi, to settle internal conflicts within the tribes and to reinforce the state.

Tragically, further fragmentation and social polarisation led to the weakening of the state, and as the raiding by the powerful Dzungars from the east grew ever more frequent,

in 1717 Tauke Khan was forced to appeal for help from the mighty Russian Empire, its neighbour to the north. At that time no actual intervention was necessary, and when Tauke Khan died in 1718, his successor did not consider himself committed to his word.

The horrific period between 1723 and 1726, when the Dzungars dealt out murder and mayhem to the peoples of Semirechye and the Kazakh Steppe, are remembered as the "Years of Great Distress". They resulted in a temporary consolidation of forces, mostly within the middle and lower stratas of the population. Abulkhair Khan of the Junior Horde and later Ablai Khan of the Middle Horde succeeded in uniting the Kazakh tribes for a short period; kurultais took place on a regular basis, and a popular defence force was formed. However, in 1731, lacking confidence in their own defences, the elders of the Junior Horde under Abulkhair Khan concluded an assistance pact with Russia and placed themselves under Russian sovereignty. It was a fateful decision: over the course of the following 150 years the entire Kazakh territory would become part of the Russian Empire and was – initially peacefully – colonized.

Top: Abulkhair Khan, the leader of the Junior Zhuz who for a short period in the early 18th century united the steppe tribes to repel the Dzungars, but who ultimately swore allegiance to the Russian Empire. Above: A statue in Astana of the "Three sages" – Kazybek Bi, Tole Bi and Ayteke Bi – who helped Tauke Khan create a new code of law for the Kazakhs to live by: the *Zhety Zhargy* or "Seven Rules"

# The evolution of Kazakh statehood

By *Meruyert Kh. Abusseitova*

The formation of the Kazakh Khanate was built on the development of pre-existing states such as Ak-Orda and Moghulistan, ruled by descendants of Genghis Khan's sons Juchi and Chagatai respectively. By the 1420s, the Great Steppe had split up into several uluses, the southern regions of Ak-Orda being ruled by descendants of the most prominent khans Urus and Barak, but in particular by the Shaybanid Abulkhair, who with his nomadic Uzbek tribes slowly built himself a new khanate through military campaigns and consolidation of the many other nomadic groups of the steppe.

This colourful 15th century miniature painting by Siya Kalem, titled "Preparation for hunting", illustrates an important element of the nomadic lifestyle – hunting with birds of prey

By the middle of the 15th century, the nomadic Uzbek state of Abulkhair's Khanate ruled the majority of East *Dasht-i Kipchak*, although his struggle with the Juchids to the north continued throughout his reign, and his power never extended to the whole of the Ak-Orda territory. Incessant wars and civil dissent were ever-present in his state, constantly weakening it, but the most significant characters were two political opponents descended from Urus Khan: the sultans Kerei (Kirey or Girei) and Janibek (Janybek or Zhanibek).

In 1459-1460, these two proud leaders decided to leave the state of Abulkhair Khan, taking with them a group of ally tribes. They moved east into the neighbouring territory of Moghulistan, which at that time was ruled by Esen Buga Khan. He received Kerei, Janibek and the other sultans hospitably, and gave them territory in the western part of Moghulistan known as "Chu and Kozy-Bashi" along the Chu and Talas rivers.

This angered Abulkhair Khan considerably, and he prepared an army to punish his former

A 15th century Timurid painting from Samarkand shows Timur's grandson Ulugh Beg with ladies of his harem and retainers (note the figures at top right with nomad caps and a falcon). Ulugh Beg ruled southern Kazakhstan until the Shaybanid Abulkhair Khan swept south to seize control and carve out his new khanate

The move by Kerei and Janibek to the Chu River region was of course an important link in the chain of political events that contributed to the formation of the Kazakh Khanate. However, this process was associated not only with the migration of the two khans, but was a result of the general economic, social and political development of the broader area of medieval Kazakhstan, and the ethnic history of the nascent Kazakh group. Kerei and Janibek's decision to leave the Uzbek Khanate of Abulkhair and find their own land outside state control simply cast a spotlight on one of the most important stages in this process.

As the 15th century ended and the 16th century began, the modern name of the Kazakh nation was established. During that period, sources from neighbouring countries and peoples began to refer specifically to the "Kazakh people". Terms such as *"Mamlakat-i Kazakh"*, *"Doulat-i Kazakh"* and *"Ulus-i Kazakh"* appeared, all meaning "the state of the Kazakhs"; and with recognition of Kazakh statehood a defined territory and a certain ethnic composition also took shape once and for all.

As ever, though, maintaining control over a wide-ranging population of nomadic tribes was a difficult feat. The strength and durability of a khan's power depended on the extent to which he met the interests of the nomadic elite. In addressing issues that affected the entire state, the khan had to deal with a council consisting of both Genghisids (sultans and *oghlans*) and representatives of clans (*biys/beys, tarkhans, bahadurs* and elders), as well as the urban nobility who controlled the cities, and the clergy.

The importance of Islam in strengthening the authority of the khans during the 16th and 17th centuries should not be overlooked. Various Sufi orders took refuge in the khans' camps and spread the faith, and the khans, seeing their value, supported them and used them for their own purposes. One significant religious figure from the 16th century was Maulan Muhammad Kazakh Rabateghi (Syradg al-Salkiman Muhammad Rakim). The Sufis were the missionaries of Islam in Central Asia. The religious writing of Khoja Ishac, who preached the doctrine of the Nashbandija order, described in detail the lives, tribal structure and politics of the Kazakh khans.

Janibek and Kerei ruled together, though Kerei was the senior leader till his death in 1470, after which Janibek ruled alone until he died in 1480. Oriental sources reveal that Baranduk (Burunduk) then inherited power, having

sultans and invade Semirechye. However, he died on this campaign in the late 1460s, and during the inevitable period of unrest that followed, a growing number of tribes adjoined themselves to the Qazaqs (Kazakhs) or "free people", as they were becoming known to differentiate them from the nomadic Uzbeks. The Kazakhs' area of control gradually expanded until as many as 200,000 people looked to Kerei and Janibek as their leaders.

## THE FORMATION OF THE KAZAKH KHANATE

A plethora of sources from the Middle East, Persia and China describe in detail the internal political struggle that raged across the territory of Kazakhstan after the death of Abulkhair Khan. But despite common opinion that the history of the Kazakhs begins with Kerei and Janibek's split with the Uzbeks and migration to a new land, it can actually be traced back much earlier. The question of the Kazakh khans' origins and blood relations can only be solved by studying the history of the Golden Horde and the states that emerged from its ruin. Numerous sources adduce the genealogy of Juchi's descendants in naming them as the Kazakh khans' ancestors.

This mid-16th century painting shows the ascension of Abulkhair Khan to the throne of his new khanate (more than 100 years earlier). Note that where other illustrations always showed nomadic leaders wearing the typical headgear of the steppes, here Abulkhair wears a crown – more common to the shahs of Persia farther south

lordship over all the other Kazakh sultans, including Janysh Sultan and his brother Tanysh Sultan (occupying the grazing pastures of Kara-Abdal), Ahmad Sultan (son of Janysh), but most importantly Kasym Sultan, Janibek's son, whose land was in the region of Balkhash Lake and the Karatal River. Each of these sultans headed separate Kazakh tribes which formed uluses – areas of grazing land granted to them by the supreme Khan, whom they all obeyed.

Kasym, however, commanded the Kazakh army and distinguished himself in battles with Muhammad Shaybani Khan, a Juchid who had been given Turkistan (formerly called Yassi) by Mahmud Khan of Moghulistan in return for assisting him in a war against Ahmed Mirza, the Sultan of Samarkand. Muhammad Shaybani Khan attempted to capture the southern areas of Dasht-i Kip-chak, but was defeated by Kasym, whose popularity and power grew so much among the Kazakh people that although Baranduk officially continued to be the senior

Khan, according to the *"Tarikh-i Rashidi"* by the military general and chronicler Muhammad Haidar he was sidelined and became increasingly unpopular.

Haidar wrote that almost a million people followed and were loyal to Kasym; the Kazakh sultans and other members of the nobility supported him because of the success of his military campaigns and the abundance of looted treasure he doled out. With each new campaign Kasym's influence grew stronger, until despite the fact that he was not the legitimate Khan, the time came when he was actually recognized as the Khan of all Kazakhs. Unpopular and with few allies, Baranduk was expelled from the steppe and died in exile in Samarkand, leaving Kasym Khan to become the sovereign ruler of Dasht-i Kipchak.

Meanwhile, the Shaybanids' power and their military successes in Mawarannahr had also increased. Sources report of four campaigns by

118   The evolution of Kazakh statehood

Muhammad Shaybani Khan against the Kazakhs; the southern Dasht-i Kipchak steppes – especially the Syr Darya region, which was rich in pastures – were constantly fought over by the two sides. The Kazakhs' need to exchange their surplus animal products for agricultural products and urban crafts created a desire to master the Syr Darya cities, but their efforts met with resistance from the Shaybanids, who wanted to block the Kazakhs out of the interregional markets.

In 1509, Muhammad Shaybani Khan's army attacked Kasym in the Ulytau Mountains of the Central Steppe and routed the Kazakhs in their wintering grounds. However, the following year Kasym defeated him in the Ulytau foothills and drove him back south; Muhammad Shaybani never recovered from this campaign, his authority weakened and he subsequently died near Merv. Kasym, however, became Khan in 1511, consolidating his domination over the vast steppe areas of the Kazakh Khanate.

When Kasym Khan died in 1518, the Kazakh Khanate fell into a time of feuding between sultans. His son Mamash Sultan became khan, but soon died of suffocation in one of many battles. After his death, Tahir Khan, son of Adik Sultan, ascended to the throne of the Kazakh Khanate. Unfortunately, during his rule the strength of the Kazakhs was noticeably shaken; Tahir suffered a series of defeats in the west by the Nogai tribes, lost nomadic territories near the Yaik (Ural) River and migrated to Kochkara. This significantly reduced the number of Tahir's subjects; while Kasym Khan was said to have

Above: An exquisitely detailed 17th century Kazakh war helmet complete with chainmail neck skirt. Left: An impressive statue of the Kazakh Khanate's founding fathers – Kerei and Janibek – stands in front of the Museum of the First President in Astana. Below left: Muhammad Shaybani Khan receives a moon-faced girl in front of his yurt, in an early 16th century painting by Mullah Muhammad Shadi of Mawarannahr

commanded an army of ten lakhs or one million warriors (many Turkic societies used the term "lakh", corresponding to 100,000 as per modern Indian usage), Tahir's reign saw a serious decline and his army was reduced to two lakhs (200,000 subordinates). Tahir never enjoyed a reputation such as Kasym Khan had had; he was a man of extreme cruelty, and according to contemporary sources, "about 400,000 people suddenly turned away from him and scattered".

After the retreat of the Moghuls into the Tarim Basin, where they continued to hold power until the late 17th century, Semirechye came under the sway of the Kazakhs and Kyrgyz. In the mid-1520s a large proportion of the Kyrgyz tribe had joined Tahir, but the alliance between the Kazakhs and Kyrgyz did not last long – some say due to Tahir's cruelty and mistreatment. Tahir died some time between 1529 and 1533; according to Muhammad Haidar, he remained among the Kyrgyz and died in conditions of great distress. Power then passed to his brother Buidash (Buydash), who ruled briefly until 1534.

## RENAISSANCE UNDER HAQ NAZAR KHAN, SHIGAY AND TAUEKEL

The 16th century saw important developments in the Kazakh state's military affairs and diplomacy, but it also suffered periods of deep crisis and decline. The Kazakhs struggled to retain lands from hostile forces that began to penetrate the steppe, creating anti-Kazakh coalitions and undermining Kazakh authority.

When Haq Nazar (Khak-Nazar) Khan came to power in 1538, however, he carried out a number of reforms that significantly strengthened the state administration system and the Kazakh military. Slowly a resumption of foreign policy and interaction occurred, and the second half of the 16th century marked a return to the Kazakh Khanate's former power. Under Haq Nazar Khan the Syr Darya cities once again became the main focus. Confrontation between the Kazakhs and Shaybanids (and later the Ashtarkhanids) flared up again, and the Kazakhs captured a number of cities and their environs, the rulers of which were forced to manoeuvre diplomatically between their more powerful neighbours.

During Haq Nazar Khan's relatively long reign, he made a peace pact between the Kazakh Khanate and Shaybanid State and established close multilateral ties. The Shaybanid Abdullah Khan II, who ruled in Bukhara, decided that the Kazakhs' military power could be used to consolidate his own reign, especially in areas

A 1572 portrait of Muhammad Shaybani Khan from Bukhara, now held in the British Museum

where his rivals had settled. Abdullah Khan II and Haq Nazar Khan therefore agreed to create an "Oath Union" committing both sides to peaceful relations, and close ties existed between the Kazakhs and the Khanate of Bukhara until 1579. After 1580 all written references to Haq Nazar Khan in the historical sources stop. His cousin Shigay was called Kazakh Khan, but although Shigay is said to have lived to about 80 years of age, only fragmentary information on him has been preserved, and he actually ruled for only two years or so.

As the 16th century came to a close, the Kazakh khans waged a life-and-death struggle for military superiority and control over the steppes of Dasht-i Kipchak. Their enemies were many and came from all points of the compass: the Russian Empire was advancing into Siberia and across the Volga to Astrakhan; the nomadic territories of the Nogais (Mangits) were spreading over the Kazakh steppe as far as the Irtysh River; a migration of Bashkirs moved south from the Siberian steppe; Oirat tribes from the east were moving into Kazakh lands; there was pressure from Chagatayid Moghul khans to the south, and the Kyrgyz were also seeking independence. Under such a weight of pressure from all sides, the Kazakhs were slowly pushed into the Semirechye region.

Seeking a way out of this situation, the Kazakh rulers turned their eyes towards southern Central Asia. Shigay Khan had been succeeded by Tauekel (Tevke) Khan in 1582 or soon after, and his early rule was characterized by preservation of positive relations with the Shaybanids. However, in-fighting began between the Kazakh sultans, whose nominal dependence on the khan hid a desire for autonomy and separatism among some, who sometimes then sided with the Kazakhs' antagonists. The result was economic disunity and fragmentation of the Kazakh state.

As the political crisis in the Khanate grew, Tauekel attempted to conquer cities in the south; the Tashkent uprising of 1588 resulted in violent suppression by the Shaybanids, but their empire was beginning to disintegrate, and the Kazakhs soon gained control over Tashkent, Andijan, Ferghana and Samarkand. In 1598, in an attempt to conquer Mawarannahr Tauekel Khan laid siege to Bukhara, but this was a step too far, and he was driven back to Tashkent, where he died soon after.

## TRADE, ECONOMY AND ADMINISTRATION AMONG KAZAKHS

At this point it is important to note that although military clashes and conflict were a regular feature of the Kazakh Khanate during this period of history, there were also periods when good neighbourly relations allowed for healthy trade along the ancient caravan routes. Kazakh history and culture developed through close interaction with both Eastern and Western civilizations – Chinese, Turkic, Iranian, Arabic and Mongol medieval written records are all valuable sources of study for Kazakh statehood and its ethno-political history.

Sources from the 16th to 18th centuries report on diplomatic negotiations between the Kazakh khans and the rulers of neighbouring Central Asian states such as Khiva, Bukhara and Kokand, but also countries much farther afield. The Kazakh Khanate had diplomatic relations with the Safavids of Persia, the Moghuls in India, the burgeoning Russian Empire and the Ottoman Empire in Turkey.

The steppe region had of course acted as a bridge between East and West for millennia, and despite the opening of the maritime trade routes

there was still much commerce across Kazakh territory in the 16th-17th centuries. Political and trade relations with the Central Asian khanates, India, Afghanistan and Russia greatly expanded under the Kazakh khans, and the exchange of diplomatic missions flourished. Archaeological evidence corroborates this through the large amounts of gold and silver coinage discovered – a vital component of interstate trade.

From the end of the 16th century the exchange in Russian-Kazakh embassies intensified, and the trade routes between the Kazakh Khanate, Central Asia and Russia played a major role in the economy and livelihoods of the regions' peoples. Kazakhs were the suppliers of camels and horses for caravans; artisans from cities supplied the passing caravans with necessary products; and security guards and guides were mainly local Kazakhs and Turkmen.

The most dynamic trade routes passed through Semirechye and southern Kazakhstan and were part of the ancient Silk Road, but there were many others; trade passed down the Syr Darya to the Aral Sea then west to the Caspian and

"A Kirghiz gathering" by Nikolai Karazin (1842-1908) appears to show a transaction between Kazakhs and Uzbeks as two girls are sold into slavery, which was rife in Central Asia in the 18th and early 19th centuries

across the sea to Astrakhan from Mangyshlak, as well as around the Caspian's northern coast. The Kazakhs also traded in livestock with the new Mughal Empire in northern India, driving cattle south through Central Asia. Written sources show that a significant number of horses (up to 40,000) were driven to India from Bukhara by Kazakh merchants – Kazakh-bred horses had an especially high value.

Kazakh merchants traded directly with China as well. The memoirs of Babur the Timurid, founder of the Mughal Empire, mention caravans returning from China in the late 15th century. He estimated the total strength of some caravans at 1,000 people, which gives an idea of the volume of trade that was conducted with China during these years. A Chinese source from the 18th century titled *Xiyu tsung chib* illustrates the flow of goods between the countries at that time, stating that a prosperous Kazakh pastoral economy allowed them to buy Chinese silk and other products in abundance.

Even during times of war trade continued, though to a lesser extent. Seid Aly Rais, the 16th century author of *Mirat al-Mamalik*, described the "Tashkent" and "Turkistan" roads, which connected Bukhara with Astrakhan via the Syr Darya cities and Saraichik on the Zhayik (Ural) River. His information on the state of cities such as Sayram, Turkistan and Sygnak provides insight into the political, cultural and economic life of both nomads and settled populations in Central Asia. At the beginning of the 16th century Sygnak was said to be the "harbour of Dasht-i Kipchak", where goods from the Volga, Mawarannahr, Kashgar, Khotan and China could be found.

Although this picture was shot in the 20th century, take away the gun and this image of Kazakhs hunting with eagles could represent a scene from 300 years ago (©MAE (Kunstkamera) RAS No: 2035-212)

The greatest khans also enacted legislation aimed at strengthening the internal foundations of Kazakh society and the development of statehood. Of these, the most important were Kasym Khan's *"Kasym Hannyn Qasqa Zholy"* ("Bright Road of Kasym Khan"), Haq Nazar Khan's *"Aq Zhol"* ("Bright Path"), Ishim Khan's *"Eski Zholy"*("Original Path") and Tauke Khan's *"Zhety Zhargy"* ("Seven Rules").

## INTERNAL STRIFE AND THE COMING OF THE DZUNGARS

During the early 17th century the Kazakh statehood was strengthened, increased trade and cultural relations with neighbouring countries took place, but there was constant military conflict with the Ashtarkhanids of Bukhara for possession of Tashkent, Turkistan, Sauran and Andijan, over which the Kazakhs' power extended at that time.

Ishim (Esim) Khan officially inherited the title of supreme leader in 1598 after his brother Tauekel's death. He ruled in Turkistan, but among the Kazakh sultans there were several competing factions headed by sultans Tursun, Abulay and Khan Zadeh. The instability of their relationships was compounded by the Ashtarkhanid Imamkuli Khan (reigned 1611-1642), who colluded and made temporary alliances to sow dissent among the Kazakhs and weaken their state.

In 1613 Imamkuli Khan took Tashkent and made Kazakh sultan Tursun its ruler. However, Tursun soon refused to recognize Imamkuli Khan's suzerainty and began to mint his own coins and

Above: A timeless image of three *begs* (local headmen) in western Kazakhstan, their clothing unchanged from centuries past (©MAE (Kunstkamera) RAS No: 136-41).
Below: A stone relief depicting the Kazakh wars with the Dzungars is part of a semicircular collection of such historic moments in Kazakhstan's history located in Almaty's Independence Square

Within the quarters of the Kazakh khans were chancelleries whose job was to prepare and send diplomatic, social and economic documents with envoys to the rulers of foreign countries. For the Kazakh Khanate, as well as every other Central Asian nomadic society that reached a certain level of development, the export of livestock was the mainstay of its economy, and was therefore a key issue. Monetary reforms were initiated – currency circulation both strengthened a khan's authority and helped to revive trade links with neighbouring countries and peoples. From the 16th century on, the role of capital cities as the centres of state coinage increased (Tursun Muhammad Khan and Tauekel Khan, among others, minted their own coins).

A bust of a Kipchak warrior with helmet and chainmail protecting the neck and shoulders.

levy his own *baj* (duty) and *kharaj* (land tax). After internecine fighting with Tursun Sultan, Ishim Khan, together with his Kazakh and Kyrgyz subject uluses, was forced to move to the region of modern-day Kyrgyzstan. At this time the Kazakhs and Kyrgyz were again allies, and in 1621 one of the largest battles between Ashtarkhanid troops and the combined forces of Kazakhs and Kyrgyz took place.

The Kazakh khans now each developed strategic alliances with different Chagatayid rulers in Moghulistan – Tursun with Abd al-Latif (Apak) Khan of Yarkand and Kashgar, and Ishim with Abd ar-Rakhim Khan, the ruler of Chalysh and Turfan (Turpan). Ishim's enmity with Tursun in Tashkent grew, and his failure to be recognized by all as the supreme khan of the Kazakhs weakened him further, forcing him at one point to move to Abd ar-Rakhim Khan's territory and contribute his own troops to that leader's cause for a period of five years or more. Ishim Khan did eventually defeat his enemies and abolish the Tashkent khanate in 1627, but according to Mahmud ibn Wali he died the following year (although some other sources allege that Ishim ruled until 1643) and was buried in Turkistan near the mausoleum of Khoja Ahmed Yasawi.

After Ishim Khan, power passed to his son Jahangir (Salqam-Jangir), but the Kazakh Khanate was once again torn by internal strife, and Abulay Sultan took control of Tashkent and the surrounding region from his base in Andijan. However, the 1630s saw a major shift in the political situation in the lands to the east

of the Kazakhs on the far side of the Altai and Tarbagatai mountains. One of the major tribes of the Mongol Oirat (Kalmyk) confederation had steadily been growing in power, and in 1635 the new Dzungar (Zhungar or Junggar) Khanate began to make incursions along the banks of the Irtysh River.

The Kazakhs' struggle against the Buddhist Dzungars for possession of valuable nomadic lands became fiercer as the years passed, and the balance of power in the seemingly ceaseless and debilitating wars was not in favour of the Kazakhs. In fighting the Dzungars Jahangir Khan enjoyed the support of Abdullah Khan of East Turkestan, but the tide of invading armies from Dzungaria (today's northern Xinjiang, China) continued throughout the middle of the 17th century, as the Dzungar leader Batur made a determined effort to wipe out the Kazakh Khanate.

Jahangir Khan was killed in battle in 1680 and Tauke Khan was elected to carry the fight to the Dzungars. But Batur's son Galdan continued where his father had left off, and slowly conquered most of Semirechye in the 1680s, forcing the Kazakhs west. When the new Dzungar chief Khuntay-shi Tsewang Rabdan took control of the Dzungar hordes, the situation for the Kazakhs deteriorated even further. Although Tauke Khan scored some successes in minor skirmishes, he could not drive the Dzungars back. One war after another followed as the 18th century began, and the Kazakhs were under serious threat from many sides, their people being enslaved, their animals driven off and whole villages and clans massacred.

In 1717 Kaip Khan and Abulkhair Khan of the Junior Zhuz led 30,000 warriors in a major campaign against the Dzungar Khanate, but they suffered a crushing defeat at Ayaguz River in the eastern Kazakh steppe. When Tauke Khan died in 1718, no leader was able to hold the failing khanate together, and power degenerated to the leaders among the three tribal unions known as the Senior, Middle and Junior zhuzes. In 1723 the Dzungars moved in huge force into Kazakh territory and the Kazakhs had no choice but to flee before them. This was the start of the "Years of Great Distress", marked by terrible losses and hardship as the conquering invaders swept murderously across the region, in the process capturing Sayram, Turkistan and Tashkent.

The only way to fight back was as a united force, and the uprising took shape under the

banners of *batyrs* (brave knights or warrior heroes) such as Bogenbay, Raimbek, Saureq and Janibeg Khan. The troops of each of the zhuzes came together and in 1726 the Dzungars were defeated in the Battle of Bulanty in the eastern Torgai steppe. Emboldened by their success and still united, the Kazakhs chose Abulkhair Khan of the Junior Zhuz as their leader, and in 1730 at the Battle of Anrakai they triumphed again, this time driving the Dzungars back to their eastern homeland.

Yet despite this success, the unity of the zhuzes did not last, and the steppe splintered into separate domains, even with the imminent danger of a renewed Dzungar invasion. With little confidence in his people's ability to withstand the next assault from the east, in 1731 Abulkhair Khan concluded an assistance pact with Empress Anna of the Russian Empire, in which the Junior Zhuz placed itself under Russian sovereignty. Sameke Khan of the Middle Zhuz subsequently also put his seal to the pact – although a young Ablai Khan did not – and in 1738 certain khans of the Senior Zhuz also signed.

This was the signal for the Russian Empire to begin its inexorable advance into Central Asia – little could the Kazakh khans have imagined of what the future held.

*Meruyert Abusseitova is the former Director of the RB Suleimenov Institute of Oriental Studies in Kazakhstan's Ministry of Education and Science. Currently she is Director of the Institute's Republican Information Centre for the Study of Historical Materials, as well as Chairperson of the UNESCO Chair in Science and Spirituality. A well-known researcher working in the field of history, historiography, historical sources and Central Asian and Islamic studies, she has authored 10 books and more than 200 articles in Kazakhstan and worldwide, and participates in numerous multinational research projects and conferences. She is President of the European Association of Central Asian Studies (ESCAS), a member of the International Institute of Nomadic Civilizations under UNESCO, and on the governing board of the OIC's Research Centre for Islamic History, Art and Culture (IRCICA).*

In the Burabay forest-steppe region north of Astana lies the "Sleeping Batyr", a mountain ridge that looks like a Kazakh warrior's head in profile (from left you can see his helmet, eyebrow, nose and mouth). The legend goes that a hero exhorted his people to fight but when none came forward, he rode out against an invading army alone. He fought bravely against impossible odds, but knowing he could not win, eventually retreated and lay down to die of his wounds, whereupon his body became a mountain that blocked the invaders' route to his people's encampment. There are many such legends from the era of Ablai Khan and the Dzungar wars

Above: An 1889 watercolour portrait of Sultan Baimuhammed by
S. Aleksandrovsky, who painted embassy members attending the
coronation of Alexander II. Top right: Kazakh tribesmen with a local
Russian governor and his family (circa 1885) in front of a yurt

# THE RUSSIAN EMPIRE:
# ACQUIESCENCE AND CULTURAL UNREST

Russia's entrance onto the Central Asian stage did not follow the historical formula of sweeping onslaughts by conquering armies that until now had characterized most invasions of the steppe. Instead, it was a slow and careful process designed to expand Russia's sphere of influence towards China and the East.

In the middle of the 16th century, after conquering the khanates of Kazan and Astrakhan, Tsar Ivan the Terrible had wooden fortifications constructed along the the western bank of the Yaik (Ural) River – the front line against the Kazakh tribes on the eastern side. The Cossacks founded the first Russian town within modern-day Kazakhstan's territory in 1613, when the frontier post of Yaitsk was built along the Yaik River (the town was renamed Uralsk in 1775 and the river became the Ural). In 1645 the Guriyev family, one of Russia's wealthy trade clans, was allowed to develop and strengthen the fort on the lower Yaik against Kalmyks, Cossacks and Kazakhs alike, and this grew into the town of Guriyev (today's Atyrau).

But it was Tsar Peter I (styled "Peter the Great") who, at the start of the 18th century recognized the full extent of the potential rewards of expansion into Central Asia. The steppe lands bordering southern Siberia and the Altai Mountains were relatively easily reached from Siberian fortresses like Tobolsk via the great Irtysh River, and over a five-year period from 1715 to 1720 forts were built along the "Irtysh Line" – first Omsk and Yamishevsk (1716), then Zhelezinsk (1717), Semipalatinsk (1718), and finally Koriakovsk and Ust-Kamenogorsk (1720). This string of fortified strongholds, all manned by Cossack forces, played a crucial role in Russia's defence against the brutal Dzungars and other would-be invaders, as well as being strategically important in the forthcoming colonization of Kazakh territory.

The political and cultural transformation of the Kazakh people took place gradually in comparison to other countries, and it took many decades before it became obvious that the 18th century khans' submission to Russia had effectively sold the Kazakh steppe to the Russians. Although this was partly due to the desperate circumstances of the times, when Russia was seen as the lesser of evils, greed and a lust for personal gain also came heavily into play amongst many of the Kazakh nobility. The Russian administrators were clever, giving power to those khans they could most easily control and paying off or emasculating those they could not. They preyed on the historical feuding and rivalries that ran through the clan hierarchy and epitomized the steppe nomads of the time.

## ABLAI KHAN: WARRIOR, LEADER AND DIPLOMAT

However, not all Kazakh leaders were dishonourable or weak. The greatest Kazakh name of the 18th century was Abulmansur Ablai (1711-1781), later known simply as Ablai Khan. He was a sultan of the Middle Zhuz who played a major role in the unification of the three Kazakh zhuzes. Descended from the 15th century co-founder of the Kazakh state Janibek Khan, Ablai proved himself to be a brave warrior from a very early age, earning the title *batyr* (hero) in battles with the Dzungars. As he grew older his talent for organizing and strategizing brought him more renown – he took part in all the major battles with the Dzungars between 1720 and 1750, and resisted swearing any oath of allegiance to Russia, diplomatically sidestepping their attempts to gain his signature and at the same time forging peaceful relations with the Qing emperor Qianlong, who in the 1750s finally crushed the Dzungar Empire and ended the Kazakhs' suffering under that particularly fearsome foe.

Above: A representation of Ablai Khan, who led the Kazakhs against the Dzungar threat. Right: A Qing dynasty painting of Emperor Qianlong's battlefield court in the Ili Valley at the end of his campaign against the Dzungars in the late 18th century, when they were finally destroyed. Below: Kazakhs present a tribute of horses to Emperor Qianlong in a painting by the Italian Giuseppe Castiglione (1688-1766), a celebrated Qing court artist

For much of his life Ablai competed with Abul Mambet Khan for leadership of the Middle Zhuz. Abul Mambet was officially named Khan of the Middle Zhuz by the Russians, while Ablai had the backing of the Chinese. In 1740, however, he was captured by the Dzungars in the Ulytau Mountains, and it was only after the intervention of a Russian embassy that he was released. As a result he finally swore allegiance to Russia, though he continued to maintain an austere and organized hierarchy of power and a strong army, and developed a network of diplomatic and commercial connections with Russia, China and the khanates of Bukhara and Khiva.

In 1771, at a *kurultai* of the three zhuzes, Ablai was elected as the Kazakh khan (a title ratified by Russia). At this point there was still some hope of creating a strong and independent Kazakh state. Ablai Khan headed the unified forces of the Kazakhs and furthered the centralization of state power in Kazakhstan, performing a political juggling act as he deftly played China off against Russia in an attempt to keep control of the steppe for the Kazakhs. (This "multi-vector" approach was mirrored more than two centuries later when Kazakhstan finally gained independence, its leader Nursultan Nazarbayev employing the same tactics to help build the nascent state's economic and political foundation.)

Ablai Khan led a number of campaigns against the Khanate of Kokand and the Kirghiz tribes in the south. During his final campaign he liberated many cities in southern Kazakhstan and even captured Tashkent. From there he proceeded into present-day Kyrgyzstan, winning a great battle against the forces of the region's Kirghiz warlords. When he died in 1781, Ablai Khan was given the high honour of interment in the Khoja Ahmed Yasawi Mausoleum in Turkistan – a fitting tribute for a leader who, despite the inexorable advance of the Russian Empire, did his utmost to preserve the ideal of the Kazakh nation.

Once it had a foothold in the steppe regions, there was no stopping Imperial Russia's advance, though many tried. The Russian Peasants' War of 1773-74, led by Yemelyan Pugachev in the grasslands astride the Ural River, was crushed by Russian troops. Rebellion flared once again in this region in the 1780s with the Kazakh Liberation Wars, when a peasant army under Srym Datov held out for 14 years against the Russian forces. But Mother Russia was not to be denied, and in 1797 Datov surrendered after discovering treachery being plotted within his own Kazakh ranks.

The khans' position and influence continued to be undermined and weakened, and in 1822 they were replaced as representatives of power by Russian governors. Popular dissent once more boiled over in 1836 in an uprising led by the poet Makhambet Utemisuly and his comrade-in-arms Issatay Taymanov. Grazing rights between the Volga and Ural rivers were at the core of the problem; for two years the area controlled by the Junior Zhuz was ravaged by insurgency, only to end with the defeat and death of Taymanov, and the murder of Utemisuly in 1846.

### KAZAKH LUMINARIES OF THE 19TH CENTURY

Concurrent with this rebellion, further protests against the weakening of the traditional patriarchal order arose over the majority of Kazakh territory, and by 1837 unrest had spread and taken on the dimension of a powerful uprising under the leadership of Kenesary Kasymov (1802-1847). A grandson of Ablai Khan, Kenesary rejected and fought against the stripping of the khans' authority and loss of fertile pastureland to Russian settlers and military forces. He led a rebellion that sought to regain independence for the Kazakhs, reinstate the Kazakh Khanate and bring power back to the beys. From 1837 he commanded a force that sometimes reached 20,000 men, and with this military might brought vast stretches of land under his control.

In 1841, in strict contradiction of Russian law he was elected Khan at a kurultai in the rebel-controlled Torgai steppe. He initiated economic reforms and attempted to settle relations with the Russians peacefully, but the Tsarist government unsurprisingly rejected him and sent a large army against him. In an attempt to mobilize the entire Kazakh population against their new masters, Kenesary resorted to punitive action against *auls* that were unwilling to submit to his vision. This was a mistake, as it made him unpopular and when some of his former allies were lured to the Russian side with offers of land and gifts, he became paranoid and suspicious of the sultans that remained around him. Eventually he was forced to retreat to a peninsula in the Ili Delta region, then to the mountains of the Kirghiz tribes. Kenesary's hopes for an independent Kazakh Khanate were dashed, and in 1847 he was captured by a Kirghiz khan who cut his head off and sent it to the Russians.

Two other 19th century Kazakhs should be mentioned in any history of Kazakhstan. The first is Chokan Valikhanov (1835-1865), a great-grandson of Ablai Khan who received a first-class education at the Omsk military academy, and whose insatiable appetite for knowledge of his homeland's history, geography and ethnography drew him into a fascinating life. Joining the Russian army at 18, he served as an adjutant to the Russian governor-general, with whom he journeyed around the Kazakh steppes, increasing his knowledge of his own people. In 1855 he met and forged a strong friendship with the great Russian writer Fyodor Dostoyevsky, who had been exiled to Semipalatinsk and who was enthralled by the young Kazakh nobleman's expansive historical knowledge and inquisitive mind.

Valikhanov spent the next few years on a diplomatic and fact-finding mission to Semirechye, the Ili Valley, Issyk-Kul and as far as Kashgar. His expertise was recognized by Moscow and he became a member of the Russian Geographical Society, giving presentations of his research

in St Petersburg and being awarded the Order of Saint Vladimir for his scientific work. When in 1864 he was asked to participate in an armed expedition to wrest control of southern Kazakhstan from the khanates to the south, he declined, horrified at the thought of the suffering it would bring on the Kazakh inhabitants, and asked for premature dismissal from the army on the grounds of his worsening tuberculosis. He retired to a remote corner of Semirechye, where he dreamed of a Turkestan liberation movement, but died before his 30th birthday.

Another great Kazakh of the late 19th century was Abai Kunanbayev (1845-1904), born Ibrahim Kunanbayev but self-styled Abai the Righteous. The son of a rich Kazakh provincial leader, he was sent to Semipalatinsk to study at a Koranic school; while in that city he came to know many exiled Russian intellectuals, took part in the many seminars and discussions they had, and was heavily influenced by them.

On returning to his countryside aul, however, Abai was conflicted by the cultural chasm between his educated world view and the old Kazakh customs. He was married against his will and was forced to bow to all his father's wishes. He decided to dedicate his life to liberating his nomadic people from ignorance; taking elements from his immediate environment, he moulded them into poetry and other literary works to which uneducated Kazakhs could relate. Abai also translated classic Russian and European literature into Kazakh, making it accessible to his compatriots for the first time. A strong promoter of Kazakh national self-consciousness, Abai advocated the benefits of education and moral integrity. His literary and philosophical masterpiece, the *Book of Words*, espoused these themes and served as a powerful impulse for the development of Kazakh writing. Today, Abai is honoured as the founder of Kazakh literature.

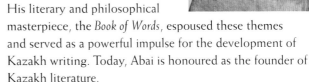

Clockwise from top left: The beautiful landscape of Burabay National Park was used as a base by Ablai Khan and the Middle Zhuz during the Dzungar wars; a statue of Kenesary Kasymov stands by the Esil River in Astana; a drawing of Abai Kunanbayev, the father of Kazakh literature; a proud statue of Abai stands at one end of the eponymous street in Almaty; Chokan Valikhanov, a Kazakh luminary of the 19th century

## RUSSIA CLOSES ITS FIST

As the second half of the 19th century began, Russian forces moved like an unstoppable tide into southern Central Asia. As the following essay by Irina Yerofeyeva explains, a string of forts were constructed along the Syr Darya River and throughout Semirechye to facilitate the annexation of the region and support the Russian troops preparing to conquer the khanates of Khiva and Kokand. In 1854 Fort Verniy was founded in the foothills of the Tien Shan on the site of the ancient settlement of Almatau (Apple Mountain). Within a year the first settlers arrived and the town of Alma-Ata began to grow; as well as Russian officials there were Cossacks and farmers from Siberia in the Greater and Lesser *stanitsa* (settlements), Tatars in their own settlement, and surrounding Kazakh auls were drawn into the gathering conurbation.

By 1860 Alma-Ata boasted a water mill, brewery, post office and hospital, and had 5,000 inhabitants living in 677 houses, of which only one was built of stone (the rest were wooden). When a 21,000-strong army from Kokand invaded Semirechye in the same year, Fort Verniy's contingent of 700 soldiers marched forth and defeated them. Alma-Ata was granted city rights in 1867 and became the centre of Semirechye province. A grand urban development plan was implemented, and by 1879 the city had 18,000 residents and a number of grandiose buildings including a cathedral and the governor's colonnaded residence. An earthquake in 1887 devastated the city, but it was rebuilt and many beautiful buildings were created, including Zenkov's all-wooden Holy Ascension Cathedral – which somehow survived another earthquake in 1911. In 1913 Alma-Ata's population was 40,000, and its position as Russia's most important city in the Kazakh territory was assured.

In 1859 Russia decreed that all slaves of the Kazakhs should be liberated and slavery abolished (though it continued in isolated incidents for some time to come). The emancipation of Russian slaves was the Tsarist excuse for invading the southern khanates, but this superficial justification was stymied by the English, who were anxious about the Russian advance towards their own empire's borders in the subcontinent and sent agents to persuade the Khan of Khiva to set free all his Russian slaves.

However, the Russian military machine was not to be halted. Tashkent was taken in 1865, Samarkand fell, and with victory over the Khanate of Kokand in 1868, when a commercial treaty made it a vassal state, Russia had conquered virtually all of present-day Kazakhstan's territory. When in 1873 first the Emirate of Bukhara, then the Khanate of Khiva fell and became Russian protectorates, Imperial Russia had finally gained complete control over Central Asia.

During the last third of the 19th century, after the abolition of serfdom in Russia in 1861, an increasing number of landless Russian peasants flooded into the Kazakh steppe. Nomads' pasturelands were confiscated, and a harsh tax system was introduced (see following essay). In this manner, livestock-breeding Kazakhs were gradually deprived of their livelihoods, and incredible poverty ensued. (Around 1890 the first oil deposits were discovered in the land north of the Caspian Sea, and early in the 20th century there was some extraction and exploitation of this resource, but at the time no one could have guessed the value this "black gold" would have for the country a century later.)

The beginning of the 20th century saw the formation of a new politicized group of Kazakh intellectuals in the Semipalatinsk region. Calling themselves Alash Orda, they remained neutral towards Russian control of the steppe, but called for greater autonomy and an end to Russian settlers being given vital Kazakh pastureland. When in June 1916 an imperial decree on the conscription of Kazakhs into war-imposed labour forces came into effect, at first Alash Orda supported the Russian administration. But for the common people this appeared to be the last straw, and under the banner of Islam, the Central Asian Revolt or "Great Revolt" broke out. Initially a united front of nomads, farmers, officials and traders, it was harshly suppressed, which prompted the majority of Alash Orda's members to abandon any association with the Tsarist authorities.

However, the events of 1917 were to change the political and social landscape of Central Asia almost beyond recognition. The Russian Revolution and abdication of the Tsar were seen by many Kazakhs as an opportunity for positive change and an end to expansionism by foreign settlers in their steppe lands. This naive hope, however, was soon to be proved very wrong.

Clockwise from far left: An old photo of Almaty in its early years; two examples of intricate 19th century Kazakh metalwork, the bracelet and ring sets from western Kazakhstan, the orb-like button from the Semipalatinsk region; Russian settlers near Petropavlovsk at the turn of the 20th century; "Tatars swearing allegiance to the Tsar", by Otto Gerlach (late 19th century); a classic portrait by Sergei Prokudin-Gorskii of Isfandiyar Jurji Bahadur, the Khan of Khiva (circa 1911)

# Tsarist strategies for the conquest of the steppe

By *Irina Yerofeyeva*

The incorporation of Kazakh territory into the Russian Empire came about as a result of much broader socioeconomic and geopolitical developments across the Eurasian landmass. The formation of a world market economy saw the major European powers vying for dominance over the various trade routes between East and West. Rivalries grew swiftly as the desire for global commercial-industrial predominance led to military-political tensions – and Central Asia was at the heart of Tsarist Russia's plans.

In the second decade of the 18th century, in order to establish a direct link by water between Russia, India and other Eastern countries, Peter I (aka Peter the Great) sent several military reconnaissance expeditions to Central Asia. Two of them were directed towards the Caspian Sea (1714-1715) and Khiva (1716-1717), and were headed by Prince Alexander Bekovich-Cherkassky; two others, under the leadership of Colonel Ivan Buchholz (1715-1718) and Major Ivan Mikhailovich Likharev (1719-1720), were sent to the upper reaches of the Irtysh

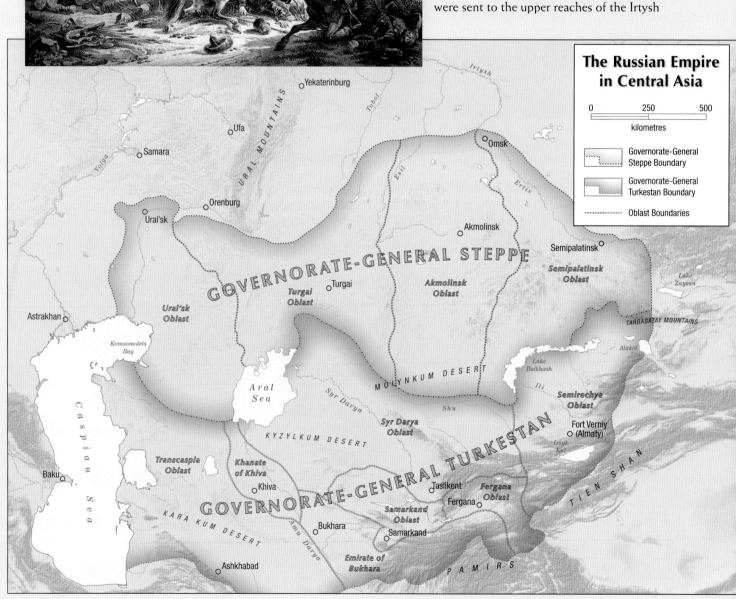

River, occupied at that time by Khan Tsewang Rabdan of the Dzungar Empire. Thus began the construction of the "Irtysh Line" of Russian military forts and administrations in eastern Kazakhstan.

In 1722, during a stay in Astrakhan on his return from Persia to St Petersburg, Peter I learned a great deal from local Russian officials about the neighbouring Kazakh lands. For the first time Peter now understood the significance of this region as an important transit route to the rich countries of Central and South Asia.

As Peter the Great's strategic thinking about the "Eastern promise" developed, it coincided with successive stages of crisis in the political life of Kazakh nomadic society, and the deterioration of the Kazakh Khanate's influence and geopolitical position within Central Asia. During the first third of the 18th century, a series of catastrophic incursions from external forces, combined with internal strife within Kazakh society, made life almost unbearable for the nomadic peoples of the steppe, and the senior Kazakh khans Tauke (1672-1715), Kaip (1715-1718) and Abulkhair (1719-1748) struggled to contain or curtail the separatist aspirations of the other khans and sultans.

The constant wars with the Dzungars – despite some impressive victories from the Kazakh popular militia led by Abulkhair Khan at Bulanty River (1727) and Anrakai (1730) – spelled disaster for the Kazakh people and they failed in their main objective of wresting back control of the southern Kazakh steppe region from the Oirats. Additionally, by the end of the 1720s and in the early 1730s the Kazakhs were involved in frequent armed clashes with the Volga Kalmyks, the Bashkirs and the Siberian and Ural Cossacks in the northwestern and northern regions. They now occupied the steppe region near Yaik, Ori and Uya, and were forced to purchase new pastures in the lower Yaik where roads to the fertile pastures of its right bank were opened, thus expanding their ties with the Russian markets.

It became obvious that the Kazakhs had to find allies or a protector in order to continue their fight with the Dzungars for the return of their ancestral nomadic territories and the Syr Darya cities in the south and southeast regions, and the political elite of the Kazakh hierarchy therefore sought assistance from the Tsarist government.

In June 1730, Abulkhair, the senior Kazakh Khan and Khan of the Junior Zhuz (Horde), sent ambassadors to the Russian Empress in St Petersburg to request assistance for his people and sue for their territory to become a protectorate of the Russian state. The answer was positive, and in February 1731 Empress Anna Ivanovna sent an embassy – led by A.I. Tevkelev, the translator of the College of Foreign Affairs – to the Junior Zhuz in order to have the Kazakhs swear allegiance to the Russian throne.

On 10 October 1731 in Manityube, the headquarters of Abulkhair Khan in the region between the lower courses of the rivers Irgiz and Tobol, an oath of allegiance to the Russian Empress was sworn by Abulkhair and a group of 30 Kazakh elders at a general gathering (*kurultai*) of the Kazakh nobility of the Junior Zhuz. This historic event marked the beginning of the long process of annexation of the Kazakh zhuzes by Russia.

The development of the Russian presence in the Kazakh steppe was challenging for many reasons, including the uncertainty of ethnic boundaries and the economic and geopolitical dependency of the steppe's agrarian regions on the imperial administrative and commercial core in Moscow and the Volga and Ural regions. In the ruling circles of the Kazakh Khanate, an understanding grew of the vital importance of trade and political ties with their powerful northern neighbour, and thus they began to develop and deepen relations with the Russian authorities in western Siberia, the southern Urals and the Volga region.

Far left: "Cossacks fighting Kazakhs", by A.O. Orlovsky (1826). Below: The now empty battlefield of Bulanty on the river Kalmakkyrgan, where a Kazakh army was victorious against the Dzungar invaders

Above: "A Kalmyk Wedding" by Baron Josef Berres von Perez in the late 19th century. The Kalmyk lands at this time were north of the Caspian Sea, but they were swiftly incorporated into the Imperial Russian province of Astrakhan. Below: A typical Central Asian tea stall in the 19th century, where locals and travellers would congregate

## THE RUSSIAN ADVANCE BEGINS

Between 1730 and 1740 Russia consolidated its formal legal sovereignty over the territory and nomadic population of the Junior Zhuz and sections of the Middle Zhuz. Following the initial oath of loyalty to the Russian throne by Abulkhair Khan and 30 Kazakh elders, the Kazakh khans and influential sultans of the Junior and Middle zhuzes took part in a series of Russian-Kazakh talks.

On 3 December 1731, Sultan Batyr of the Junior Zhuz took the same oath, followed on 19 December by Sameke Khan of the Middle Zhuz (ruled 1724-1738). The next political interaction between imperial officials and

the ruling elite came on 28 November 1740 at the newly established Orsk fortress on the northwestern border of the Kazakh nomads' land, when Abul Mambet, the new khan of the Middle Zhuz (ruled 1739-1771), and the influential Sultan Ablai (ruled 1771-1780), swore an oath of allegiance to the Russian empress.

Following these negotiations, the Russian protectorate was widened to include the pasturelands of Sultan Barak (died 1750), the ruler of many of the Middle Zhuz's Naiman clans, who grazed their herds in regions to the south and northeast. By the mid-1740s, almost all the khans and influential sultans of the Junior and Middle zhuzes had formally come under the patronage of the Russian throne, and the sphere of control of the Tsarist border authorities in the southern Urals and western Siberia was expanded legally to cover the northwestern, central and eastern regions of modern-day Kazakhstan.

However, trying to get the Kazakh rulers to fulfil their political commitments to the Russian crown – which included protecting trade caravans as they passed through the desert or steppe, controlling the raiding of neighbouring nations' pasturelands, and protecting the region's Russian subjects – was almost impossible for the Tsarist government, whose powers over the khans were limited because of a lack of any real coercive capability. Added to this was the fragility of internal control between khans

and influential sultans and between sultans and tribal elders. The result was a wholly ineffective system and the imperial authorities quickly realized this, but they did not yet possess sufficient military, administrative and economic strength to officially take control of the Kazakh zhuzes as a full suzerain.

In the decades following its creation, therefore, being a Russian protectorate did not entail any significant or rapid transformation in Russian-Kazakh relations. These evolved over the years, mainly through individual contact between the imperial border administrations and certain Kazakh rulers, the cultivating of whom – through political favours, preferential treatment and gifts – allowed the Russians to influence the traditional institutions of power among the nomads, and slowly but surely incorporate them into the bureaucratic administrative system of the empire.

While this process was slow to take effect, the legalisation of the Russian patronage over the Junior and Middle zhuzes did allow the Tsarist government to strengthen its position in the northern and northeastern borderland steppes. The construction of new towns and forts went ahead between the 1730s and 1750s – forts at Orenburg, Novo-Ishim and Kolyvan-Voskresensky were built and this created the conditions for trade development with neighbouring Asian countries. The towns of Orsk (founded in

1733), Orenburg (1743), Petropavlovsk (1752), Semipalatinsk (1776) and others became major centres of contact between Russia and the peoples of Central Asia beyond the Kazakh nomads.

## THE NOOSE TIGHTENS

Now began the transformation of Kazakh territory into a genuine protectorate of the Russian Empire. On 5 October 1748, at the suggestion of the Russian authorities Nuraly, the eldest son of Abulkhair Khan and the elected Khan of the Junior Zhuz, requested from Empress Elizabeth the "highest" approval of his khan title. The publication of the decree by the Russian empress was issued on 10 July

Above: A Kazakh woman wears a traditional large white headdress, while a wandering musician poses for a Russian photographer. Below: Kazakh chiefs and *begs* in the 19th century, when Russia was gaining strict control over political and administrative life for the Kazakh communities

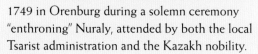

Portraits of both wealthy and poorer residents of the steppe region at the turn of the 20th century. Note the high pointed *saukele* hat worn by the woman in the centre picture, and the heavily embroidered and fur-lined finery of the rich compared to the far simpler clothing of the man above

1749 in Orenburg during a solemn ceremony "enthroning" Nuraly, attended by both the local Tsarist administration and the Kazakh nobility.

In a sly strategic move, this had been preceded by a special decree on 13 April 1749 that had momentous consequences for Central Asia's nomadic inhabitants. Elizabeth created a historical precedent with a procedure called "confirmation of the new Khan elevated to the rank of legislative principle", which gave him regulatory power over the Kazakh pasturelands. According to this principle, among all the legitimate rulers of the steppe clans – of which there were many – St Petersburg now recognized only those "elected" representatives to the khanate, officially approved by the Russian throne. All other steppe rulers had no right to the title of "khan" and were henceforth called "sultans" by the Russian officials.

A new type of vassal relationship now developed between Russia and the traditional pastoral ruling elite, as prerogatives and power were conferred on a select few Kazakh leaders whose "legitimization" left them indebted to and dependent on their Russian superiors. The Russians could now direct their political activities, and effectively take control of the steppe – which they did from administrative centres in Orenburg and Siberia. These significant changes to the traditional rights and privileges of the Kazakh khans led to a system of direct control over both their external relations and internal affairs.

The Tsarist government now sought, through the redistribution of the khans' power and by

directly changing and influencing the traditional pastoral power structure, to disavow the tradition and institution of a khan's political position and thereby pave the way for its abolition as a legislative power. To achieve this goal, the administrative authorities in Orenburg and Siberia proceeded on a number of different fronts.

First came the process of official approval of the Kazakh khans, in particular Ablai (1771-1780), Vali (1781-1821) and Bukey (1816-1819); internal political strife was encouraged by assisting certain leaders against their political enemies (for example their support of Bukey against his rival Vali Khan). Next came a strategy of selecting only easily influenced and obedient leaders to give the title of khan, such as the senile Eraly (1791-1794) and Aishuak (1797-1805), the weak-willed Esim (1795-1797) and Zhantore (1812-1809), and the incompetent Shergazy (1812-1824). At the same time the most powerful and influential Kazakh rulers, including the sultans Kaip (died 1789), Karatai (lived 1772-1826) and Aryngazy (1785-1833), were purposely overlooked and ignored. Any strong, self-sufficient leaders who might potentially claim independence from St Petersburg (Aryngazy in particular fitted this description) were actively removed from power.

As a result of this constant political interference, by the end of the 1820s all the necessary conditions for the liquidation of the institution of a khan's power had been created, and deep sociopolitical reorganization in the region could now begin.

## THE NEW ADMINISTRATIVE SYSTEM

The period from 1820 to 1855 was one of profound reform. The traditional power structure in the steppe now changed, with Kazakh society becoming more involved in the bureaucratic structure of the Russian Empire, and a system of territorial administration taking over the Kazakh lands. This strengthened the grip of the Tsarist authorities over the Junior and Middle zhuzes, and allowed them to use their territories as a base from which they could make further inroads into southeastern Central Asia.

In 1822, by special decree of Emperor Alexander I, the institution of the khan's power was dissolved in the Middle Zhuz Khanate. In 1824 the khan's power was also abolished in the Junior Zhuz, and in 1845 the Inner or Bukey Horde – which had been founded in 1801 – also suffered the same fate.

Control over the nomadic populations of northern, central and eastern Kazakhstan now passed into the hands of the West Siberian General governorship through a series of decrees: in 1822, the "Charter relating to the Siberian Kirghiz" (as the Kazakhs were known); in 1838, the "Regulations Concerning the Separate Management of the Siberian Kirghiz";

in 1854, the "Provision on the Management of the Semipalatinsk Region", as well as a number of other regulations.

The Kazakh population of the western region came under the authority of the military governor of Orenburg, developed and enacted through the following decrees: in 1824, the "Opinion of the Committee of Asian Affairs concerning the reform management of the Orenburg region"; in 1844, the "Regulations Concerning the Administration of the Orenburg Kirghizs"; and in 1859, the decree "On the renamed steppes of the trans-Ural Kirghizs called Small Horde, on the Kirghizs of the Orenburg province and on the new order of administration of this area".

The provincial authorities of Orenburg and Siberia now implemented territorial divisions within the land inhabited by Kazakhs, organizing the middle and lower echelons of its management in an idiosyncratic fashion. In the Orenburg jurisdiction, consisting of the Kazakhs of the Junior Horde and the western clans of the Middle Horde, new Eastern, Central and Western sections (*distance*) were created, subdivided in turn into smaller districts. In much of the Middle Horde territories, under the jurisdiction of the West Siberian governor-generalship, eight external and four internal autonomous districts (*okrug*) were created.

Each distance and okrug included an average of 15-20 rural districts (*volost*) consisting of 10-12 administrative villages (*aul*). In each village were 50-70 tents (*kibitka*). The heads of each autonomous okrug/distance

Below: Officers of the Imperial Russian postal service beside their wagon in southern Kazakhstan. Bottom: A district governor and his wife pose for a photo surrounded by local Kazakhs

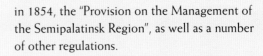

included "senior sultans", a staff of functionaries (two assessors, an interpreter, clerk, treasurer, etc) and small coercive detachments of 200-300 armed Cossacks. The volosts were headed by sultans, the auls by elders.

The creation of a public administration management system now allowed regular taxation of the nomadic population. From the 1830s to 60s, the Kazakhs of the Siberian division had to pay a so-called *"Yasachnaya* tribute", a progressive tax of 100 head of cattle, whilst the Kazakh population of the Orenburg region paid a *"kibitochnaya* tribute", a fixed tax amount from each "tent", meaning any dwelling must provide 1.5 roubles in silver annually to the state. In the Inner Horde, the nomads initially gave cash payments called *"zyakst"* and *"sogum"* to the state treasury, then from 1860 on they had to pay "emoluments".

The previous levies and duties paid to the khans and sultans of the Kazakh Khanate had mostly been of a voluntary character, and were irregular, small and collected in different seasons of the nomadic cycle from the tribes located close to the Khan's headquarters. Now, however, the state established a strict fiscal dependence on all groups of Kazakh society. Through this tax system, the Russian government drew several hundred thousand, then millions of roubles from the steppe regions, used primarily for the maintenance and needs of the local administrative staff, regular troops and other requirements of the imperial government.

## CONQUERING THE SOUTH

The implementation of Russian state structures and imperial taxes on the Kazakhs generated a hostile response among the Kazakh population, but it also set alarm bells ringing to the south in the neighbouring khanates of Khiva, Kokand and the Emirate of Bukhara. These states still controlled the south and southeastern regions of the Syr Darya plain and the "Land of Seven Rivers" (Semirechye in Russian, Zhetisu in Kazakh), and their antagonism towards Russia led to the acceleration of its advance into the south.

During the 1840s and 50s, the Orenburg authorities built a chain of strongholds in the valleys of the rivers Irgiz and Torgai, and at the mouth of the Syr Darya. Here they placed Cossack settlements around the fortifications of Raim and Karabutak, located in the traditional land of the lower Syr Darya Kazakhs. In the summer of 1853, a Russian military force of more than 2,000 men under the command of

the Orenburg Military Governor General V.A. Perovsky stormed and took the fortress Ak-Mechet, an outpost of the Kokand Khanate on the Lower Syr Darya; it was subsequently renamed Perovsk for a time, and eventually became modern-day Kyzylorda.

Concurrently from the Siberian side, the West Siberian governor G.H. Gasford launched an active offensive against the Kokand forts in the southeast. In 1854 and the years that followed, Siberian detachments erected first the fort of Kopal in the upper course of the Kyzyl-Agach River, then the fortresses of Sergiopol (Ayaguz), Lepsinsk, Verniy (Almaty) and other strongholds in Semirechye. This expansion of controlled territory stabilized and strengthened Russia's strategic position over the Middle and Junior zhuzes, whose winter camps were in Semirechye and the Syr Darya region.

The pincer-like extensions of fortification lines from Perovsk upstream on the Syr Darya and from Verniy in Semirechye towards the southwest now enabled the Russian Empire to master all of southern Kazakhstan. In 1863 a Russian military unit took the Kokand fortresses

Above: Russian steamboats at the mouth of the Syr Darya River, an illustration made between 1847 and 1865 to describe Russian naval activity in the Aral Sea. Below: An early 20th century photograph of the town of Turkistan, with the Mausoleum of Khoja Ahmed Yasawi in the background

Above: Shymkent at the end of the 1800s. Below: An illustration from Charles Marvin's "Reconnoitring Central Asia" (1886) shows a Kazakh horseman encountering the modern world in the form of a steam train – the construction of rail tracks across Central Asia heralded the dawn of a new technological world order

– Orenburg, Western Siberia and Turkestan – which were divided into six provinces (*oblasts*): Uralsk, Turgai, Akmolinsk, Semipalatinsk, Semirechye and Syr Darya. The first four provinces were divided in half between the Orenburg and West Siberian governorates, but in 1882 they were grouped together in the newly formed Governorate General of the Steppe, which was administered from Omsk. Semirechye and Syr Darya provinces became part of the Governorate General of Turkestan, which also included the oblasts of Fergana, Samarkand and Transcaspia, as well as the Khanate of Khiva and the Emirate of Bukhara.

Each province was divided into several districts (*uezd*); in turn the districts were split into rural areas (volosts), and the rural areas into administrative villages (auls) comprising an average of 100-200 tents (kibitka). The oblasts were led by military governors appointed directly by the Tsarist government, the uezd were headed by county commanders appointed by the military governor, the volosts were led by rural managers and the villages by aul elders.

During 1867 and 1868 a unified tax system was introduced throughout Kazakhstan, the "kibitochnaya tribute" that was an annual fixed tax levied in cash on each tent. However, the Kazakhs had to make other tax payments as well, and in this way the Russian authorities extracted any surplus products from the nomads and ensured a continuous chain of communication from grassroots Kazakh society right through to the supreme power of the state.

However, despite the large-scale and dramatic administrative changes the Russian authorities imposed on the Kazakh steppe, the socioeconomic relations of nomadic society were not overly affected, and existing forms of social consciousness continued to prevail among Kazakhs. The right of appeal by each individual to the traditional values of his or her clan and tribal ideals still dominated, and all attempts by the Imperial government to reform the traditional power relations in nomadic society ultimately failed in the pre-revolutionary period, because the tribal organization of the Kazakhs, deeply rooted in nomadic culture, adapted quite successfully to the changes.

*Irina Yerofeyeva is a historian and researcher at the Nurbulat Masanov Social Foundation in Almaty. She was formerly director of the Kazakhstan Scientific Research Institute on the Problems of the Cultural Heritage of Nomads.*

of Dzhumagal, Kurtka and Suzak (near the northern slopes of the Karatau mountains) with barely a fight. In 1864, military troops commanded by Colonel P.L. Verevkin took Turkistan while Colonel M.G. Chernyaev captured the cities of Aulye-Ata (Taraz) and Shymkent, finally linking the Orenburg and Siberian lines. With this military operation the southern Kazakh territories were finally annexed to Russia.

In July 1867, Emperor Alexander II issued a decree on the establishment of the Governorate General of Turkestan, which included the newly annexed territories of the Senior Zhuz, of northern Kyrgyzstan and of the former Central Asian khanates (Semirechenskaya and Syr Darya provinces). The implementation of the Russian legislation and tax system on the southern parts of Kazakhstan was the final step in their inclusion in all aspects of the empire. Kazakhstan's accession to Russia was over, and it had become part of the Russian state.

The governance of the region – which previously had been undertaken in a variety of fashions in different areas – was now unified and a common system of administration for all Kazakhstan was developed. Its territory was initially split up into three governorate generals

Top: Miners at the workface in the Karaganda region during the early 20th century – the transition from life as a nomadic herdsman to mining underground must have been traumatic. Above: The school of cutting and sewing at a collective farm in the Enbekshi-Kazakh district in 1931. Right: Guests are served drinks in a yurt in the early 1900s – the ornate boxes and other accoutrements mark this as a relatively wealthy family (©MAE (Kunstkamera) RAS Nos: 1905-60; 1905-48; and 1199-1 respectively)

# THE SOVIET ERA: COLLECTIVIZATION, EXILES AND THE "KAZAKHSTAN TRAGEDY"

The 1916 Central Asian Revolt, or "Great Revolt", was played out on a stage where other momentous happenings were already taking place: the Russian Empire was at the point of collapse, whilst World War I was forever changing the face of Europe. With the downfall of Tsarism the following year, the newly formed Kazakh Alash Party (Alash Orda) – based in Semipalatinsk (modern-day Semey) – was deprived of its adversary, but suddenly had hope for the independent development of a democracy in the Kazakh steppe.

In October 1917, at the first All-Kazakh congress, which took place in Orenburg in present-day Russia, the first provisional autonomous people's council of Kazakhs was appointed, with Alikhan Bokeikhanov as its president. Orenburg (spelt Orynbor in Kazakh) became the first capital of the Kazakhs. Unfortunately, as the Russian "Red" Bolsheviks and "White" Tsarists fought throughout the former empire, Kazakhs too were split in their allegiances, and the economic deprivations in the region continued and even worsened. In 1920, the new Soviet government established the Kyrgyz Autonomous Soviet Socialist Republic, which in 1925 changed its name to the Kazakh Autonomous Soviet Socialist Republic and then to the Kazakh Soviet Socialist Republic (SSR) in 1936.

By this time Joseph Stalin had consolidated himself as the undisputed leader of the Soviet Union. Stalin's cult of personality and incredibly destructive ideology are well documented, but his nationalities and collectivization policies had a particularly devastating effect on Kazakh territory. The reorganization of Central Asia, a markedly multinational region that had not known any fixed borders for centuries, had a professed goal of national

delimitation, but in the end was based on political and economic calculation, and resulted in the creation of the republics of Uzbekistan, Turkmenistan, Kyrgyzstan, Tajikistan and Kazakhstan.

As in the case of all nomadic nations within the Soviet realm, Stalin's policies inflicted horrors on the Kazakhs. Under the pretence of liberation from the yoke of backwardness, Kazakhs were prohibited from following a unique culture and way of life adapted to the conditions. Not only the rich *biis* (*beys*) and *beks* (*begs*), but also many of the elders and respected persons in *auls* (villages), themselves in possession of smaller herds, were dispossessed and deported.

The "Kazakhstan Tragedy", as the dramatic events of 1929-1933 are called, reached its peak during the collectivization of the semi-nomadic population ordered by the Communist Party. Pastoral families, who could not survive without moving their herds from one place to another on the scanty steppe soils, were forced to settle in designated areas and surrender most of their livestock to hurriedly established collective farms. As a result of administrative arbitrariness and mismanagement, the majority of the previously well looked after animals died of sickness, malnutrition, or by compulsory slaughter. This lunatic policy led to the death by starvation of an unknown but horrifying number of people (possibly more than one million), with hundreds of thousands more fleeing the country. Today, most of the latter live in China's Xinjiang province, but also in Mongolia, Iran, Afghanistan and Turkey. The Kazakh diaspora of more than five million people now lives in more than 40 countries.

In the process of forced collectivization, the Kazakhs had lost a significant proportion of their population. Convicts, settlers and people exiled from their homelands for various reasons were now placed in the abandoned territories in random fashion. In the years preceding and during World War II, entire peoples were deported to the vast lands of the Kazakh steppe. Volga Germans, Koreans, Chechens, Crimean Tatars, Kalmyks, Greeks, Balkarians, Ingush and other ethnic groups suspected by Stalin of collaboration with the enemy were sent there. Many died of starvation or froze to death, and it is only thanks to the Kazakhs' readiness to help (hospitality towards strangers is a cultural imperative among Eurasia's nomads) that tens of thousands survived – in the Kazakhs' yurts and clay huts, and in the huts and refugee camps built with their help. Prison camps (*gulags*) were also established in inhospitable areas of Kazakhstan; entire economic sectors rested on the shoulders of the people detained in them, who lived in appalling conditions of cruelty and suffering.

Above right: A *gulag* labour camp near Karaganda housed prisoners who lived in appalling conditions. Left: The traditional way of life – eagle hunting, felt making and embroidery, weaving and pastoralism in small communities or *auls* – still existed for Kazakhs in the early years of Soviet control. But this was about to change...

Stalin died in 1953 and the following year, now with Nikita Khrushchev at the helm, the Soviet state unleashed a new economic programme on the steppe that was to cause lasting devastation over a vast area of Central Asia: the Virgin and Idle Lands Project. The cultivation of huge swathes of "unused" land (much of it was in fact valuable pasture) was designed to feed and clothe (with cotton) the whole Soviet Union, and therewith an influx – this time predominantly voluntary – of young people and adventurers from the other republics began. Professor Sabol's essay (see page 148) explains this misguided programme in greater detail, but today it is universally accepted that the Virgin Lands programme, with its short-lived economic effect, inflicted irreversible damage both to the steppe's vulnerable ecosystem and to traditional extensive livestock breeding. Additionally, the massive human migration also led to organizational, social and cultural problems.

However, the war also had an unexpected consequence for the Kazakh SSR, as many important enterprises and industries were evacuated from the European part of the Soviet Union to the far side of the Urals to keep them out of the hands of the Germans. All of a sudden, the Central Asian republics were playing a vital role in supplying the front, and providing for the other Soviet republics. But at the time this did little to improve life for the masses, and agricultural productivity continued to decline.

Two other catastrophes – one environmental, the other human – should be highlighted from this period. The fate of the Aral Sea has been called one of the planet's greatest environmental disasters. Once the fourth largest inland water basin in the world, with a surface area of 65,000 square kilometres, it boasted immense fishing resources, abundant wildlife and had a moderating effect on the harsh continental climate. However, the massive irrigation works created during the Virgin Lands programme in the 1950s

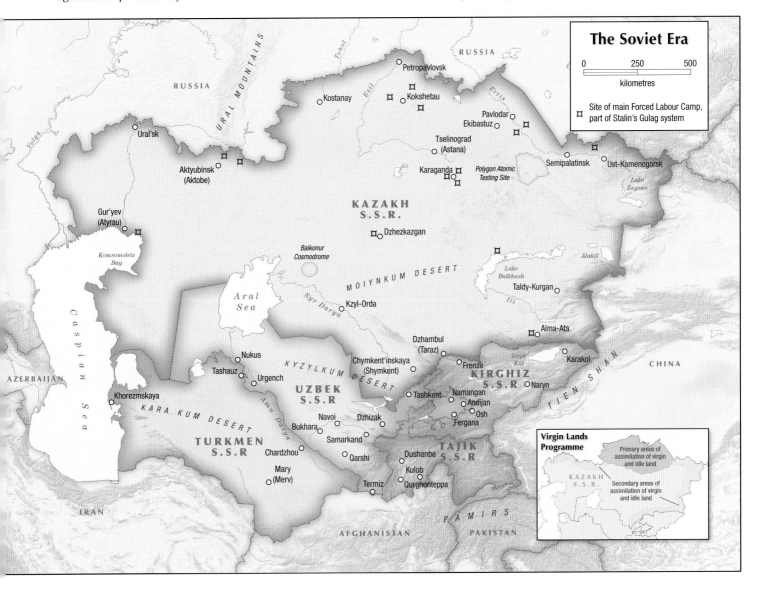

and 60s drained the Syr Darya and Amu Darya rivers to provide water for the thirsty state cotton farms in south Kazakhstan and Uzbekistan. So much water was siphoned off – through terribly inefficient canals – that each river's flow into the Aral Sea was reduced to the point that for much of the year they petered out before ever reaching their deltas.

During the 1960s the Aral Sea began to shrink, and continued to do so until the beginning of the 21st century, when only two partial lakes remained – the North Aral Sea and a crescent-shaped stretch of water near the old western shore. A 50,000-square-kilometre desert, dubbed the Aralkum, now covers the former seabed, its thick salt layers mixed with the remnants of the fertilizers, herbicides and insecticides used in the cotton fields. These are often whipped up into devastating toxic dust storms, while the climate has become much harsher without the water's tempering effects. (However, a dam project funded by the Kazakhstan Government and World Bank was completed in 2005 on the Syr Darya in an attempt to save the North Aral

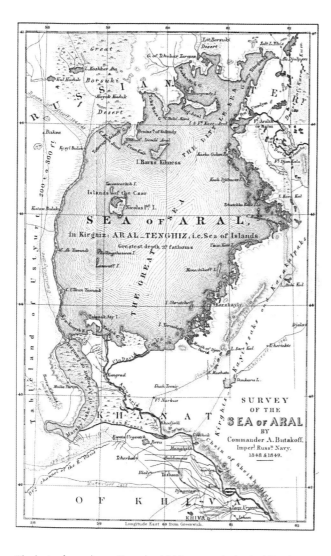

Clockwise from above: From the 1960s onwards the Aral Sea began to shrink. The map shows the Aral as it was in 1853; the top satellite image was taken in 1964; the bottom shot was taken in 2012 – the light-green expanse of water in the centre is no longer permanent, but the "North Aral Sea" segment is at least stable. Below: Oil extraction in the Caspian region began early in the 20th century, but its full potential was not yet realized

Sea, and by 2008 the water level in this lake had risen by 12 metres. Salinity has dropped, and fish are again found in sufficient numbers for some fishing to be viable.)

In 1949 an area of steppe near Semipalatinsk in the country's northeast was designated as a testing ground for atomic bombs. A series of huge test explosions were detonated above ground until 1963, and continued underground thereafter. This was an example of Stalinist ideology and its contempt for human life; in the name of Soviet wellbeing, entire communities were sacrificed, and this appalling situation was compounded by the arms race that developed during the period of the Cold War. However, by the late 1980s a series of campaigns by the human rights movement Nevada-Semipalatinsk protested against and lobbied for the cessation of nuclear testing. It was president-elect Nursultan Nazarbayev who took the courageous step in 1991 – even before Kazakhstan became independent – to sign into law the decision to finally close the testing ground.

Kazakhstan's economy continued to stagnate through the 1970s and 80s, despite an increase in high-ranking Kazakh members of the CPK (Kazakh Communist Party), orchestrated by First Secretary Dinmukhamed Kunayev, and the many monumental buildings commissioned by him for the capital Alma-Ata, which had grown from a sleepy town into a major Soviet capital since the opening of the Turkestan-Siberian Railway or Turk-Sib in 1930.

Finally, after almost 20 years of economic crisis, the coming of perestroika saw a major political shift for Kazakhstan. Social movements and informal organizations emerged, culminating in demonstrations by thousands of students in Almaty's main square on 16 December 1986, after Kunayev had been replaced by Gennady Kolbin, who was from Russia and knew nothing about Kazakhstan. As they demonstrated in Almaty's main square the students were shot at; the number of dead has never been officially declared, although it is estimated that more than 200 people died, and hundreds were arrested.

Since that infamous day, 16 December has been celebrated as a National Memorial Day – and it was telling that when Kazakhstan finally gained independence, President Nazarbayev intentionally chose 16 December 1991 as the day for the Law on Independence to be adopted. Also very significant was the fact that Almaty was chosen as the location to officially declare the dissolution of the Soviet Union, with the signing of the Alma-Ata Declaration on 21 December 1991, less than a week later. Kazakhstan was the last member state to leave the USSR – taking into account its close economic relationship with Russia, this was by no means an easy step.

Left: "The Turkestan-Siberian Railway", a painting by Ablaikhan Kasteyev (1904-1973), a master of the realism genre who documented Kazakhstan's 20th century development through his paintings. Below: The construction of railway tracks across Central Asia was a difficult and demanding undertaking

# Communism and the effects of the Soviet experiment

*By Steven Sabol*

T he history of Kazakhstan during the Soviet era is complicated, often tragic and frequently bewildering, but rarely uneventful.

The decade before the 1917 Russian Revolution witnessed the emergence of a relatively small, but active, Kazakh sociopolitical movement called Alash Orda ("The Horde of Alash"). It was led by prominent Kazakh intellectuals, most notably Alikhan Bokeikhanov, Akhmet Baitursynov and Mirzhaqyp Dulatov. Alash was the most important modern political force among the Kazakh people in this era; it was decidedly neutral to the Tsarist colonial regime, but hostile to many of the policies that its leaders believed impoverished the majority of Kazakh nomads and illegally confiscated land and property from the rightful Kazakh owners.

Alash's chief goals, most often expressed in the pages of its newspaper, *Kazakh*, were for greater cultural and social autonomy, the cessation of Russian settler expansion in the steppe and Semirechye, and the expansion of Kazakh economic, education and political opportunities. During the first two years of World War I, Alash's leaders supported the Tsarist government's fight against the Central Powers, and in 1916 it supported the government's decision to conscript Kazakhs and other Muslim Central Asians into the army. The 1916 Central Asian Revolt compelled many Alash leaders to abandon their support for the Russian government, as they complained bitterly about the violent and harsh measures taken by the military and local Russian officials to suppress the revolt. When news reached the Kazakh steppe in February 1917 that the Tsar had abdicated, few Kazakhs mourned the regime's passing.

Below: A young pupil of a Soviet state school puts books in order in the "Red Corner". Bottom: A young Kazakh woman in traditional clothing looks suspiciously into the camera lens

The 1917 February Revolution was welcomed by Kazakh intellectuals, many believing it represented a new era in Kazakh-Russian relations. Alash's leaders quickly embraced the Provisional Government's programmes and policies to suspend Russian colonization in the steppe, to abandon tsarist "Russification" policies that repressed Kazakh economic, social and cultural representations, and to expand native political participation.

Many Kazakhs, however, quickly became disillusioned with the Provisional Government's failure to resolve land disputes between Kazakhs and Russian peasants, the continued economic dislocation and depredations in the steppe caused by the wartime necessities, and its inability to resolve the so-called nationalities question by extending constitutional and civil liberties. By the autumn of 1917, Alash's leaders were vacillating between cooperation and resistance; however, the Bolshevik seizure of power in late October forced Alash Orda to proclaim independence and Bokeikhanov was elected president of the first modern Kazakh state.

Alash Orda's declaration of independence did nothing to alter the terrible economic deterioration in the steppe. Moreover, many Kazakh intellectuals rejected Alash's programme and formed opposition parties, most notably Ush Zhuz ("Three Hordes"), which aligned with the Bolsheviks. The Civil War in the steppe was brutal, rife with atrocities, and further worsened economic conditions for the vast majority of Kazakhs.

During the Civil War, Alash Orda aligned with White Forces, including Admiral Kolchak's Siberian Army. Kazakhs were essentially caught between the Bolshevik Red Army and the "Whites", neither of which professed a programme that matched Alash's vision for an independent Kazakh republic. Kazakhs suffered during the difficult Civil War, often

Above: Alikhan Bokeikhanov, a prominent member of Alash Orda. Below: Life for poor Kazakhs on the open steppe was hard at the best of times, but under Soviet policies it became almost unbearable (©MAE (Kunstkamera) RAS No: 3862-12 upper left; No: 2833-5 lower left)

finding themselves caught between competing Red Army and White Forces trying to conscript men or confiscate livestock. Scholars are still uncertain how many perished during this period, but there is no doubt that it cost thousands of lives and ruined the steppe economy. By mid-1920 the Red Army's victories against Kolchak and others forced Alash's leaders to seek peace in the steppe.

## A NEW KAZAKH REPUBLIC

Following Alash Orda's capitulation, the Soviets managed to consolidate control in the steppe and incorporated the various factions into new political structures. Implementing a policy of *korenizatsia* ("nativization"), the Soviets assimilated hundreds of Kazakh intellectuals into the newly established Kazakh Communist Party (CPK). Opposition remained in the southern steppe regions and Semirechye, chiefly affiliated Basmachi rebels, but in general korenizatsia provided greater integration of local Kazakh leaders into the government and fostered some sense of participation in the decision-making process.

Economic recovery from the years of war, revolutions and civil war was slow and sporadic. Land disputes between Russian settlers and Kazakh nomads took time to resolve, but the Soviet New Economic Policy (NEP) introduced some stability into the system between 1921 and 1927. Kazakhs without livestock were provided with land to farm, despite the fact that few (if any) had the seed, the tools or the

skills to exploit the land as agriculturists and the state failed to provide the material assistance necessary. Subsistence farming became the rule in the steppe.

Many Soviet leaders perceived NEP as a temporary system that facilitated land redistribution, although little was done in this regard because Kazakhstan lacked enough arable land to redistribute equitably and the Soviet government was never inclined to remove Russian peasants from the steppe. At best, impoverished Kazakhs acquired some livestock, migrated shorter distances (if at all), and built permanent structures on small parcels that enabled them to survive. NEP stabilized the economy; however, it was not, in the minds of many Soviet leaders, the remedy to long-term economic and industrial progress.

In 1925 the Soviets delimitated Central Asia into separate republics, constructed from the four Tsarist Steppe Governor-Generalship *oblasty* (Ural'sk, Turgai, Akmolinsk and Semipalatinsk) and two oblasty from the former Turkestan Governor-Generalship (Syr Darya and Semirechye). Kazakhstan, at first an Autonomous Soviet Socialist Republic (initially called the Kirghiz ASSR – prior to the revolutions Kazakhs were referred to as "Kirghiz" and the Kirghiz people were called "Kara Kirghiz" or "Black Kirghiz"), became an All-Union Kazakhstan Soviet Socialist Republic in 1936. Critics have often condemned the delimitation as Soviet "divide and rule"

imperialism; however, they fail to acknowledge that many Kazakh intellectuals, including former members of Alash Orda, were involved in the debates and negotiations that constructed the borders that constituted the new Kazakh ASSR. Not all Kazakhs were included in the new republic; many resided around Tashkent and further north in the steppe where other Kazakh territories remained part of the Russian Federation.

This new Kazakh Communist Party cadre was instrumental in the efforts to establish institutions of higher education, many became teachers, helped eradicate illiteracy, established health clinics, worked in factories and mines, and generally cooperated with the Soviet government to introduce modern technologies, education and health care to the Kazakh people. Kazakh art, culture and literature was promoted by the Soviet government, reflecting earlier Soviet korenizatsia policies. In the 1920s the Soviets' nationalities policies also standardized written Kazakh using a modified Arabic script – although in 1929 a Latin script was introduced and in 1939 the Soviet government decreed that written Kazakh use a Cyrillic script. The power struggle within the Bolshevik party following Lenin's death in 1924, however, dramatically altered the meagre economic recovery of the 1920s and Kazakhstan was not spared from the turmoil that followed.

## COLLECTIVIZATION, PURGES AND FORCED RESETTLEMENT

The 1930s was an extraordinarily painful decade in Kazakhstan. Collectivization, the purges, the radical struggle against *kulaks* (wealthy landowners), and the Sovietization of Kazakh society resulted in horrific demographic decline and the complete surrender of Kazakh cultural, economic and political sovereignty. These trends were already evident in the mid-1920s, as former Alash leaders, most notably Baitursynov and Bokeikhanov, were expelled from the Communist Party, generally charged with exhibiting nationalist tendencies. By the time the First Five-Year Plan (1928) introduced plans to collectivize agriculture in the republic, many Kazakh leaders were being targeted as traitors and counter-revolutionaries. They were subsequently linked to the first disastrous collectivization efforts in 1929; Baitursynov, for example, was arrested and charged with trying to overthrow the Soviet regime.

Resistance to collectivization was widespread throughout the republic. Kazakhs withheld their livestock from officials, farmers (Kazakhs and Russians) refused to surrender their surplus crops, and many violently resisted the confiscation of property. Kazakhs slaughtered their livestock rather than submit to the government's collectivization demands. By late 1931, several hundred thousand Kazakhs and Russians faced famine conditions unless some relief was quickly forthcoming – but the central Soviet government determined to collectivize agriculture in Kazakhstan regardless of the consequences. The Kazakh Communist Party First Secretary, F.I. Goloshchekin, blamed the resistance on excessive nationalism, counter-revolutionaries, former Alash leaders and some amorphous reactionary elements in the steppe. These excuses did little to satisfy Soviet leaders and Moscow dismissed Goloshchekin and numerous other CPK functionaries from their positions, blaming them for the resistance and the horrific famine that ravaged the republic in 1933-34.

Best estimates suggest that roughly one-quarter of the republic's population died or fled between 1926 (the First Soviet Census) and 1939; numbers fell from 3.9 million to 3.1 million, many Kazakhs crossing the border into China to flee the violence and oppression. It will probably never be known how many starved to death during the famine, but the census data reveals a significant population decrease. In addition, after the 1937 CPK congress mass arrests of nationalists, kulaks and those deemed disloyal or counter-revolutionary resulted in thousands of convictions and either execution or long prison terms in the gulags. Baitursynov, Bokeikhanov and other Alash members died during these purges.

All levels of the government and party were purged, resulting in the loss of a generation of leading Kazakh intellectuals, writers, scholars, administrators, journalists and others; significant names include Turar Ryskulov, Saken Seifullin and Mirzhaqyp Dulatov. On the eve of World War II, Kazakhstan was decimated by collectivization and the purges, while its political and cultural leadership had largely disappeared. But the impending global conflict was to provide a new twist to the tale.

Kazakhstan changed

A 1950s image from the Ili Valley shows a daughter helping her mother process milk. The milk from horses, sheep, goats and camels is used to make cheese and various drinks, and has been a staple of nomadic life for millennia

Top: The impressive memorial to General Ivan Panfilov and his 28 brave guardsmen in Almaty's Panfilov Park; they destroyed 50 German tanks in the battle of Volokolamsk Shosse near Moscow but were killed in the process. Above: Kazakhs work a tractor as they plough a beet field on a collective farm

dramatically in the 1940s and 50s. World War II forced Soviet leaders to relocate war-related industries and manufacturing to the republic, to distance it from the front lines. There was also a dramatic demographic shift caused by the Soviet government's decision to resettle thousands of potentially disloyal peoples in the steppe, including more than 400,000 Volga Germans and large numbers of Crimean Tatars. Near the end of the war, the Soviets also transferred thousands of Korean and Japanese prisoners of war to Kazakhstan.

During the war, more than 450,000 Kazakhs (and Slavs – Russians, Ukrainians and Cossacks – from Kazakhstan) served in the Red Army, including in the famed "Panfilov Division", which defended Moscow against the German invasion (a memorial to those that died is located in Almaty's Panfilov Park).

Wartime necessity led to the Soviet government relying on Kazakhstan's agricultural and livestock production, its labour and natural resources. What was untapped before the war was maximized during it, for example coal production tripled by 1945. Soviet collective farms, however, struggled to meet the state's needs during the war; agricultural production actually fell because labour resources were diverted to other essential war-related activities,

leaving farms to be operated by women and children. The Soviet government failed to mechanize Kazakhstan's agricultural sector before the war and was unable to supply Kazakhstan's farmers with the necessary resources during the war to supplant that which was lost. As a result, Kazakhstan's agricultural sector declined. In addition, some scholars have claimed that harsh winter weather during the war affected crop harvests significantly.

Following the war, Kazakhstan's agricultural productivity continued to decline in some areas or remained static in others. The Soviet government blamed poor management of the collective farms and strongly criticized the republic's political leadership. By 1949, agriculture and livestock production was less than that produced in the late 1920s, all this despite the fact that the ploughed acreage had increased by more than 40 percent. Nothing was done about this state of affairs until after Stalin's death in 1953; however, a far-reaching and drastic new programme was just around the corner.

## THE VIRGIN LANDS AND ATOMIC TESTING

In 1954 Nikita Khrushchev introduced a new agrarian programme that dramatically altered the steppe environment and Kazakhstan's demographics. The "Virgin and Idle Lands Project", often referred to simply as the "Virgin Lands", was designed to utilize vast swathes of untilled soil in the steppe regions that border Kazakhstan and Russia (see map on page 145). Hundreds of thousands of young people, chiefly Russians, settled on newly established collective farms in order to exploit the more than 255,000 square kilometres of untapped land. The goal was to make the Soviet Union agriculturally self-sufficient; however, the programme rarely fulfilled the promises made, and ultimately had disastrous ecological consequences. Khrushchev selected Leonid Brezhnev to administer the programme, and despite its disappointing results he was eventually called back to Moscow to serve on the Politburo.

Under the Virgin and Idle Lands Project, thousands of Russians and other nationalities were settled in the northern parts of the republic; many were enticed to move there with the offer of housing, financial bonuses, etc, and many more were resettled in Kazakhstan to work in the extensive coal, oil and gas industries. In addition, in the late 1940s and early 1950s tens of thousands of Uighurs from Xinjiang, China fled across the border during the Chinese Civil War, settling chiefly in the

Above: A 1932 picture of Karaganda's "top miners" (©MAE (Kunstkamera) RAS No: 1905-14). Below: The Soviet policy of collective farming and technological advancement had high ideals, but ultimately was a disastrous failure

southeastern regions of the republic. As a consequence, this immigration to Kazakhstan resulted in a dramatic demographic shift. In the 1959 census, Kazakhs made up only 30 percent of the republic's population, with Russians constituting more than 42 percent. That demographic disparity meant that by the 1970s, the Kazakh SSR was the only Soviet republic in which the eponymous nationality remained a minority in their own republic.

Another catastrophic development added to this demographic shift. In the late 1940s the Soviet government selected an area in the northeast region of Kazakhstan to conduct secret tests for its atomic bomb programme. In 1949 the Soviets successfully tested their first nuclear weapon near the city of Semipalatinsk. Throughout the 1950s the Soviet government continued above-ground testing there, ending the programme only in 1963, at which time tests were continued but underground. The consequence for Kazakhstan has been, and continues to be, horrific. Thousands of children

were born prematurely or with terrible birth defects, and thousands of people suffered from radiation poisoning or other illnesses caused by exposure to the testings' aftereffects. By the 1970s and 80s, testing was often suspended but the testing facilities near Semipalatinsk remained operational.

The economic revitalization efforts during the 1950s and 1960s failed to raise Kazakhstan's economic prosperity, but they did integrate Kazakhstan's economy more fully into the Soviet economy and, perhaps more importantly, those efforts elevated Kazakhstan's political leadership and administration within the USSR's governing assemblies. Moscow did not put resources solely into the Virgin and Idle Lands Project, but into education and social services, transportation and communication infrastructure as well. In addition, the Soviet government expanded industrial enterprises and mining in the republic. Nonetheless, Kazakhstan's economy stagnated in the late 1950s and by 1959 agricultural output in the republic was worse than the year before.

## STAGNATION AND PERESTROIKA

Following the CPK Congress in 1959, First Secretary N.I. Beliaev was replaced by Dinmukhamed Kunayev, who was briefly supplanted in 1962, but returned to power in 1964. Kunayev remained First Secretary until December 1986. He was a staunch supporter of Brezhnev and strong advocate for continued improvements in Kazakhstan's agricultural and industrial sectors, significantly expanding the number of large collective farms throughout the republic during his tenure. Accordingly, the Soviet Union's 8th Five-Year Plan, announced in 1966, proposed several guiding principles to strengthen land reclamation and irrigation, expand industrial agriculture (such as food processing and fertilizers), and to increase livestock production. All subsequent Five-Year plans reiterated these guiding principles, but the perennial results were notable more for their failures than any demonstrable or prominent achievements.

The 1960s and 70s were sometimes mockingly referred to as the "cult of stagnation", in which few personnel were replaced or held accountable for the poor results, despite repeated demands at party meetings or in the Soviet media for discernible advances in agriculture and industry.

If anything, the 1970s was a decade in which the Kazakh republic ossified; agriculture continued to stagnate, industrial output barely

Top: The first Soviet nuclear test, code-named "First Lightning", was a plutonium bomb detonated in the Semipalatinsk region on 29 August 1949. Above: Residents and sympathizers united in a movement that protested loudly against the horrific effects of the many hundreds of atomic and hydrogen bombs that were set off both underground and on the surface between 1949 and 1989

increased, GDP grew insignificantly, and Kunayev remained in power. About the only thing that grew in this decade was the Kunayev patronage system. More and more Kazakhs joined the CPK; by the mid-1970s Kazakhs comprised more than 50 percent of the delegates to the party congresses, Kazakhs headed collective farms – except in the Virgin Lands oblasts in the north – Kazakhs led the universities and academies of sciences, and other political and economic posts. Despite the economic stagnation of the 1970s, by the end of the decade Kunayev was perhaps one of the most powerful and influential non-Russians in the Soviet government. But that was about to change.

The 1980s was a decade of turmoil and squandered opportunities. The death of Leonid Brezhnev in 1982 marked a surprising turning point in Soviet history. Kremlin-watchers recognized that a younger generation of leaders would ascend, but it created a rather chaotic environment in the republics as the "old guard" clung to power. Kunayev managed to remain

CPK First Secretary, despite the emergence of Yuri Andropov and his reform agenda. It was not until Mikhail Gorbachev emerged as the CPSU's leader in March 1985 that Kunayev's grip weakened significantly, although not completely. Gorbachev's reform programme, centred on two key components – *perestroika* and *glasnost* – revealed a clear rupture between Kunayev and Moscow.

Between March 1985 and December 1986, Gorbachev openly and frequently criticized the Kazakh leader, noting that decades of maladministration, nepotism and corruption had impoverished the republic and undermined Soviet authority. Several oblast first secretaries, most appointed by Kunayev during his long grasp on power, were denounced in the press and in Gorbachev's speeches, and the majority were replaced. There was little doubt that the republic's economy, which was the third largest in the USSR, had fallen in the 1970s; labour productivity was down, agriculture was mired in inertia, and the black market was siphoning off millions of roubles in materials and income. In fact, per capita income had declined precipitously in the previous decade, a statistic evident throughout the USSR.

On 17 December 1986, Kunayev was finally ousted. Gorbachev appointed Gennady Kolbin, who had no connection to the Kazakh SSR, to lead the republic. Kolbin was an ardent supporter of Gorbachev's reforms, whereas Kunayev often found it difficult to acknowledge that economic and administrative reforms were necessary. Moscow was, however, caught completely off guard by the hostile reaction in Kazakhstan and the seemingly feverish nationalism among Kazakhs who rejected the appointment of someone from outside Kazakhstan to the top post in the CPK.

## RIOTS AND A NEW LEADER

The December 1986 Alma-Ata Riots remain a controversial episode in Kazakhstan's recent history; scholars are still unable to determine the causes and reports vary widely about the number of protesters, the number killed, arrested, even executed, during the ensuing weeks and months. Some scholars argue that the riots were spontaneous, inspired by a sincere protest against the ham-handed manner in which Kunayev was ousted – it was originally reported that he was retiring for health reasons – and replaced by an outsider with no understanding of Kazakhstan's people, its economy or its needs. Other scholars have claimed that the riots were orchestrated by Kunayev loyalists, many of whom stood to lose their positions, their influence and their illegal (ie black-market) incomes if Kolbin successfully rooted out the nepotism and corruption. What scholars and others do not dispute is that Moscow was clearly not expecting such vociferous opposition to Kunayev's forced departure, or that officials in Alma-Ata knew how to quell the volatile situation.

When protestors, the majority of whom appeared to be Kazakh university students, marched into Alma-Ata's central square, many carried signs in support of Kunayev and chants rang throughout the area demanding that Kunayev be reinstated. Local officials tried to calm the demonstrators, but by the third day of protests Soviet officials dispatched armed police and army units to disperse the increasingly large and vocal crowds.

Official reports claim the demonstrators sparked the violence; many witnesses blamed the police and army. Reports, official and unofficial, suggest that anywhere from three to 200 protesters were killed during the clashes; hundreds were arrested and sentenced to long prison terms for their roles in the demonstrations. Many teachers, deans and university rectors were dismissed from their posts for failing to stop the students from marching on the square. In the end, the protests were suppressed, but Kolbin never enjoyed any serious support in the republic and in June 1989 he was eventually replaced as First Secretary by Nursultan Nazarbayev, a Kazakh who had been chairman of Kazakhstan's Council of Ministers since 1984.

The five years between the Alma-Ata Riots and the collapse of the Soviet Union in December 1991 were marked by increased Kazakh nationalism and economic dislocation for many in the republic. For example, one debate that raged in the local media was about a proposed language law that would make Kazakh the "official" language of the republic. Russians, and others, opposed the law, but it passed in 1989. In addition, Kazakhs demanded great economic, social and political autonomy over the republic's territory, its natural resources and its economy. Kazakhs further demanded a new constitution for the republic and an investigation into what many referred to as the "white pages of history". In 1989, the Soviet government "rehabilitated" hundreds of Kazakhs who died during the purges, clearing the names of notables such as Bokeikhanov and Baitursynov (many Kazakhs had also been "rehabilitated" in the 1950s during the Khrushchev "thaw", including Saken Seifullin,

but not leaders of Alash Orda).

In March 1990 competitive elections for a new legislature were held in the republic for the first time since 1925; Kazakhs won a majority of the seats despite only representing about 43 percent of the republic's total population. Nazarbayev had to walk a fine line between supporting the Kazakh nationalist agenda, which was ardently pushing cultural, economic and political programmes, while simultaneously trying to avoid alienating the large Russian population that looked to Moscow to protect its interests and prerogatives in an increasingly tense environment.

Nazarbayev continued, as well, to be a supporter of Gorbachev, at least rhetorically. During negotiations for a new union treaty that would hold the Soviet Union together, Nazarbayev was one of the strongest advocates. He recognized that land-locked Kazakhstan's transportation, communication and economic connections to Russia, in particular, were its Achilles heel in the event that the Soviet Union collapsed. As a consequence, when some Soviet hardliners attempted to remove Gorbachev from office in August 1991, Nazarbayev initially remained silent.

When it became clear that the coup would fail, Nazarbayev once again supported the idea of some sort of new union treaty that would protect Kazakhstan's interests but perhaps extend even more autonomy and independence than what had been envisioned in the earlier negotiations. Nazarbayev signed legislation that abolished the CPK and in December 1991 he won an uncontested election to become Kazakhstan's first president – a post he has held ever since.

Above left: An early picture of Dinmukhamed Kunayev. Above right: Nursultan Nazarbayev in 1991 before he presided over Kazakhstan's independence. Below: Nazarbayev with Boris Yeltsin of Russia, Leonid Kravchuk (left) of Ukraine and Stanislav Shushkavid of Belarus at the signing of the protocol establishing the CIS (Commonwealth of Independent States)

Just a week later, the three Slavic republics – Russia, Ukraine and Belarus – announced the creation of a new federation, the Commonwealth of Independent States (CIS) which excluded Kazakhstan. In a matter of days, however, Kazakhstan was invited to join the CIS, which it did. The Soviet Union survived, at least in principle, until 21 December 1991 when 11 leaders of the former Soviet republics met in Kazakhstan's capital to sign the Alma-Ata Declaration, effectively dissolving the USSR. Kazakhstan's Soviet experiment was over and a new independent chapter for Kazakhstan and the Kazakh people was beginning, but history bequeathed a powerful, troublesome, complex and contested past.

## THE SOVIET LEGACY

Kazakhstan's inheritance was a republic that had more than 100 different nationalities residing within its borders, an archaic centralized economy that was in disarray, decaying transportation and communications infrastructure, and environmental disasters at the nuclear testing sites near Semipalatinsk and the Aral Sea. Scholars are still assessing the environmental and health consequences around the Semipalatinsk site, which is larger than the American state of New Jersey, but it is believed that elevated rates of cancer and thyroid conditions among the local population are directly attributable to both forms of nuclear weapons testing that contaminated local water and soil resources. During the Soviet era,

Below: Olzhas Suleimenov led the Nevada-Semipalatinsk movement that campaigned successfully for the closure of the nuclear testing site in the Semipalatinsk region. Bottom: The large-scale farming of the Virgin Lands programme had terrible social and environmental consequences for Kazakhstan

the local population, mostly Kazakhs, was unprotected and uninformed about the prospective consequences of irradiation. In 1989 the Kazakh "Nevada-Semipalatinsk Anti-Nuclear Movement", named to show solidarity with similar movements in the United States, formed to organize petitions and protests to close the site to any further testing. Led by the Kazakh writer Olzhas Suleimenov, it garnered international attention, which compelled Soviet and helped Kazakh authorities to permanently close the site in 1991.

Another major environmental disaster, the region around the Aral Sea, was devastated by Soviet irrigation practices, which were instituted to provide water for the extensive cotton cultivation in Uzbekistan, Turkmenistan and southern Kazakhstan. Siphoning water from the Syr Darya gradually reduced the Aral Sea's level, shrinking the sea and salinizing the local soil. The sea continued to contract throughout the 1980s, despite Soviet and later international efforts to protect the world's fourth largest inland body of water. By the end of the century, it was roughly one-third its 1950s size.

However, it is important to note that there were some positive consequences for Kazakhstan during the Soviet era; it was not one uninterrupted catastrophe. Kazakh art, music and literature flowered during the different phases of the Soviet experience. The Soviet space programme, located at Baikonur Cosmodrome in Kazakhstan, remained active following Kazakhstan's independence and continues to be essential to the international space station and its astronauts. Education and science, archaeology, history and anthropology all made significant contributions to the world's knowledge about the region. When the Soviet Union collapsed, Kazakhstan was a literate, well-educated, multinational society that possessed abundant natural resources and ample opportunities to grow and thrive.

*Steven Sabol is an Associate Professor of History at the University of North Carolina at Charlotte. He has lived and worked for many years in Central Asia, chiefly in Almaty. His first book, Russian Colonization and the Genesis of Kazak National Consciousness, was published in 2003. His next book project compares Russian colonization of the Kazakhs and American colonization of the Sioux in the 19th century. He has published numerous scholarly articles, including in Central Asian Survey, Problems of Post-Communism and the Western Historical Quarterly.*

# A NEW NATION:
# INDEPENDENCE AND FIRST STEPS
# INTO A MODERN WORLD

The Republic of Kazakhstan was officially born on 16 December 1991. As an impoverished former Soviet republic it was eyed with caution by developed countries in both East and West – as were the other new Central Asian states that emerged from the wreckage of the USSR. But a number of key factors helped alter those negative impressions as far as Kazakhstan was concerned. First, its new leader, President Nursultan Nazarbayev, was a thoughtful, talented diplomat and a tough but inspirational leader. Second, the country was blessed with prodigious wealth in natural resources: it is the ninth richest country in terms of oil reserves, and has vast deposits of natural gas, coal, copper, uranium, zinc, wolfram, silver, gold, lead... the list goes on.

Combine these features with the fact that the people of the steppe are survivors, born and bred to be strong and hard working, and it is easier to understand that although the early years of independence were always going to be challenging, Kazakhstan as a nation was well conditioned to survive and prosper.

The 1990s was a tough period, both for the Kazakhstani people and their government. Nazarbayev was tasked with leading the painful transition from a centrally controlled economy to a free-market economy, while at the same time creating a new political structure, maintaining social stability, and formulating strategic policies for developing international relations. The breakdown in economic ties with neighbouring ex-Soviet republics did not help (suspicion and internal power plays were rife), and Kazakhstan's economic relation with Russia was closer than the others, which required skilful diplomacy.

Nazarbayev made the decision to focus clearly on building a strong economy first and foremost, reasoning that the stability this brought to Kazakhstan would stand it in good stead in the long term. It would of course take time and be a bumpy road – but when and where has this not been the case? Leveraging the country's exceptional mineral resources would be the foundation for success, but this could only be achieved through tight control by a powerful government. Understanding that, the constitution drawn up in 1992

An aerial view of downtown Almaty, Kazakhstan's initial capital city. The Holy Ascension Cathedral can be seen in the foreground and the TV Tower on the slopes of Koktobe Hill in the background. The built-up area of high-rises at top right is part of the newly developing uptown Financial District. Right: Almaty's Independence Monument is crowned by a statue of a Saka warrior holding a falcon and bow and standing on the back of a winged snow leopard

in November 1993 a new national currency, the tenge, was introduced, the value of people's rouble-denominated accounts was reduced to virtually nothing.

By 1996 the situation in Kazakhstan had hit its nadir. Unemployment was dangerously high, the loss of state funding in rural areas was creating desperate conditions, and a lack of skills and education among the population needed to be addressed if Kazakhstan was to develop and grow. The government therefore implemented new economic reforms, amending the privatization policies and encouraging small and medium-sized enterprises (SMEs).

Trade and services began to flourish, and a spirit of entrepreneurialism began to develop. The global financial crisis and the depreciation of the rouble in 1997-98 were a setback, since the tenge also had to be devalued, but after a short period of shock, this actually brought about the stimulus for the economy's revival. It became economical once more to process commodities within the country, and agriculture, food processing and light industry profited from this. (However, throughout the 1990s agricultural output was poor, and investment in this sector was very low, partly because of the much safer revenue-earning capacity of the energy and mining industries.)

gave the president sole authority over the prime minister and Council of Ministers – and a constitution amendment in 1995 reinforced and extended that power. This did not go down too well with some international observers, but Nazarbayev chose to follow his own path, looking east to the tiger economies of Asia for inspiration.

In 1992 Kazakhstan joined the United Nations and other international organizations, beginning the process of integration into the global community. Political stability and economic potential attracted foreign investors, in particular multinational oil companies, but the closure of state enterprises led to mass unemployment. The liberalization of the economy also resulted in enormous inflation and the disappearance of external trade, and when

Slowly at first, then with gathering pace the economy began to grow – helped in no small part by rising international oil prices. In 1997 President Nazarbayev unveiled the "Kazakhstan-2030 Strategy", a roadmap for long-term development of the country aimed at transforming it into "one of the safest, most stable and ecologically sustained states in the world with a dynamically developing economy". By the end of the decade a middle class was beginning to emerge, the energy sector was providing financial stability, and in spite of some friction with separatist movements among portions of the ethnic Russian population in the early years of its nationhood, Kazakhstan was generally free of the communal tensions that troubled other former Soviet republics.

The Russian separatist issue and proximity to the Chinese border, among other factors, could account for the unusual decision in 1997 to move the nation's capital from Almaty to a small, innocuous riverside town in Kazakhstan's northern central Great Steppe region. Many thought

Khan Shatyr is a 150-metre-high, futuristic leisure and shopping complex designed by Norman Foster to be reminiscent of a nomadic tent – the transparent plastic compund of its outer skin keeps the interior at a steady 26°C whether the temperature outside is baking under the summer sun or well below freezing in the depths of winter

staunchly secular Kazakhstan government and the unstable and religiously militant countries to the south might have been a factor as well.

From the start the government worked hard to ensure its secular authority and religious tolerance – in a country with around 130 different ethnic groups and followers of many religions, this was vital to social stability. This standpoint was also frequently presented to the world; the striking Palace of Peace and Accord, or "Pyramid", was built in Astana to be a focal point for the country's focus on religious equality, hosting annual conferences for leaders of the world's religions. Kazakhstan's strong support of nuclear non-proliferation initiatives was also an early banner under which it set itself on the world stage.

When Kazakhstan entered the international arena as an independent state, President Nazarbayev wisely chose what he called a "multi-vector" approach to foreign policy. The country's geographical location, midway between East and West in a region full of tension in the 1990s, meant it was of interest to many other influential countries, especially given its oil and gas resources. Nazarbayev therefore had to perform a skilled balancing act in relations with Russia (its most important economic partner), China, the USA, Western Europe and the Middle East, including Turkey.

Throughout the first decade of independence, Kazakhstan joined many international trade and security organizations, including the Economic Cooperation Organization (ECO), the Organization for Security and Co-operation in Europe (OSCE), the Organisation of Islamic Cooperation (OIC) and the Shanghai Cooperation Organization (SCO). This assisted its economic growth so that, by the turn of the millennium, it was able to reduce its dependence on international institutions and begin implementing its own economic and political reforms to meet the requirements of a rising player on the global stage. As the 21st century began, the scene was set for Kazakhstan to take a giant leap forward on the path to becoming a successful modern democracy.

President Nazarbayev was committing political suicide by forcing this move, but the town, called Akmola, was renamed Astana (meaning "capital") and swiftly began to be developed into a gleaming metropolis, with impressive architectural gems such as the Baiterek tower, KazMunaiGaz building, Presidential Palace and the pyramidal Palace of Peace and Accord all sprouting up in the new city area south of the Esil (Ishim) River.

As a statement of intent it spoke loudly of Kazakhstan's aspirations (and new wealth), but by relocating the centre of governance and administration to the north, Nazarbayev brought about a better-balanced ethnic mix (historically Kazakhs generally populated the south while the north was a stronghold of Russians and Ukrainians), thus cooling Russian separatist tendencies, and also narrowed the financial gap that had grown (Almaty had become the overwhelming centre of money circulation) and improved the prospects of the northern provinces. It may also be that Almaty's location in an earthquake zone was cause for concern, whilst putting greater distance between the

Baiterek Tower is the 97-metre-high centrepoint of Nurzhol Boulevard in Astana. It symbolizes the "Tree of Life", with the golden egg of the legendary Samruk bird nestling in its upper branches. Visitors can take an elevator to the golden sphere, from where there ia a superb 360° view around the city

# The creation of a sovereign state: 1991–2000

By *Didar Kassymova*

W hen the former head of the Kazakh Communist Party Nursultan Nazarbayev was elected to be the first president of the newly independent Republic of Kazakhstan in December 1991, liberal nationalist trends prevailed in the political leadership and among the general public, and numerous political movements emerged. Kazakhstan entered independence as a relatively liberal, stable and pluralistic state, due in part to the legacy of the late Soviet period and also the innate nature of a society based on liberal models of communal development.

The building of a new nation in the post-Soviet period proceeded after a critical assessment of the region's recent history and recognition of both the achievements and errors of the past. A gradual replacement of key elements in its political and economic foundations began, with modernized economic blocks and ethnocratic pillars (Kazakh history, language and culture) being implemented; however, this was framed by the political and economic necessities of the immediate future, which meant first and foremost to ensure social stability and shore up the economic situation using state resources.

repatriation policy to handle a host of domestic and international challenges.

The economic situation was critical in the early years due to the collapse of state funds and a break in the previously important economic ties

The national flag reflects elements of Kazakhstan's nature and culture – a golden sun and soaring eagle on a sky-blue background, with a geometric Kazakh design on its left side. Kazakhstan's national emblem shows two winged unicorns flanking a shangyrak, the roof opening of a yurt

Kazakhstan's nascent leadership faced a wide range of issues: it needed to build a new economy and financial system, adopt a national currency, create a defence infrastructure, maintain education and health-care sectors, and formulate foreign policies and national security frameworks for both domestic and international arenas. The demise of the USSR had created a window of opportunity for Kazakhstan, but the way forward led down a long and difficult path.

## ECONOMY AS PRIORITY

In 1991 Kazakhstan was one of the most ethnically diverse post-Soviet republics; the titular ethnic group, Kazakhs, were a minority in their own land, representing only 35 percent of the total population of 16 million (Slavic groups made up 60 percent) and mostly living in rural southern areas. A massive exodus of the Russian-speaking population after 1991 statistically upgraded the Kazakh demographic, but at the same time depopulated the country's northern areas and created serious demand within the qualified labour force. The government therefore introduced an ethnic

with the former soviet republics. In response, Nazarbayev and his ministers chose an "economy comes first" approach to prioritize and tackle the many problems, with the understanding that a focus on politics would follow once the economy had stabilized. However, the economic situation deteriorated throughout 1992 and 1993; many enterprises were closed down, the liberalization of the economy led to uncontrolled inflation (2,400 percent in 1993), and external trade dropped drastically. The government began to build a mixed economy in several stages, slowly regulating market development, adopting legal mechanisms, helping domestic business to mature and involving the Kazakhstani economy in global economic networking. It was a tough and painful process.

November 1993 saw the introduction of a national currency, the tenge. A monetary model called "shock therapy" was introduced (designed by World Bank and International Monetary Fund experts); based on full trade liberalization and a tough credit policy, it resulted in galloping inflation, financial deficits

along with unregulated taxation and money outflow. Unemployment grew from virtually zero in 1991 to an official figure of 11-13 percent between 1992 and 1999 (though the real figure was much higher, as many unregistered people survived on seasonal or *ad hoc* jobs alone). By 1996 the official number of Kazakhstanis below the poverty line was 34.6 percent; unofficial figures claimed about 60 percent. Kazakhstan was listed as a developing country, and pinned its hopes of macroeconomic stability on gradual and strategically planned reforms, liberalization of trade, a favourable external environment and rising prices in raw commodities such as oil, gas and uranium within the global market.

The liberal economic policies had been set during the transition process to statehood, but Kazakhstan now faced serious problems in budget shortfalls as its tax base deteriorated. This was a precarious situation and a very tough time for the people of Kazakhstan, whose rouble-denominated bank savings had been reduced to almost no value. However, external funding from the IMF and the World Bank proved to be a turning point; although it made the economy dependent on foreign direct investment (FDI), especially in the hydrocarbon sector, the government adopted a policy of diversification of FDI sources and transit routes to the world markets. This astute strategy brought swift dividends, and once Kazakhstan's immense mineral resources began to be more fully exploited, steady economic growth was assured. (In fact, Kazakhstan was

able to repay its US$385 million debt to the IMF by May 2000, before the due date – an unusual and impressive feat.)

In the mid-1990s the IMF and World Bank's credits and loans were used to cover policies aimed at social assistance programmes, pension reforms and the like, in order to avoid sociopolitical disasters at a crucial time when the general populace was struggling but brighter times could be seen on the horizon. Nazarbayev's government borrowed the economic reform model from East Asian tiger economies such as Singapore, which promoted openness for foreign capital and market reforms.

Meanwhile, the economy was growing heavily dependent on the oil industry. In the early 1990s the government had signed agreements with Western states on oil exploration and development; this was driven primarily by a need for foreign investment in order to develop technically difficult oil fields, but also to secure access to world markets and avoid dependence on only a few partners. Kazakhstan avoided conflict with interested parties over its energy resources without allowing itself to become dependent on any one of them. One of these deals was the US purchase of Kazakhstan's Caspian oil share – dubbed the "sale of the century".

State Committee on Privatization of state-owned businesses. This took place in an unsystematic, uncompetitive and non-transparent way through transfer of small and medium-size enterprises (SMEs) to insiders, with government retaining a minority interest. The overall goal was to create a market economy and allow a middle class to emerge. In the early 1990s the government also promoted private foreign ownership in order to generate revenues quickly and accumulate resources to help stabilize the economy and facilitate foreign debt payment. By 1993, 7,000 enterprises had been privatized (the process was completed by 1997).

The general aim of the privatization process was to give members of the public the chance to have real ownership in a business, even if only as a small shareholder. The state designed and orchestrated the move to private ownership as a democratic way of providing collective ownership to a populace who had never known such entitlement. Unfortunately, the mechanism was corrupted by influential people, who used non-transparent tenders, corruption and abuse of power to grab what they wanted, and as a consequence the general population profited little.

Payment for buying shares in private businesses was in the form of cash or coupons. The people

Above: The impressive curving façade of the KazMunaiGaz building in Astana. Below: "Nodding donkey" oil well pumps in western Kazakhstan – the oil industry has been instrumental in the country's economic stability

Among the first foreign companies to invest in the Kazakhstani economy were Philip Morris, Coca-Cola and Daewoo, the latter owning 40 percent of Kaztelecom. Throughout the 1990s the government courted foreign investment, and it was possible for multinationals and foreign states to gain control over many hugely attractive resources and assets, in particular in the mining and energy sectors. Regional elite individuals and families were also given the opportunity to attain controlling power over resources, and by the mid-1990s had grown strong enough economically to challenge the central authorities. The central government circumvented this potential problem by co-opting most of the regional elite into top administrative positions.

## THE PRIVATIZATION PROCESS

One of the key requirements of the IMF was privatization, which began in 1991 with a

were allotted coupons related to their housing and the enterprises where they worked (urban citizens received 100 coupons and those in rural areas 120). These could be pooled together in stock to buy large property shares or invest in shareholdings. Privatization Investment Funds (PIFs), of which there were 170, were designed to accumulate enough coupons to acquire large stakes in companies to control the management process. But although the government issued a total of 1.7 billion non-transferable coupons, only 1.1 billion were redeemed.

In 1993, therefore, a Second National Programme of Denationalization and Privatization was initiated. This followed a more systematic model in three segments, comprising small-scale enterprises with less than 200 employees; mass privatization of businesses employing between 200 and 5,000 workers (strategic industries omitted); and case-by-case privatization of large and strategic enterprises. (Companies handling major natural resources were set apart; these were dealt with in non-competitive, non-transparent tenders.) However, it is fair to say that once again, relatively few people benefited significantly. In 1996-1997 economic reforms were initiated to support small business growth; this had a positive effect, resulting in a rise in the number of small shops and catering and services firms, so that by 2003 small businesses contributed 25 percent of Kazakhstan's GDP.

State-orchestrated privatization had created the basics for a market economy and a foundation for the emergence of a middle class. The government had denationalized most of its key economic sectors – barring those with vital social significance such as health care and education. In the mid-1990s they adopted a complex Anti-crisis Programme aimed at creating favourable investment opportunities for external and domestic producers on a competitive basis. Private business became the major driver in the national economic process, and the next stage of economic reforms was remarkably successful due to one particularly favourable external economic situation: the rise in the price of oil.

Focusing on long-term economic success proved to be the most effective way of maintaining internal stability and balance during an acutely difficult period for Central Asia's ex-Soviet states. External politics in both regional and global contexts were highly complex, and suspicion and cynicism about the region's newly independent nations was the order of

Bogatyr Strip Mine in the Ekibastuz region is one of the largest open-cast coal mines in the world

the day. However, under Nazarbayev and his government, Kazakhstan began to develop in an impressive and comparatively controlled manner.

In 1997 the president's Strategy-2030 plan was adopted. It defined key priorities including internal stability and an integrated society through realization of shared objectives in the economic sphere and improvements in the social sphere. One of the most serious problems to emerge from the focus on economic development was that the tempo of socioeconomic change was much faster than the ability of legislation and administrative control structures to monitor the positive and negative effects on society. The transfer of financial mechanisms from a central budget to local administrations created fertile ground for corruption and favouritism, rendering local administrations devoid of resources to meet the needs of economic and social reforming.

Cultural conditions and Kazakhstan's historical legacy meant that the majority of the population suffered from a lack of skills and education. In rural areas families survived by raising cattle, farming, gardening and small trade, as well as providing minor services to the community. Previously, the major source of cash income for a rural population had come from state-run offices and pensions. By the mid-1990s the loss of state funding for rural areas and the subsequent launch of free market mechanisms, along with unregulated privatization, resulted in a fall in agricultural output of about 30 percent (and 60 percent for livestock). Thus, outside the major towns and cities, the first decade of Kazakhstan's independence must have seemed to many like a return to the much harsher times of old.

## THE MOVE TO DEMOCRACY

When independence was declared, the Kazakhstani leadership outlined a path of gradual democratization, though initially the strength of an authoritarian regime was necessary – and easy for a populace used to Soviet power to accept. Kazakhstan's multiethnic composition (about 130 ethnic groups) created a natural constraint on the power balance; a central tenet of the leadership was to have an intra-ethnic balance of political and economic representation in order to meet international expectations from Russia and the West. The political system was shaped by two constitutions (created in 1992 and 1995), meeting the model of a centrally managed state led by the president and his office, and backed by two other elected bodies – Parliament and

the Assembly of the People of Kazakhstan, balanced by the Supreme Court and the Constitutional Court. The first constitution made the country a parliamentary republic; the second gave more powers to the president as a guarantor of stability. The leadership ignored Washington-consensus recommendations for policy reforms and developed its own model – the Kazakhstani way to democracy, stability and prosperity.

The presidential team manoeuvred skilfully through the political minefield of competing elites, thus saving the country from the social and political chaos that could have occurred in a rush to grab national assets. Political reforms were initiated to balance the central role of presidential power with elected representatives. President Nazarbayev retained broad powers, supervising all activities of the three branches of power under the constitution (as he continues to do today), but in the 1990s his authority was unchallenged at all social levels and by all ethnic groups, as he was viewed as the country's best hope for progress and stability.

Kazakhstan's division of power – legislative, executive and legal – was designed to provide a system of counterbalance. A two-chamber parliament was set up: the Senate or Upper House, and the *Majilis* or House of Representatives. Thirty-two senators are elected by assemblies of local representatives through secret ballot, while 15 are nominated by the president. The majority membership of the Majilis (98 representatives) are elected through general, equal and direct voting by secret ballot based on party lists, while nine Majilis members are elected by the Assembly of the People of Kazakhstan (a consultative organ appointed and headed by the president). The president was also granted the right to appoint the chairman and supreme judge of the Supreme Court.

The Chamber of the *Majilis*, the House of Representatives or Lower House, which comprises 107 members

The country was divided into 14 administrative *oblasts*, classified as donors and recipients of state funding. These varied widely in terms of population and economic potential – some being rich in mineral resources but with low populations of mostly poor inhabitants. About 30 towns were recognized as being heavily depressed (comprising about 17 percent of the country's population); these were part of the old Soviet industrial and military complex. Without state support rural areas – accounting for 45 percent of the population – had limited resources to cope with their problems, resulting in dramatic social, economic and cultural degradation.

Throughout the 1990s investment in the agricultural sector was very low as it was considered to be risky. Agrarian development fell into serious crisis (and it wasn't until well into the 21st century that a revival took place). As had been clearly proven by the catastrophic failures of the Soviet agrarian programmes, climatic conditions and the poor soil quality of the steppe lands only allow cultivation of some crops (wheat, rye, barley and oats) in limited areas as centrally managed irrigation systems are needed. The majority of the steppe zones are only viable for livestock farming – a fact clearly illustrated by the nomadic cultures of millennia past.

The dissolution of state control and patronage over the agricultural sector led to the emergence of private ownership on land and cattle breeding. Two types of producer developed in this market – individual households (usually garden-type produce) and cooperatives (larger-scale grain and meat produce). But between 1990 and 2001, overall agricultural output dropped from 34 percent of GDP to 8.7 percent, making the country deficient in domestic food requirements. Previously used land went untouched, and the state was forced to create several strategic programmes in an attempt to upgrade rural areas and develop agriculture. It was a long, slow process that continues to the present day.

An inevitable phenomenon now occurred, common to most developing countries. This was the steady migration of people from rural areas to major towns and cities. The urban/rural disparities could not be hidden, and urbanization posed serious social challenges. In response, the government set up initiatives to fight poverty and unemployment through creation of jobs, re-training to meet market demands in professional or qualified positions, and a benefits system.

## TRADE ROUTES, EDUCATION AND CIVIL SOCIETY

The transportation system inherited from the Soviet era was costly and very Russia-centric, so soon after independence work began on several domestic lines to connect areas of the country both economically and socially, and stimulate economic activity along them. President Nazarbayev knew the importance of Kazakhstan's geopolitical location, and the development of transit transport corridors between China and Europe was high on his list of projects to roll out.

In 1993 the government signed on as one of 14 states to be part of the TRACECA (Transit Corridor Europe-Caucasus-Asia) programme, an ambitious transport initiative designed to develop the Black Sea and Caspian Sea trade route by road, rail, sea and air. Kazakhstan's participation in several other international transit corridors – the northern Trans-Asian railway linking western Europe with China and the Korean Peninsula, and a southern route from southeastern Europe to China and Southeast Asia via Turkey, Iran and Central Asian states – illustrated the importance of developing trade links between East and West, and this strategy was further expanded in the decades to come (see following chapter).

By the latter stages of the 1990s, the stable political rule that had been ensured by one-party support, a centralized administration and investment in the social, cultural and intellectual spheres, was bearing fruit for the country and its global prospects. Reforms in public administration were initiated to decentralize certain areas of administrative activity – although the main decision-making powers were retained by the presidential office. In 1997

The entrance to Nazarbayev University, which opened in June 2010 as part of the president's vision to create "a prestigious world-class university" in Astana

the media came under tight state control; the concept of freedom of speech was typical for a transitional democratic country, meaning the authorities were mostly concerned with providing reliable but socially and politically correct information.

A vital area needing reform was the education system. This needed to be transformed from the Soviet state-controlled system, and gradually a private education system was introduced on three levels – pre-school, secondary and tertiary. Higher education institutions began a process of modernization to meet national and international standards, and in 1993 the Bolashak Presidential Scholarship Scheme was introduced, providing grants for the most talented students to study in universities around the world. This tied in with the country's need to develop an effective pool of top-class managerial, technical, scientific and scholarly workers as quickly as possible.

Although social traditions based on family, clan or ethnic ties and communal networks remained strong and even boasted a resurgence in newly independent Kazakhstan, a Western-style civil society began to emerge. Non-governmental organizations (NGOs) began to proliferate, but these often differed from the goal-centred Western model and were instead focused around a founder-individual or sponsor's ad-hoc personal interests. Significant financial support from international funding agencies saw the number of NGOs in Kazakhstan grow from 400 in the early years to 1,600 by 1997, and after that a gradual consolidation of the NGO sector and formal arrangements for cooperation with the government resulted in more growth (the present-day figure is more than 3,500) – though the legal difficulties and other obstacles often hampered the overall benefits.

As had been planned from the beginning, the development of democracy needed to progress hand-in-hand with the building of the state. Guaranteeing equal status to all ethnic groups and cultures was imperative; constructive policies of integration were built on respect for the history and heritage of every ethnic group and focused on tolerance, dialogue and accord. Kazakhstan is home to around 130 ethnic groups and cultural issues are very sensitive, so monitoring and tackling them in a compassionate way was vital.

The Assembly of the People of Kazakhstan (or People's Assembly) was set up in 1995 to assess the ethnic policies and handle inter-ethnic relations. Under the constitution all

ethnic groups enjoy equal rights before the law; cultural centres were built to ensure the realization of ethnic groups' cultural needs, from providing education in the mother tongue to maintaining cultural practices. But state law prohibited the creation of ethnically oriented public associations and political parties. Nazarbayev's doctrine of national unity emphasized the strengthening of Kazakhstani identity based on the historical ethnic pluralism of its society, so the government was – and continues to be – staunchly secular.

## A REGIONAL LEADER AND GLOBAL PLAYER

In March 1992 Kazakhstan joined the international community as a member of the United Nations; it also signed security agreements with NATO and Russia-centred blocks. Nazarbayev decided on a pragmatic "multi-vector" approach to international relations due to the country's geographical location and the obvious benefits of maintaining good relations with Russia, Western Europe, the Middle East, Iran, India, China and the US.

The nuclear testing site at Semipalatinsk had been shut down in 1991 by President Nazarbayev's firm decision with the support of two years of protests by the anti-nuclear movement "Nevada-Semipalatinsk", led by the renowned author and poet Olzhas Suleimenov. The Kazakhstani leadership adopted non-nuclear status, assured by security guarantees from the US, Russia and China, and joined the

Astana's monumental Presidential Palace is a marble splendour, topped by a blue dome and golden spire that reaches 80 metres into the sky. It is situated on the left bank of the Esil River at the eastern end of Nurzhol Boulevard, the new city's huge central quadrangle, and is the president's official workplace

NNPT (Nuclear Non-Proliferation Treaty). The government participated in a number of international projects aimed at providing a stable platform for peaceful coexistence of countries with different political regimes and positions in the global arena. Among these were initiatives such as conferences on confidence-building measures in Asia, Eurasian integration mechanisms with geo-cultural and geo-economic components at their core, a regular congress of world religions, and anti-nuclear initiatives.

At the same time, the government implemented human rights protection mechanisms designed to meet international standards, set up a national commission on family issues and gender policy, a committee on the protection of children's rights under the Ministry of Education, and ratified most of the international conventions on human rights protection. Opposition leaders who claimed breaches in these conventions and criticized the president and his officials were generally co-opted into state services to ensure their compliance.

Kazakhstan took the lead in several initiatives aimed at integrating the Central Asian countries into a cohesive group, but most of these failed, largely because of political inertia among the other regional leaders and their dependence on external aid, which impeded the creation of a regional bloc. Relations between the former Soviet republics were tested by the loss of economic relations, a breakdown in security obligations, and the denial of their common Soviet heritage. However, deep-rooted memories of a common cultural heritage, as well as recognition of common security threats, stopped any rifts from growing too wide. (Kazakhstan and the other Central Asian "stans" had signed the Alma-Ata Protocol to join the CIS on 21 December 1991, and in May 1992 Kazakhstan joined the Collective Security Treaty Organization with five post-Soviet states.)

Relations with the Russian Federation were paramount for Kazakhstan – it was and continues to be its most significant strategic partner. In July 1998 the two countries signed an Agreement on Eternal Friendship, and in October 2000 Kazakhstan joined the Eurasian Economic Community (with Russia, Belarus, Kyrgyzstan and Tajikistan) in order to develop economic cooperation and prepare for a unified customs tariff and free trade regime.

However, Kazakhstan was also looking east towards the growing economic giant of China. In April 1996, as a result of border negotiations with China, a mutual-security organization between five states – China, Kazakhstan, Kyrgyzstan, Russia and Tajikistan – was created and called the Shanghai Five. By 2001 this had evolved into the Shanghai Cooperation Organization, at which time Uzbekistan joined.

Nazarbayev's multi-vector approach to foreign policy during Kazakhstan's first decade of statehood provided the country with a strategically solid but flexible standpoint from which to select allies and partners in regional or global situations. In choosing to pursue its own unique policy for economic, political and social growth, the Kazakhstan government took a bold risk and endured hard times during its early years of independence, but ultimately built an idiosyncratic political and institutional structure that provided political stability, economic progress, and the promise of greater success at the start of the 21st century.

*Didar Kassymova is a full-time Senior Lecturer at KIMEP University, Almaty. She is a Fulbright scholar of the Jackson School of International Studies, University of Washington, USA, and a member of CESS (the Central Eurasian Studies Society). She has written a number of papers on Kazakhstan's relationship with its Central Asian neighbours and its significance on the global stage, and is co-author of* A Historical Dictionary of Kazakhstan.

President Nursultan Nazarbayev in deep discussion with President Barack Obama of the United States

# THE NEW MILLENNIUM: MEETING THE CHALLENGE OF GREAT POTENTIAL

At the turn of the 21st century, Kazakhstan began to record economic growth on a scale that few nations could match – in 2003 GDP had reached US$30.8 billion, but by 2009 it had more than quadrupled to US$134 billion. The tremendous value of the country's natural resources quickly became apparent, and the extraction of oil, natural gas, coal, uranium and a host of other ores and minerals was accelerated through the injection of foreign investment and skilled labour.

The government now began a renationalization process in order to regain control over its energy related sectors – it had necessarily had to make major concessions to the multinational oil (and other) companies whose capital had allowed Kazakhstan's resources to begin to be exploited. New institutions set up by the government were designed to provide long-term funding for major projects, effective management of the economy, as well as diversification of economic sectors.

This last point was of great importance to President Nazarbayev, who knew that modernization and a diversified economy – that did not depend solely on one industry sector – was vital to creating sustainable economic growth. The first decade of independence had focused on creating a solid foundation of political, social and economic stability; the second decade must now consolidate this but at the same time begin to branch out into areas such as finance, service industries, research and development, and alternative energy sectors.

Consolidation of the vital energy sector began in 2002 when Kazakhoil and Oil and Gas Transportation were merged to form the state-owned umbrella company

KazMunaiGaz, which grew to encompass many subsidiaries controlling exploration, production, refining and shipping of oil and gas. Although diversification was the buzzword, it was still important to develop the cash-cow energy sector – and in particular to expand it in the president's "multi-vector" way so as not to be over-dependent on Russia or any other country. Where pipelines initially were concentrated on providing for Russia's needs, new deals were made with European buyers, then in the mid-2000s with China.

Kazakhstan's oil and gas is now brought to the world market through pipelines from Atyrau to both the Russian Black Sea port of Novorossiysk, and Samara to the north, as well as from Baku to Ceyhan (oil is shipped from Aktau to Azerbaijan on tankers). A pipeline linked Atasu to western China in 2006, and in 2011 a Central Asian gas pipeline began delivering Turkmenistan's and Kazakhstan's gas from the Caspian Sea to China.

Also necessary at this point in the country's development was political reform, which had taken a back seat to the economy in the first decade after independence. Nazarbayev retained a tight hold over the government, but he had always declared a philosophy of "economy first and

Above: The Kashagan oil field in the north Caspian Sea was discovered in 2000 and is the world's biggest offshore oil discovery in a generation, with potentially 13-15 billion barrels of recoverable oil

Right: A stylized statue of a camel carrying a *shangyrak* (the circular roof opening of a yurt) stands in Astana's Nurzhol Boulevard. In the background is the KazMunaiGaz building and behind it Khan Shatyr

then politics", and now was the time to begin implementing democratic reforms to decentralize state administration and give more power to local government. Reforms began to enhance the effectiveness, transparency and accountability of the executive branch and to combat corruption. This, of course, was easier said than done, but the fact that process was beginning sent a message to the world that Kazakhstan's democratization was ongoing.

Slowly the old practices of nepotism and recruiting based on political loyalty began to change to a meritocracy where professional expertise and dedication to service were valued higher. An Ombudsman office was set up in 2003 to investigate citizens' complaints of human rights violations, and other anti-corruption protocols were initiated; however, inevitably corruption proved hard to eradicate in the administrative and business spheres.

Compared to other Central Asian countries, though, Kazakhstan was a beacon of stability and the regional success story by the mid-2000s. During the US-led Afghan war in 2002, it was a strategic partner, cooperating over counterterrorism initiatives, providing assistance to the security forces and subsequently creating a US$50 million scholarship fund for young Afghans to study at Kazakhstan's universities.

In 2004 Kazakhstan and Russia came to an agreement over Baikonur Cosmodrome, the secret rocket-launching facility that had been the USSR's Space Race centre during the Cold War. Russia continued the lease on the large area of semi-desert to the east of the Aral Sea for another 50 years, but within that Kazakhstan set up its own National Space Agency – called Kazkosmos. In June 2006 it launched *KazSat-1*, its first communications satellite, and with its own advanced research centres, it plans to offer commercial satellite launch services to other countries and is developing a more environmentally friendly rocket to launch from its new "Baiterek" site.

By now the country's comparatively high quality of life within Central Asia was attracting migrant workers as well as investors; these workers helped facilitate the construction boom that was happening in Almaty, other regional centres, and most of all in Astana. The capital's new city area on the left bank of the Esil River continued to grow apace; amazing edifices such as Khan Shatyr, the Palace of Independence, the Concert Hall and the National Library, among many others, served to raise Astana to the level of Dubai or Hong Kong in terms of architectural innovation and "wow" factor.

Meanwhile, in Almaty a new financial district with its own gleaming towers was emerging to the south of the old city centre, and an underground train network called the Metro was being built (it took 23 years to construct but the first line finally opened in 2011). This highlighted the fact that Almaty, having lost its role as capital and therefore centre of governance and administration, was reinventing itself as a finance hub within Central Asia.

Nonetheless, Kazakhstan still faced many challenges, including a legacy of pollution from the Soviet period. One of its leading concerns was the drying-up of the Aral Sea and its catastrophic climatic, social and environmental consequences (see chapter on the Soviet period for the sad tale of the Virgin Lands programme). In 2005 the decision was made to give up on the main southern portion of the lake and try to save the "North Aral Sea". Financed by the World Bank and Government of Kazakhstan, a 13-kilometre barrier dyke was built at the mouth of the Syr Darya, thus preventing water loss to the south and increasing the water level in the North Aral Sea. As a result the salinity began to decrease and fishing once again became viable (though only in a comparatively small capacity).

A new attitude to the environment was beginning to come into focus now, partly due to the impetus from the government to develop alternate energy sources, but perhaps also because the Soviet-era disasters of the Virgin Lands programme and the nuclear testing site near Semipalatinsk were strong in the minds of the nation's people. In 2006, with help from the United Nations Development Programme (UNDP) Kazakhstan launched a solar energy project in the Almaty region, and a solar energy development concept worth US$90 million was approved in 2009. In 2007 a three-year programme to develop a wind-based energy industry was launched, and the country plans to build 500 megawatts of installed wind power capacity by 2030.

Above: A Russian Proton-K rocket is launched from the Baikonur Cosmodrome in 2000. This particular rocket was carrying the Zvezda service module to the International Space Station

and macroeconomic reforms to fight unemployment through state-funded projects that accelerated industrial development. The major sponsor of these projects was a sovereign wealth fund and joint stock company called "Samruk-Kazyna" or the National Welfare Fund. This was set up in October 2008 and controlled all the most important national companies, as well as institutions aimed at economic development; total capitalization was set at US$45 billion.

In 2010 Kazakhstan joined with Russia and Belarus to form a Customs Union, an alliance designed to ensure regional economic prosperity. The Union created a common market of 170 million people with a total GDP of US$42 trillion, and this tied in with the government's desire to develop cross-border trade and build the country's credentials as a Eurasian trade hub.

A step up on the sporting stage occurred soon after, when Kazakhstan hosted the 2011 Asian Winter Games in and around Almaty and Astana. Held primarily in the Shymbulak ski resort and Medeu ice-rink stadium in the Tien Shan south of Almaty, this was a chance to showcase the country's natural beauty and increasing ability to host large-scale international events, and was seen as a comprehensive success.

The year 2006 also saw the release of a film that initially caused indignation and concern within Kazakhstan, but eventually had a curiously beneficial effect. *Borat: Cultural Learnings of America for Make Benefit Glorious Nation of Kazakhstan* was, at first, thought to be an offensive attack on the Kazakhstani people. However, fairly quickly it became obvious that the butt of the joke was in fact elements of American society, and the official line soon changed to one of "it's a comedy, let's laugh at it". Kazakhstan had been chosen by the film's producers simply because it was so little known by the general world populace, and therefore Borat could say outrageous things about it without people knowing he was lying. But the unexpected result of the film's success was a sudden and huge surge in interest in Kazakhstan from all around the world. This was a boon both to business but especially to the tourism industry, which was underdeveloped for such a naturally and culturally diverse country.

The constitutional amendment of 2007 gave strong veto powers to the president over parliament, but overall state bureaucracy at all levels had been rationalized and modernized, anti-corruption measures were beginning to be enforced, and central control in the lower tiers of government had been devolved. Within the private business sector traditional democratic values were generally observed, and effectiveness, transparency, accountability and professionalism was on the rise.

The global financial crisis that hit in 2007-2008 put the brakes on economic development, forced the devaluation of the tenge by 20 percent, and pushed financial institutions into bankruptcy. The real-estate market collapsed and construction sites were frozen – but Kazakhstan fared better than most countries because of a national oil fund it had established in 1999 for just such an emergency, which was now worth US$40 billion (today the fund is valued at US$76.6 billion). A stabilization programme was launched, including the tenge devaluation

Top: Hazrat Sultan Mosque opened in 2012 in Astana and is Central Asia's largest mosque. Above: Zhumbaktas, or Riddle Rock, with the cliff face of Okzhetpes (Unreachable by Arrows) behind. Burabay National Park is northern Kazakhstan's premier tourist attraction

President Nazarbayev called an early presidential election in 2011, where he garnered 95.5 percent of the votes. Many international organizations criticized the country's elections, accusing them of failing to meet international standards, but close analysis revealed that each election (1991, 1999, 2005 and 2011) had shown improvements over the previous one. After the 2011 election the Independent International Observer Mission stated that: "Commitment of the Kazakhstanis to a democratic future of the country was evident on election day."

Top: The Mausoleum of Khoja Ahmed Yasawi in South Kazakhstan is a religious focal point but also one of the country's greatest cultural draws for the tourism industry. Above: Astana's Palace of Peace and Accord is an amazing architectural showcase for the city

The president's own attitude to democratic change is that a gradual process of organic political reform against a background of economic growth provides the best guarantor of a sustainable democracy. For Nazarbayev, economic prosperity should come before full democracy. "Without such strength, as we have seen repeatedly around the world, stability is put at risk and democratic reform can flounder," he wrote in the *Washington Post* in 2011. In his view it is unreasonable for foreign observers to expect his country to complete overnight processes that in the West took hundreds of years. He takes care to stress that his country's democracy remains in its infancy, might easily be damaged by hasty or ill-considered decisions and should not be regarded as the finished political article.

As is the case with many countries experiencing rapid growth, some disparity in standards of living took place. When in December 2011 riots broke out in the oil town of Zhanaozen in the western region of Mangystau, the government needed to react quickly, transparently and effectively because the world was watching. The oil workers had gone on strike for unpaid danger money and better working conditions, then been sacked and fired on by riot police when they demonstrated in the main square. Nazarbayev visited the town and subsequently dismissed his son-in-law from his position as head of Samruk-Kazyna (which owned the oil company), as well as the heads of KazMunaiGaz and its production unit, and several local officials for their roles in the events leading up to the strike, demonstration and deaths of protestors. The police officers charged with firing at the protestors were also arrested.

It was clear that the will to enforce anti-corruption measures was strong within the presidential office. A growing disparity in wealth within the population, especially between urban and rural communities, resulted in a 2013 rehabilitation programme for 30 towns in depressed rural areas, where poverty is twice as high as the average, but there is still much to be done to prevent further destabilizing events. In the second decade of the 21st century, long-term stability and economic growth in Kazakhstan hinges on continuing political reform, enlightened policies on education, intelligent economic diversification into light industry, banking and other promising sectors with high net returns, and the development of trade, both regional and intercontinental.

The announcement in November 2012 that Astana would host the World EXPO-2017 international exhibition was a significant nod to the country's growing stature on the global stage, and in the same year President Nazarbayev set out a new Kazakhstan-2050 Strategy, calling for better governance, improvement of the welfare and tax systems, support for SMEs and development of infrastructure. Ranked at that time 51st most competitive

country in the world, Nazarbayev's goal is for it to be ranked among the 30 most advanced nations by 2050. Talks over accession to the WTO (World Trade Organization) membership began as far back as 1996, but the process was slow; the Working Party held promising talks in July 2013, and the signs are good that Kazakhstan will sooner rather than later enter the WTO fold.

Intrinsic to Nazarbayev's strategy for a sustainable economy is Kazakhstan's aspirations to be a major part of the "New Silk Road", a road and rail transit link between Europe and the Far East that will provide much shorter travel times for cargo than shipping by sea, and at lower costs. As part of this strategy Kazakhstan has improved its relations with China, settling border issues, encouraging economic cooperation and developing a strategic partnership. The potential of this modern trading route is immense, but there are obstacles to its realization, as the following essay explains in detail. In a sense, Kazakhstan can be said to be returning to its ancient Silk Road roots, making use of its position between East and West to establish itself as a centre of international commerce.

Above: President Nazarbayev addresses his political party members at the 2011 Nur Otan ("Light of the Fatherland") Congress. Below: An architect's drawing of the EXPO-2017 site, which will be constructed from scratch. Inset: Another artist's impression of the huge spherical hall that will be the hub of the enormous complex

# Eurasian hub on the modern Silk Road

By *Richard Weitz*

As the first decade of the 21st century began, Kazakhstan had become the most influential Central Asian country to emerge from the wreckage of the multinational Soviet empire. This was a remarkable achievement for a state whose leaders opposed the USSR's disintegration in 1991, due to fears about the viability of their country to survive without subsidies from other parts of the Soviet Union, and with such a large ethnic Russian minority that might easily have sought to join the new Russian Federation by splitting off parts of northern Kazakhstan.

A view of the Presidential Palace, or Akorda, from the right bank of the Esil River. The Palace faces west down the huge Nurzhol Boulevard, which is flanked by an impressive array of buildings

The leaders of Kazakhstan had overcome many challenges and accomplished a triple transformation, moving from an integrated socialist economic and political system to one characterized by newly independent states with varying degrees of free market economic and pluralistic political systems. In these efforts, Kazakhstan benefited from skilful leadership, a balanced and non-threatening foreign policy, the country's vast energy resources, and a moderate Muslim population that supported the government's policy of religious tolerance.

From independence, a key tenet of Kazakhstan's foreign policy was to promote integration within Central Asia. Kazakhstani officials strongly believed that their country as well as others would greatly benefit from enhanced ties among Eurasian countries – through increased trade, investment, incomes, as well as enhanced diplomatic influence and, ironically, national autonomy due to their elevated ability to deal with extra-regional powers such as Russia and China.

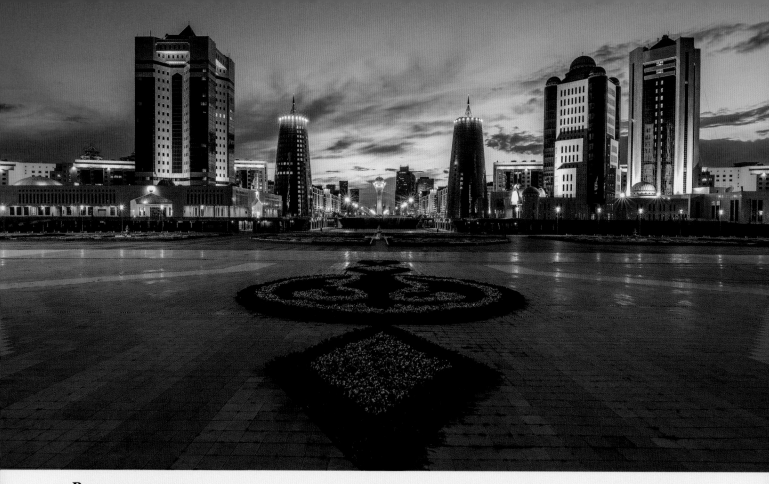

## BUILDING BRIDGES

Living in the largest landlocked country in the world, the Kazakhstan government was eager to deepen its foreign trade and transportation links. In the early 2000s it emphasized that, thanks to the country's strong economic development, successful imposition of market reforms and commitment to regional prosperity, Kazakhstan could become a driver in regional economic integration mechanisms. Since then, Kazakhstani officials have promoted closer commercial integration among Eurasian nations at multiple levels, with priority given to improving regional transportation, pipeline and communication networks, reducing customs and other manmade barriers to trade, encouraging tourism and other nongovernmental exchanges, while strengthening regulations governing labour mobility in Eurasia, and promoting Kazakhstani private investment in other Eurasian economies, especially through joint ventures.

President Nazarbayev's opinion was, and still is, that strong regional cooperation – ideally with a degree of integration that would both help harmonize regional economic policies and promote political, security and other forms of collaboration – would further their economic development and international competitiveness. It would allow Kazakhstani businesses to access new markets and exploit superior economies of scale from the resulting increase in labour, capital and other factors of production. Moreover, by reducing interregional tensions

and promoting deeper economic integration, Kazakhstani experts believed that these countries would become more attractive to foreign investors and enhance their collective leverage with external players.

Despite efforts throughout the first dozen years of the new millennium to diversify economic partners, Kazakhstan's economy today remains heavily dependent on foreign companies for capital and technology. Greater regional integration would allow Kazakhstan and its neighbours to better exploit the natural resources, economic comparative advantages, and pivotal location of Central Asia and the Caspian Basin region as natural transit routes for commerce between Europe and Asia. Kazakhstan's ability to realize its potential as a natural crossroads for east-west and north-south commercial links depends on reducing manmade political and economic obstacles to the free flow of goods and people among Eurasian nations. As the Kazakhstan government knew, and Nazarbayev planned for, an increase in regional prosperity – predicted by economists – would ensue from greater regional integration, and would help Kazakhstan expand its economic activities into new horizontal and vertical markets.

During the Soviet period, the central government ministries in Moscow controlled Kazakhstan's foreign economic activity as well as that of the other Central Asian republics. This situation allowed Soviet planners to

Nurzhol Boulevard provides a colourful counterpoint to the deep-blue sky as the sun sets over Astana, which aspires to take a central role in the future of intercontinental trade across Eurasia

dispose of the territory's rich natural resources unilaterally, directing many Kazakhstani products to other Soviet republics or to the USSR's fellow socialist countries within the Council of Mutual Economic Assistance. When Western countries purchased Kazakhstan's exports, Moscow-based planners used the hard-currency revenue for whatever schemes the Soviet government supported at the time.

However, the disruption of economic ties that followed the breakup of the USSR triggered a collapse in trade among the former Soviet republics. This development proved especially traumatic for Kazakhstan. In 1992, 92 percent of Kazakhstan's exports and 85 percent of its imports involved these other republics. This disruption of Soviet-era commerce induced Kazakhstan's government and business leaders to broaden their economic intercourse to encompass a larger number of countries.

Since then, the economies of many of the former Soviet republics have rebounded. Kazakhstan's trade flows with its former Soviet neighbours typically now exceed Soviet-era levels. Nevertheless, since the USSR's collapse, the countries of the region have found it difficult to cooperate with one another. These states share unresolved disputes over borders, trade, visas, transportation, illegal migration, and natural resources such as water and gas. The poor state of their mutual relations in recent years has meant that these countries regularly enjoy closer ties with external actors (through bilateral and multilateral mechanisms) than with each other. Unlike Kazakhstan, the other Central Asian governments place more emphasis on their relations with extra-regional powers like Russia, China and the West than on developing mutual ties among themselves. Central Asia contrasts with the experience of other former Soviet bloc countries, such as the Baltic States and the Vizegrad countries, where regional cooperation is better.

## THE CASE FOR INTRA-REGIONAL COOPERATION

Most economists today believe interstate commerce throughout Eurasia remains considerably below optimal levels, with bilateral and multilateral relationships characterized by widespread "undertrading" due to poor policy choices, excessive customs duties, weak regional economic infrastructure, and the absence of a comprehensive free-trade zone or common membership in the World Trade Organization (WTO). The region's countries would benefit from improvements in East-West transportation, communications and energy links connecting Asia and Europe as well as the harmonization of their border transit police forces.

Perhaps the most serious problems are Eurasia's undeveloped transportation, communications and commercial networks and the lack of uniform trade and tariff conditions, which result in lengthy paperwork and other wasted time and resources when goods and people move across national borders, making transit times and import and export times much higher than those along other routes or in more developed countries. Much of the infrastructure that does exist is oriented in a north-south direction due to the legacy of the integrated but autarchic Soviet economic model.

An added obstacle to progress on this front is many Central Asians' concern that economic integration could weaken their newly found political independence, national identity and economic autonomy, again resulting in foreign domination. At present, poor infrastructure and storage capacity impedes even simple agricultural trade in fresh fruits and vegetables.

These and other problems initially discouraged foreign direct investment (FDI) into Central Asia – although Kazakhstan was the frontrunner in attracting FDI and from the early 2000s to the present day has slowly built up its credentials. Foreign companies often do not learn about many local public sector investment opportunities due to lack of advance notice of tenders, short bidding windows, and a perceived non-transparent selection process for many public contracts. They also complain about poor protection of intellectual property rights, lack of legal bases for technology transfer, and judiciary systems whose members are ill-equipped to adjudicate commercial disputes.

Many foreign firms have a "wait and see" stance at this point, awaiting evidence that the countries will cooperate sufficiently to create a larger market of potential clients, resulting in economies of scale. If it could overcome these intra-regional barriers, Central Asia could collectively offer outside investors a potential market of 80 million people, the size of Germany's population. Foreign investors would also like to see Central Asian countries develop their specific areas of comparative advantage, rather than competing to sell the same products, before making major investments. For population and logistical reasons, they want to use one country to export to others. Franchisers need to ensure uniform quality control and proper branding, so they want a master franchise for the entire region.

Above: Harvesting machines at work in a massive field in northern Kazakhstan. Grain production has been ramped up to reinvigorate the country's agricultural sector. Right: A worker wears protective headgear to ward off the intense heat at a smelting factory. Mining and metallurgy have a long heritage in Kazakhstan that stretches back thousands of years

President Nursultan Nazarbayev lamented this failure to achieve deeper economic ties, which threatens to deny Kazakhstan its natural status as Eurasia's commercial linchpin as well as collectively weaken Central Asia's economic and diplomatic potential. In February 2005, the president argued that a failure of the Central Asian states to improve their economic integration would invariably leave them too weak to resist falling under the control of yet another extra-regional power, stating: "We have a choice between remaining an eternal supplier of raw materials for the world economy and waiting patiently for the arrival of the next imperial master or pursuing genuine economic integration of the Central Asian region. I propose the latter."

Nazarbayev emphasized that, thanks to Kazakhstan's strong economic development, successful imposition of market reforms and commitment to regional prosperity, the country could become a driver in regional economic

integration mechanisms among Eurasian states. Such a process, in the view of the Kazakhstan government, would in turn promote Kazakhstan's own development by making the country a more attractive market for foreign investors as well as by increasing the number of possible consumers of Kazakhstan's goods.

## A NEW ERA IN CROSS-CONTINENTAL TRADE

But Nazarbayev's ambitions extend beyond that to making Kazakhstan a hub of global commerce and investment. In 2005, he told attendees of an international conference that, "I see Kazakhstan as a junction country in the Central Asian region, an integrator of intra-regional economic ties, a centre of gravity of capital and investments, and a location of regional production or the subsidiaries of the world's major companies aimed at the Central Asian market and international services." But in time, he added, "Kazakhstan might perform the function of an important link, a transcontinental economic bridge, for interactions between European, Asia-Pacific and South Asian economic regions".

At a May 2012 plenary session of the Foreign Investors Council, Nazarbayev launched a Kazakhstan-New Silk Road project to encourage investment in those programmes needed to make Kazakhstan a key transportation and business hub in Central Asia and a key transit link between Europe and Asia. Current priorities have focused on the East Gate programme supporting the Khorgos International Cross-border Cooperation Centre bordering China, the Khorgos Free Economic Zone, and in the Western Gate expansion of the Aktau seaport.

Almost from independence in 1991, Nazarbayev began calling for a union of Central Asian states that could entail the sharing of water and energy resources; improvements in regional transportation infrastructure; establishment of common customs and trading tariffs; mechanisms to respond collectively to environmental threats and natural disasters; and support for region-wide tourist networks. Despite obstacles, Kazakhstani experts considered the deeper integration of Central Asian countries a natural process that accords with the genuine national interests of these nations, which share historical and cultural ties as well as common borders and economic incentives for collaboration. They envisaged an evolutionary path from a free-trade zone to a customs union to an economic union with ancillary political and other institutions. In this regard, Kazakhstan supported various regional integration initiatives to remedy this situation.

For example, in 1997 Afghanistan, Azerbaijan, China, Kazakhstan, Kyrgyzstan, Mongolia, Pakistan, Tajikistan, Turkmenistan and Uzbekistan, as well as six multilateral

Right: A newly laid road crosses Kazakhstan's huge expanse of steppe. More and more are being constructed to help kick-start a "New Silk Road" of intercontinental land trade

institutions (the Asian Development Bank, European Bank for Reconstruction and Development, International Monetary Fund, Islamic Development Bank, United Nations Development Programme and World Bank), pooled their resources to establish the Central Asia Regional Economic Cooperation (CAREC) Programme. This informal grouping of 10 countries and six multilateral institutions has funded to date more than 100 projects focused on promoting energy, transportation and trade facilitation in Central Asia.

These projects are valued at more than US$21 billion; CAREC's multibillion-dollar Transport and Trade Facilitation Strategy foresees substantial infrastructure investments to improve the flow of goods along six main transnational corridors – including both road and rail links – connecting countries within the region as well as with the rest of Eurasia. According to the ADB, as of mid-2013, CAREC had already built around 4,000 kilometres of roads, 3,200 kilometres of railways, 2,400 kilometres of power transmission lines, and achieved a 50 percent reduction in transit time for moving goods and vehicles across Eurasian borders.

In a more recent initiative, Kazakhstan partnered with Azerbaijan, Georgia and Turkey in the joint Silk Wind Project, which aims to construct a high-speed multimodal container transportation system for freight shipments between the countries of Europe, the Caucasus and Asia. According to the Ministry of Transport and Communications of Kazakhstan, the participating countries plan to introduce a single tariff for the transportation of goods within the project as well as share more preliminary information between their customs authorities and rail operators.

The Silk Wind Project was initiated in the Transport Corridor Europe-Caucasus-Asia (TRACECA) framework, an EU-sponsored project created two decades ago to promote the economic and political development of the Black Sea, Caucasus and Central Asia region by improving the transportation corridor between Europe and Asia through these countries. The main initial task for the Silk Wind Project was to complete construction and modernization of the Baku-Tbilisi-Kars railway line, which was scheduled to open in 2014. In an effort to supplement its export routes through Russian territory, Kazakhstan plans to convey grain products and oil from its Kashagan field by train through Azerbaijan and Georgia onward to European markets. President Nazarbayev has called on the partners to work on the "principle of 5Cs" (from Russian): speed, service, cost, safety and stability. KazTransOil has acquired controlling shares in Batumi Sea Port and Batumi oil terminal in support of this project.

## STRATEGIES FOR THE ROAD AHEAD

Kazakhstan is eager to realize its potential as a land-based transportation hub connecting Europe and Asia. The government would like to double freight and passenger transit from Europe to Asia via Kazakhstan by 2020 and multiply it tenfold until 2050. Kazakhstan participates in many other international transportation initiatives. These include the Euro-Asian Transport Links Project, the International Transport Consortium, the Common Transport Policy, and the North-South Meridian Transport Corridor agreement (a Russian-Indian-Iranian project that Kazakhstan joined in 2003). Astana has also supported related initiatives within the Eurasec, the OSCE, the SCO, and other multilateral institutions. Inside Kazakhstan, during the last decade various complementary public and private efforts have constructed new railway lines to integrate its disparate regions with each other as well as these emerging international transportation lines.

Kazakhstan's future prospects of becoming a Eurasian hub for broader East-West commerce partly rest on the success of the Western China-Western Europe International Transit Corridor, which aims to improve the efficiency and safety of the main roads between China and Europe. Construction and other project-related activities occur along the 8,445km route (2,233km in Russia, 2,787km in Kazakhstan and 3,425km in China) running from St Petersburg in Russia to China's eastern port of Lianyungang. The Kazakhstani portion of the highway corridor should reach completion in 2015. The goal of the corridor is to increase commerce by accelerating the movement of goods between Europe and Asia while reducing transportation costs.

Nazarbayev has called the Western Europe-Western China corridor the "construction of the century". The project will provide many economic benefits to Kazakhstan. The route encompasses some of the least developed areas of Kazakhstan, with decaying rural roads built in Soviet times that now see many accidents. The new roads will be safer, more durable, capable of carrying heavier vehicles, and allow for faster driving speeds. They will also make their regions better able to trade with other parts of Kazakhstan as well as abroad, making them more attractive to investors. The construction process will itself generate investment, manufacturing and many jobs.

Kazakhstan is also helping to develop a longer 10,800-kilometre fast rail link between Chongqing in southwest China and Duisberg, Germany via Kazakhstan, Russia, Belarus and Poland. This "Silk Road" China-Europe railway, which began limited operation in 2011, is still under construction. The annual volume of freight turnover totalled about two million metric tonnes in 2013 and is planned to increase to some 15 million metric tonnes annually in coming years. Thanks to strong government support, Kazakhstan expects to finish its share of this track by 2015, the original deadline.

All these projects aim to increase East-West trade by accelerating the movement of goods between Europe and Asia while reducing transportation costs. At present, businesses seeking to send goods from China to Europe face a dilemma. They can send items by the existing Trans-Siberian Railway, which normally requires 14 days, but this means of transport is costly. Or they can send goods by sea, through the Suez Canal, which costs less but is three times longer and takes on average 45 days. Thus far, some 80 percent of China's manufactured goods reach Europe via this sea route. The proposed Eurasian corridor aims to allow shippers to send goods even faster by land, using roads as well as railways, and at a considerably lower cost, resulting in more businesses using the land route.

Besides providing Kazakhstan with major economic gains, these projects – many of which have been carefully formulated and implemented over the course of the last 12-14 years – all help to advance Nazarbayev's vision of his country as

a nexus of international commerce and his goal of promoting greater regional integration within Central Asia and beyond. In 2007, he called for a Eurasian transport corridor that would eventually "connect the Persian Gulf on one end and the Baltic Sea on the other" through "the creation of a high-tech system that includes railroads, highways, power transmission lines, gas and oil pipelines". These projects also align well with Kazakhstan's multi-vector foreign policy of developing strong ties with all the major powers in order to avoid becoming overly dependent on any one of them. The Nazarbayev administration has encouraged Kazakhstanis to engage in regional commerce as well as wider economic intercourse in order to limit Kazakhstan's dependence on any single supplier, customer, investor or market. Nazarbayev has warned that, "The destiny of all Central Asian peoples depends on this most important factor – whether we can become a transportation route of global significance or will be pushed off to the side of the road again."

*Richard Weitz is Senior Fellow and Director of the Center for Political-Military Analysis at Hudson Institute. Dr Weitz is a graduate of Harvard College (BA with Highest Honours in Government), the London School of Economics (MSc in International Relations), Oxford University (MPhil in Politics) and Harvard University (PhD in Political Science), where he was elected to Phi Beta Kappa. He has authored or edited several books and monographs, including* China-Russia Security Relations, Kazakhstan and the New International Politics of Eurasia *and* Revitalising US–Russian Security Cooperation: Practical Measures.

President Nazarbayev in a meeting with Lorenzo Simonelli, president and CEO of GE Oil & Gas

# Our past is prelude to our future: Kazakhstan's continuing modernization and leadership

By *Kairat Umarov*

Kazakhstan has come a long way in just 23 years since gaining independence. In this relatively short time it has achieved what most nations aspire to: stability, security, prosperity and peace. As with all nations at the moment of their independence, Kazakhstan was founded on the promise of a better future. If we take inventory of all that Kazakhstan's people have accomplished in just two decades, and consider the goals that have been established for the decades ahead, it is hard to be anything but optimistic for our young nation.

Kazakhstan today is strong, and its future is bright. Let me offer a review of some of the country's top domestic and international priorities, which will help to explain the dynamic trajectory of our plans for future development.

## Kazakhstan 2050 Strategy

The Kazakhstan 2050 Strategy is a comprehensive national development plan presented by President Nursultan Nazarbayev in his 2012 State of the Nation address. It seeks to position Kazakhstan as one of the world's 30 most developed and

Left: Astana's architecturally stunning modernist skyline skilfully incorporates motifs and themes from Kazakhstan's legends and traditions. Below left: An early 20th century photo of a nomad and packed camel ready to move to new pastures (© MAE (Kunstkamera) RAS No 1199-167)

President Nursultan Nazarbayev has guided Kazakhstan on its journey from Soviet republic to independent state, and is now setting out the roadmap for its future success

modernized countries by the year 2050. The new strategy includes broad-ranging developments in industrialization, infrastructure, asset management, investment, competitiveness, entrepreneurial projects, economic diversification, agriculture, exports, energy, natural resources and employment. Buttressing the 2050 Strategy, the government has laid the basis for accelerated diversification of the economy through industrialization. According to President Nazarbayev, "Strong and powerful countries are formed on long-term vision and stable economic development. The Kazakhstan 2050 Strategy outlines a modernization path for all areas to provide sustainable growth. It is a big challenge, which will test and strengthen our country, our unity, our courage and our efforts."

As Foreign Minister Erlan Idrissov says, it is "a powerful, large-scale document for the future... It is a call to the younger generation of the people of Kazakhstan to continue along the highway of our development, focusing on the establishment of a self-sufficient, modern, secular and democratic state with stable institutions and a strong economy."

## KAZAKHSTAN'S CANDIDACY FOR A SEAT AT THE UNSC IN 2017-2018

Based on its high record of development and proactive diplomatic efforts, Kazakhstan has announced its bid for non-permanent membership in the United Nations Security Council (UNSC) for 2017-2018. As an important partner in the Council's spheres of interest, "Kazakhstan wishes to bring its unique experience and expertise to bear on some of the pressing challenges currently facing the UNSC". Home to over 130 different nationalities and ethnic groups, "Kazakhstan is nothing less than a microcosm of the United Nations," as Kazakhstan's Foreign Ministry puts it.

In considering Kazakhstan's credentials for a UNSC seat, one should take into account Kazakhstan's recent contributions to international security:

- **Afghanistan:** Astana continues to play an active and important role in the Istanbul Process on Afghanistan and hosted the Istanbul Process Ministerial meeting in 2013. Kazakhstan has assumed a critical supportive role in NATO-led operations to stabilize Afghanistan logistically and provide much-needed humanitarian assistance to the country.

Kazakhstan was the first to support the Northern Distribution Network, to promote the New Silk Road initiative, and provide scholarships to 1,000 Afghans at the best Kazakh universities as part of a US$50 million educational programme. Today, we are establishing the Kazakhstan Agency for International Development (KazAID), with the focus on Afghanistan and Central Asia. As it moves forward in its mission to provide technical assistance to the countries of this region, the geographical scope of KazAID's activities may expand slowly over time.

- **Leadership in non-proliferation:** Kazakhstan has been an active proponent and regional leader in the nuclear disarmament movement, making the strategic decision to eliminate its own arsenal of nuclear weapons immediately after achieving independence from the Soviet Union.

- **Iran talks:** Kazakhstan provided a platform for two rounds of the P5+1 negotiations on Iran's nuclear programme, paving the way for the subsequent international talks in Geneva.

- **Congress of Leaders of World and Traditional Religions:** Astana hosts this triennial Congress to promote inter-faith dialogue, religious tolerance and harmony by spreading a message of peace between the world's religious leaders and their followers.

- **CICA:** Kazakhstan initiated the Conference on Interaction and Confidence Building Measures in Asia (CICA) in October 1992. The CICA initiative's main idea is to conduct CBMs in Asia to enhance trust among the members, help foster economic development in these countries and prevent conflict in the region. After Turkey's successful chairmanship from 2010 to 2014, China has taken over chairmanship for the 2014-2016 period, and promises to help grow the initiative and promote peace and development in Asia.

- **OIC:** Kazakhstan successfully chaired the Organisation of Islamic Cooperation (OIC) in 2011-2012, during which it placed such priorities as progressive development, science and technology firmly on the OIC agenda under the motto "Peace, Cooperation and Development".

- **OSCE:** Kazakhstan successfully chaired the OSCE (Organization for Security and Co-operation in Europe) in 2010 and hosted a historic Astana Summit of the organization. Its chairmanship was conducted under a motto of four "Ts": "Trust. Tradition. Transparency. Tolerance".

• Kazakhstan has vast experience in chairing **regional organizations**, for example the Shanghai Cooperation Organization (SCO) in 2010-2011 and the Collective Security Treaty Organization (CSTO) in 2012.

Kazakhstan's membership in the UNSC will be based on four pillars: food security, water security, energy security and nuclear security – all areas in which Kazakhstan has valuable experience, and through which it will contribute to ensuring security on the world stage.

## Astana Expo-2017

Awarded the title "City of Peace" by UNESCO, Astana is preparing to host the World's Fair: EXPO-2017. The theme of the expo will be "Future Energy" and it will showcase the world's greatest innovations in global sustainability and energy efficiency. Kazakhstan stresses the importance of future environmental initiatives and hence will be promoting the use of renewable energies and technologies at EXPO-2017, which is expected to attract over five million attendees. This important global event will advocate initiatives for alternative and efficient use of sustainable energy in order to provide for future world demands.

In the same vein, Kazakhstan has developed the Green Bridge Initiative to foster international cooperation by creating a platform for knowledge and technology transfer necessary for making the transition from current conventional development patterns to "green growth". The initiative enjoys widespread support from developing countries and international organizations, including the UN and EBRD (European Bank for Reconstruction and Development). Through such an initiative, Kazakhstan is contributing to sustainable development designed to prevent economic growth from harming our environment.

## Dynamic economic development

Kazakhstan's business and investment environment has improved at an impressive rate in the past two decades, providing positive momentum for investment, and the current trends point to further progress in the next couple of years.

Kazakhstan has systematically fostered a favourable business environment by eliminating bureaucratic obstacles to investment, creating structures to support investors – including KazNexInvest, the Foreign Investors' Council and Investment Ombudsman – as well as provision of significant preferential treatment. These measures have earned Kazakhstan 50th place in the World Bank's Ease of Doing Business rankings, 22nd place in the Investor Protection Index, and 50th place in the World Economic Forum's Competitiveness Ranking. Kazakhstan receives about 80 percent of Central Asia's FDI inflows. Kazakhstan has abolished visa requirements for 10 countries – the United States, the Netherlands, the UK, France, Germany, Italy, Malaysia, the United Arab Emirates, South Korea and Japan – as a one-year pilot project, starting from 15 July, 2014, to encourage investment and cooperation with its significant partner countries.

Having such a beneficial investment climate, Kazakhstan can serve as a gateway for foreign investors to the huge market of the Eurasian Economic Union (EEU), which will be created in 2015 and will facilitate international transport corridors connecting Western China with Western Europe through Kazakhstan by cutting the shipment time to only 10 days compared to 45 days via sea. This is possible because the trucks and trains will not need to stop at the borders between EEU member countries. Connectivity is very important to us as a landlocked nation, and by creating the EEU we are turning landlocked into "land-linked".

Kazakhstan is also now in the final stage of talks on accession to the World Trade Organization (WTO), a significant economic step that will provide a considerable boost to importers, exporters, and producers of goods and service.

## A hospitable nation

Kazakhstan boasts a multiethnic society with a long tradition of tolerance, secularism and inter-faith dialogue. In particular, Muslim, Russian Orthodox, Roman Catholic, Jewish and many other representatives contribute to building a single united home, where every citizen feels empowered and enjoys the benefits of high economic growth and greater integration to the world.

This book reveals Kazakhstan's rich past and highlights its ancient civilizations, telling the story of a nation whose roots delve deep into world history, but which has its eyes fixed firmly on the future. To experience this land where historical wealth blends with dynamic future plans, I invite citizens from around the world to visit us and experience a unique destination that offers developed infrastructure, natural beauty and renowned hospitality. Welcome to Kazakhstan, an ancient nation and forward-looking country!

*Kairat Umarov is Ambassador of the Republic of Kazakhstan to the United States of America.*

A replica of the Saka-era Golden Man stands as the centrepiece in the main hall of the Presidential Cultural Centre's musem of history

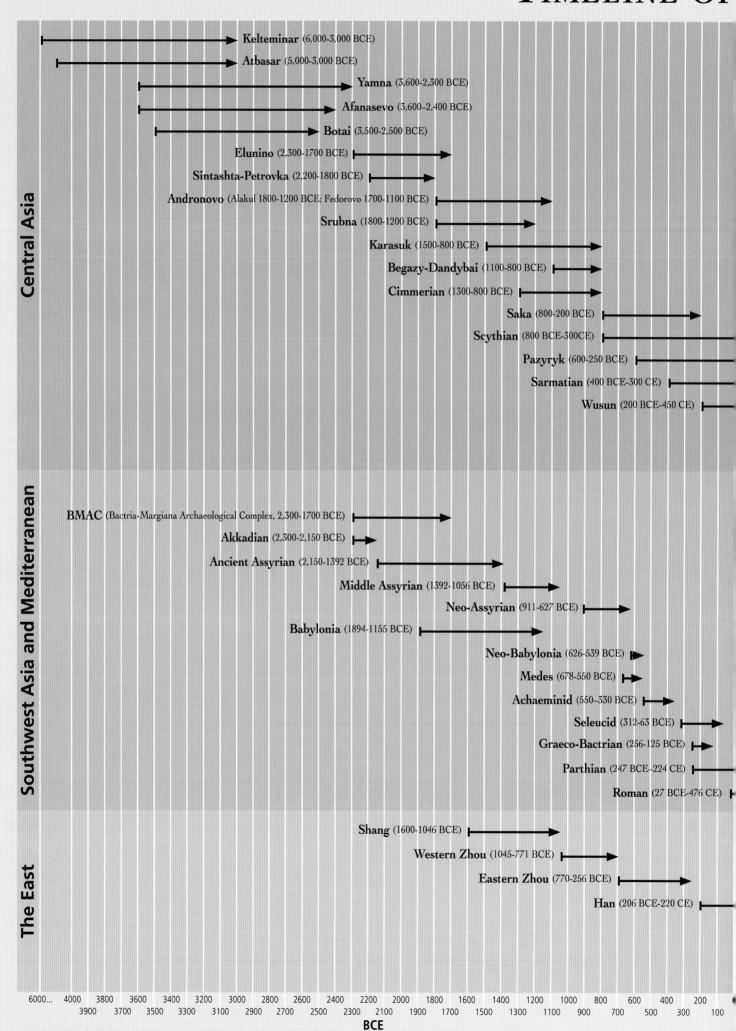

**Central Asia**

Kelteminar (6,000-3,000 BCE)

Atbasar (5,000-3,000 BCE)

Yamna (3,600-2,300 BCE)

Afanasevo (3,600–2,400 BCE)

Botai (3,500-2,500 BCE)

Elunino (2,300-1700 BCE)

Sintashta-Petrovka (2,200-1800 BCE)

Andronovo (Alakul 1800-1200 BCE; Fedorovo 1700-1100 BCE)

Srubna (1800-1200 BCE)

Karasuk (1500-800 BCE)

Begazy-Dandybai (1100-800 BCE)

Cimmerian (1300-800 BCE)

Saka (800-200 BCE)

Scythian (800 BCE-300CE)

Pazyryk (600-250 BCE)

Sarmatian (400 BCE-300 CE)

Wusun (200 BCE-450 CE)

**Southwest Asia and Mediterranean**

BMAC (Bactria-Margiana Archaeological Complex, 2,300-1700 BCE)

Akkadian (2,300-2,150 BCE)

Ancient Assyrian (2,150-1392 BCE)

Middle Assyrian (1392-1056 BCE)

Neo-Assyrian (911-627 BCE)

Babylonia (1894-1155 BCE)

Neo-Babylonia (626-539 BCE)

Medes (678-550 BCE)

Achaeminid (550–330 BCE)

Seleucid (312-63 BCE)

Graeco-Bactrian (256-125 BCE)

Parthian (247 BCE–224 CE)

Roman (27 BCE-476 CE)

**The East**

Shang (1600-1046 BCE)

Western Zhou (1045-771 BCE)

Eastern Zhou (770-256 BCE)

Han (206 BCE-220 CE)

6000... 4000 3900 3800 3700 3600 3500 3400 3300 3200 3100 3000 2900 2800 2700 2600 2500 2400 2300 2200 2100 2000 1900 1800 1700 1600 1500 1400 1300 1200 1100 1000 900 800 700 600 500 400 300 200 100

**BCE**

# CULTURES AND EMPIRES

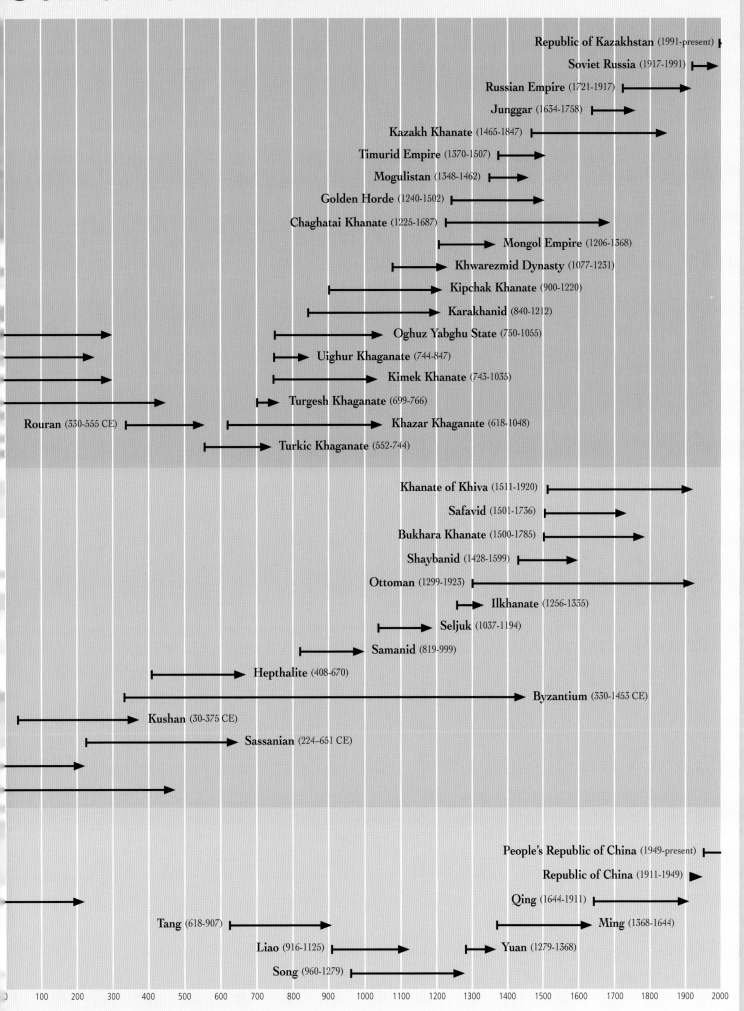

Republic of Kazakhstan (1991-present)

Soviet Russia (1917-1991)

Russian Empire (1721-1917)

Junggar (1634-1758)

Kazakh Khanate (1465-1847)

Timurid Empire (1370-1507)

Mogulistan (1348-1462)

Golden Horde (1240-1502)

Chaghatai Khanate (1225-1687)

Mongol Empire (1206-1368)

Khwarezmid Dynasty (1077-1231)

Kipchak Khanate (900-1220)

Karakhanid (840-1212)

Oghuz Yabghu State (750-1055)

Uighur Khaganate (744-847)

Kimek Khanate (743-1035)

Turgesh Khaganate (699-766)

Rouran (330-555 CE)

Khazar Khaganate (618-1048)

Turkic Khaganate (552-744)

Khanate of Khiva (1511-1920)

Safavid (1501-1736)

Bukhara Khanate (1500-1785)

Shaybanid (1428-1599)

Ottoman (1299-1923)

Ilkhanate (1256-1335)

Seljuk (1037-1194)

Samanid (819-999)

Hepthalite (408-670)

Byzantium (330-1453 CE)

Kushan (30-375 CE)

Sassanian (224–651 CE)

People's Republic of China (1949-present)

Republic of China (1911-1949)

Qing (1644-1911)

Tang (618-907)

Ming (1368-1644)

Liao (916-1125)

Yuan (1279-1368)

Song (960-1279)

0   100   200   300   400   500   600   700   800   900   1000   1100   1200   1300   1400   1500   1600   1700   1800   1900   2000

CE

# FURTHER READING

**Abazov, Rafis**, *The Palgrave Concise Historical Atlas of Central Asia* (Palgrave Macmillan, 2008)

**Abusseitova, Meruyert Kh**. and **Dodhudoeva, L.N.**, *History of Kazakhstan in Eastern Miniatures* (Daik-Press, 2010)

**Aitken, Jonathan**, *Nazarbayev and the Making of Kazakhstan* (Continuum, 2009)

**Akiner, Shirin**, *The Formation of Kazakh Identity: From Tribe to Nation-State* (Royal Institute of International Affairs, 1995)

**Anthony, David W.**, *The Horse, the Wheel, and Language: How Bronze-Age Riders from the Eurasian Steppes Shaped the Modern World* (Princeton University Press, 2010)

**Barysbekov, Berik**, *Kazakhstan from the Sky* (Central Asia Production, 2011)

**Baumer, Christoph**, *The History of Central Asia: The Age of the Steppe Warriors* (I.B.Tauris & Co Ltd, 2012)

**Beckwith, Christopher I.**, *Empires of the Silk Road: A History of Central Eurasia from the Bronze Age to the Present* (Princeton University Press, 2011)

**Bolton, Roy**, *Russian Orientalism & Constantinople* (Sphinx Books, 2009)

**Bonora, Gian Luca, Pianciola, Niccolo** and **Sartori, Paulo** (editors), *Kazakhstan: Religions and Society in the History of Central Eurasia* (Umberto Allemandi & Co, 2009)

**Boulnois, Luce**, *Silk Road: Monks, Warriors & Merchants* (Odyssey Books & Guides, 2012)

**Bregel, Yuri**, *An Historical Atlas of Central Asia* (Brill Academic Publishers, 2003)

**Cummings, Sally N.**, *Understanding Central Asia: Politics and Contested Transformations* (Routledge, 2012)

**Di Cosmo, Nicola, Frank, Allen J.** and **Golden, Peter B.** (editors), *The Cambridge History of Inner Asia: The Chinggisid Age* (Cambridge University Press, 2009)

**Dundas, Lawrence John Lumley (Marquess of Zetland)**, *On the Outskirts of Empire in Asia* (Ulan Press, 2011)

**Fitzhugh, William, Rossabi, Morris** and **Honeychurch, WIlliam**, *Genghis Khan and the Mongol Empire* (Arctic Studies Center, Smithsonian Institution, 2013)

**Golden, Peter B.**, *Central Asia in World History* (Oxford University Press, 2011)

**Grigoriev, Stanislav A.**, *Ancient Indo-Europeans* (Institute of History and Archaeology, Chelyabinsk Scientific Centre, Ural branch of the Russian Academy of Sciences, 2002)

**Hanks, Bryan K.** and **Linduff, Katheryn M.**, *Social Complexity in Prehistoric Eurasia: Monuments, Metals and Mobility* (Cambridge University Press, 2009)

**Hiro, Dilip**, *Inside Central Asia: A Political and Cultural History of Uzbekistan, Turkmenistan, Kazakhstan, Kyrgyzstan, Tajikistan, Turkey, and Iran* (Overlook Duckworth, 2011)

**Hopkirk, Peter**, *The Great Game: The Struggle for Empire in Central Asia* (Kodansha International, 1992)

**Kassymova, Didar** and **Kundakbayeva, Zhanat**, *Historical Dictionary of Kazakhstan* (Scarecrow Press, 2012)

**Knobloch, Edgar**, *Russia & Asia: Nomadic & Oriental Traditions in Russian History* (Odyssey Books & Guides, 2007)

**Kohl, Philip L.**, *The Making of Bronze Age Eurasia* (Cambridge University Press, 2009)

**Kuidin, Juri**, *Kazakhstan Nuclear Tragedy* (Humanist Institute for Cooperation with Developing Countries Netherlands and United Nations Office, Almaty, Kazakhstan, 1997)

**Kulchik, Yuriy, Fadin, Andrey** *and* **Sergeev, Victor**, *Central Asia After the Empire* (Pluto Press, 1996)

**Kundakbayeva, Zhanat**, *History of Kazakhstan in the Late Medieval Period of the XIII – First Third of the XVIII Centuries* (Al-Farabi Kazakh National University, 2011)

Opposite: Kazakh nomads begin a migration to new grazing lands, a grandmother and two children perched atop felts and carpets on one of their camels

**Kuz'mina, Elena E.** (edited by **J.P. Mallory**), *The Origin of the Indo-Iranians* (BRILL, 2007)

**Kuz'mina, Elena E.** and **Mair, Victor H.**, *The Prehistory of the Silk Road* (University of Pennsylvania Press, 2007)

**Liu, Xinru**, *The Silk Road in World History* (Oxford University Press, 2010)

**Loveday, Helen, Wannell, Bruce, Baumer, Christoph** and **Omrani, Bijan**, *Iran – Persia: Ancient and Modern* (Odyssey Books & Guides, 2010)

**Manz, Beatrice F.** (editor), *Central Asia in Historical Perspective* (Westview Press, 1998)

**Marozzi, Justin**, *Tamerlane: Sword of Islam, Conquerer of the World* (HarperCollinsPublishers, 2004)

**Martin, Virginia**, *Law and Custom in the Steppe: The Kazakhs of the Middle Horde and Russian Colonialism in the Nineteenth Century* (Routledge, 2001)

**Marvin, Charles**, *Reconnoitring Central Asia: Pioneering Adventures in the Region Lying Between Russia and India* (Forgotten Books, 2012)

**Minns, Ellis Hovell**, *Scythians and Greeks: A Survey of Ancient History and Archaeology on the North Coast of the Euxine from the Danube to the Caucasus* (Cambridge University Press, 2011)

**Nazarbayev, Nursultan**, *The Kazakhstan Way* (Stacey International, 2008)

**Olcott, Martha Brill**, *The Kazakhs* (Hoover Institution Press, Stanford University, 1995)

**Pierce, Richard A.**, *Russian Central Asia 1867-1917: A Study in Colonial Rule* (University of California Press, 1960)

**Rashid, Ahmed**, *The Resurgence of Central Asia: Islam or Nationalism?* (Oxford University Press, 1994)

**Roy, Olivier**, *The New Central Asia: The Creation of Nations* (I.B. Tauris, 2007)

**Sabol, Steven**, *Russian Colonization and the Genesis of Kazak National Consciousness* (Palgrave Macmillan, 2003)

**Samashev, Zainolla** and **Stollner, Thomas**, *Unknown Kazakhstan: Archaeology in the Heart of Asia* (Deutsches Bergbau-Museum Bochum)

**Schreiber, Dagmar** and **Tredinnick, Jeremy**, *Kazakhstan: Nomadic Routes from Caspian to Altai* (Odyssey Books & Maps, 2012)

**Schuyler, Eugene**, *Turkistan: Notes of a Journey in Russian Turkistan, Kokand, Bukhara and Kuldja* (F.A. Praeger, 1966)

**Shayakhmetov, Mukhamet**, *The Silent Steppe* (Stacey International, 2006)

**Soucek, Svat**, *A History of Inner Asia* (Cambridge University Press, 2000)

**Stark, Sören** and **Rubinson, Karen S.** (editors), *Nomads and Networks: The Ancient Art and Culture of Kazakhstan* (Institute for the Study of the Ancient World at New York University and Princeton University Press, 2012)

**Starr, Frederick S.**, *Lost Enlightenment: Central Asia's Golden Age from the Arab Conquest to Tamerlane* (Princeton University Press, 2013)

**Teissier, Beatrice**, *Russian Frontiers: Eighteenth-century British Travellers in the Caspian, Caucasus and Central Asia* (Signal Books Ltd, 2011)

**Thubron, Colin**, *The Lost Heart of Asia* (Harper Perennial, 2008)

**Tredinnick, Jeremy**, *Xinjiang: China's Central Asia* (Odyssey Books & Guides, 2012)

**Wardell, John**, *In the Kirghiz Steppes* (The Galley Press, 1961)

**Whitfield, Susan**, *Life along the Silk Road* (University of California Press, 2001)

**Wood, Frances**, *The Silk Road: Two Thousand Years in the Heart of Asia* (University of California Press, 2004)

Opposite: A bronze tray on a conical stand dates to the fifth-third centuries BCE and was discovered by chance in the Almaty region. The seated man holds a cup and faces a standing horse, highlighting the close bond between the ancient nomads and their most prized and revered animals

# PHOTOGRAPHY AND ILLUSTRATION CREDITS

Courtesy of Meruyert Abusseitova/The British Museum: 120

Courtesy of the Academy of Sciences of Uzbekistan: 99; 118; 119 (bottom)

Courtesy of Astana EXPO-2017 National Company: 173 (middle and bottom)

Courtesy of Dina Astayeva: 165

Courtesy of Alan Aydakhar: 8; 80; 83 (top); 88 (top); 92 (top)

Courtesy of Karl M. Baipakov: 1; 55 (top right); 56 (top); 59 (bottom); 60 (top); 61 (x3); 62 (x3); 63 (top and middle illustration); 64 (bottom left); 68-69; 74 (top and bottom right); 76 (x3); 78 (middle and bottom); 79 (top and bottom); 85

Courtesy of Berik Barysbekov / CAPro (Central Asia Production): 20-21; 26; 29; 82; 100-101; 156-157; 163; 168; 178 (top)

Courtesy of Dobdoyin Bayar: 90 (top left)

Courtesy of Napil Bazylkhan: 89 (top left); 91 (top left); 93 (image and illustration)

Bibliothèque nationale de France: 97 (top)

Courtesy of the Central State Archive of Cinema-Photo Documents and Sound Recording of the Republic of Kazakhstan: 146 (bottom right); 147 (bottom); 152 (bottom); 155 (bottom); 161 (bottom); 189

Courtesy of Central State Museum of the Republic of Kazakhstan: 12 (bottom); 52 (inset top left and right); 59 (top); 63 (bottom); 64 (top); 78 (top); 119 (top right); 132 (top right and middle right); 144 (x4); 148 (bottom); 190

Courtesy of the Committee of the Monuments of South Kazakhstan (Architectural and Archaeological Heritage of South Kazakhstan Oblast): 34

Jean-Marc Deom: 39; 41; 43; 45; 47; 48

Labgeoarch (Laboratory of Geoarchaeology of the Department of History, Archaeology and Ethnology at the Al-Farabi Kazakh National University): 28; 31; 32; 34

Edinburgh University Library, Special Collections Department, Or. Ms.20 f.124v: 106 (top)

Courtesy of the website of the Embassy of Kazakhstan in Japan:

Freer Gallery of Art, Smithsonian Institution, Washington, D.C.: Purchase F1946.26: 117

Freer Gallery of Art, Smithsonian Institution, Washington, D.C.: Gift of Eugene and Agnes E. Meyer, F1968.46: 94-95

Freer Gallery of Art, Smithsonian Institution, Washington, D.C.: Gift of Martha Mayor Smith and Alfred Mayor in memory of A. Hyatt Mayor, F2000.3: 112

Courtesy of the Institute for the Study of the Ancient World at New York University: 13; 52 (main picture); 54 (middle); 55 (middle); 56 (bottom – After Walser 1966, pl.18); 58 (left and below right); 65 (A. Ongar top right and Y. Cherkashin bottom right); 67 (top and bottom)

Courtesy of Altynbekov Krym/Ostrov Krym Laboratory: 54 (bottom)

Courtesy of Juri Kuidin (from the book *Kazakhstan Nuclear Tragedy*): 153 (top); 155 (top)

Courtesy of NASA: 146 (top right and middle right); 170

Courtesy of the National Library of Russia Manuscripts Department: 126

Courtesy of the Nazarbayev Center, Astana: 3; 58 (above right); 66 (top right)

The Palace Museum, Beijing: 128-129 (top)

Peter the Great Museum of Anthropology and Ethnography (Kunstkamera) of the Russian Academy of Sciences: 10-11; 12 (top); 18; 122; 123 (top); 142 (top and bottom); 143; 148 (top); 149 (middle left and bottom left); 150; 151 (bottom); 152 (top); 183 (bottom)

RMN-Grand Palais (Museé Guimet, Paris): 128-129 (bottom)

Renato Sala: 36; 49 (top right); 60 (bottom); 73; 135

Courtesy of Zainolla Samashev: 64 (bottom right); 65 (top left and middle right illustration); 66 (bottom left illustration and image); 88 (bottom)

Courtesy of the Shaanxi Provincial Institute of Archaeology: 2; 87; 91 (bottom right)

Courtesy of Vitaliy Shuptar/Avalon HGS: 51

Shutterstock Images (shutterstock.com): Ruta Production: 14; Kristina Postnikova: 24-25; Maxim Petrichuk: 35; Elimoe: 50 (bottom); ppl: 158; Steshkin Yevgeniy: 162 (bottom); Kristina Postnikova: 166; Azat Khayrutdinov: 171 (top); Sfam-photo: 174-175; Nutexzles: 176; Im Perfect Lazybones: 179

Courtesy of Sphinx Fine Art: 75; 81; 89 (bottom); 95 (bottom); 121; 133 (bottom); 136 (top)

Courtesy of Kuatbek Tabaldiyev: 89 (top right)

Courtesy of A.T. Toleubaev: 53 (top and bottom)

Topkapi Palace Museum, TSMK. H.2160, fol.84a "Preparation for hunting": 116

Jeremy Tredinnick: 6; 9; 15; 16; 17; 37; 44; 46 (top and bottom); 49 (top left, middle and bottom right); 50 (top); 54 (top); 72 (top and bottom); 77; 83 (middle inset and bottom); 84 (right); 92 (bottom); 101 (bottom); 105 (top and bottom); 115; 119 (top left); 123 (bottom); 125; 130; 131 (top left and middle right); 132 (middle left); 147 (top); 151 (top); 157 (right); 159; 162 (top); 169; 171 (bottom); 172 (top and bottom); 182-183; 185; 193

Courtesy of the US Library of Congress (LOC), Prints & Photographs Division: 5 (above and below); 127; 132 (bottom, Prokudin-Gorskii Collection); 133 (top, Prokudin-Gorskii Collection); 136 (bottom); 137 (top left and right); 138 (x4); 139 (top and bottom); 140 (bottom); 141 (top); 149 (middle right and bottom right)

Courtesy of the Walters Art Museum: 109; 110

The following images are used under licence by Creative Commons Attribution-Share Alike (CCAS, http://creativecommons.org): Tim Evanson/CCAS2.0: 23 (below left and right); Firespeaker/CCAS3.0: 84 (left); Cicero Moraes/CCAS3.0: 23 (top left); PHGCOM/CCAS3.0: 90 (bottom right); 104; RIA Novosti archive/Dmitryi Donskoy/CCAS3.0: 154 (bottom); Silar/CCAS3.0: 100 (left)

*Opposite: A Kazakh grandmother and her young granddaughter in traditional dress in the Altyn Emel National Park region of Zhetisu*

# INDEX

## A

Abai the Righteous, *see* Kunanbayev, Abai
Abashevo culture, 37, 42, 44
Abbasid Caliphate, 82, 90
Abd al-Latif Khan, 124
Abd ar-Rakhim Khan, 124
Abdullah Khan, 120, 124
Ablai Khan, 3, 115, 125, 128, 130, 131, 136, 138
Abulay Sultan, 123, 124
Abulkhair Khan (Junior Zhuz), 124, 125, 135
Abulkhair Khan (Uzbek leader), 19, 101, 110, 113, 115, 116, 117, 118, 136, 137
Abulkhair Khanate, 101, 110, 111, 113, 116
Abul Mambet Khan, 130, 136
Abulmansur Ablai, *see* Ablai Khan
Achaemenid Empire, 16, 55, 59, 60, 76
Acheulean culture, 28, 30, 32
Afanasevo culture, 37, 41
Afghan war, 170
Agreement on Eternal Friendship (Russia-Kazakhstan), 167
agricultural sector, the, 158, 165, 178
Ahmad Sultan, 118
Ahmed Mirza, 118
Aisha (Bibi), 85
Aisha Bibi Mausoleum, 84, 85
Aishuak Khan, 138
Ak-Allah (burial site), 76
Ak-Beshim (Suyab), 73, 84
Akishev, Professor Kimal A., 60
Ak-Mechet fortress, 140
Akmola (town), 159
Akmolinsk Oblast, 141, 149
Ak-Orda (White Horde), 98, 107, 108, 109, 110, 111, 116
Aktau, 168, 179
*akyn*, 10-11
Alakol Lake, 73, 110
Alakul culture, 37, 42, 44, 46, 49, 51
Alanliao (tribe), *see* Alans
Alans (tribe), 73, 88
Alash Orda, 133, 143, 148, 149, 150, 154
Alexander I, Tsar, 139
Alexander II, Tsar, 126, 141
Alexander the Great, 56, 59, 60, 75
Alexandria Eschate, 56
Alexis, Metropolitan of Russia, 98
Al-Farabi, 84, 104
Al-Farabi Kazakh National University, 35, 51
All-Kazakh Congress, 143
Alma-Ata, *see* Almaty
Alma-Ata Declaration, 147, 155
Alma-Ata Protocol, 167
Alma-Ata riots (1986), 147, 153, 154
Almalyk, 73, 108
Almatau, 108, 132
Almaty, 73, 132, 147, 156, 158, 159, 170, 171
Al-Omari (Arab writer), 102, 111
Altai Mountains, 13, 16, 17, 26, 30, 40, 41, 42, 45, 48, 50, 51, 54, 56, 58, 59, 64, 65, 69, 76, 85, 93, 97, 102, 104, 107, 124, 127
Altyn-Emel National Park, 62
Altyn-Emel Pass, 73
Altyn Tamgan Tarkhan, 91, 93
Amangeldy culture, 49
Amu Darya, 24, 34, 41, 44, 51, 59, 84, 102, 107, 146
Anagui Khagan, 80, 88
Anatolia, 40, 44, 75
Andijan, 121, 123, 124
Andronovo culture, 41, 42, 44, 46, 48, 49, 50, 75
Andropov, Yuri, 153
An Jia sarcophagus, 3, 87, 91
An Lushan rebellion, 82
Anna, Empress of Russia, 125, 135
Anrakai, Battle of ,125, 135
Anthony, D.W., 42

Anti-crisis Programme, 163
Apar (tribe), *see* Avar
Apsheronian period, 27
*Aq Suyek*, 115
Aralkum, 146
Aral Sea, 19, 26, 29, 55, 56, 59, 66, 67, 72, 73, 75, 85, 100, 102, 110, 113, 121, 170
    environmental disaster of, 145, 146, 155, 170
    North Aral Sea, 146, 170
Aras River, 59
Aravalli polymetallic district, 44
Argippaeans (tribe), 59
Argu-Talas, 79
Argyn (tribe), 114
Arimaspians (tribe), 59
Aristan Bab, 100
Arkhangai province (Mongolia), 90
Arsubaniket, 74
Aryans, 44
Aryngazy Sultan, 138
Arystandy, 27, 30, 32, 33
Arzhan (kurgan), 16, 54, 76
Ashina clan, 80
Ashnas, 103, 106
Ashtarkhanids, 120, 123, 124
Asian Development Bank (ADB), 180
Asian Winter Games (2011), 171
Assembly of the People of Kazakhstan, 164, 166
Assyrian Empire, 44, 60
Astana, 159, 170, 171, 183
Astrakhan Khanate, 108, 110, 111, 127
Astrakhan (town), 107, 108, 120, 122, 135, 136
Atasu, 168
Atasu culture, 49
Atbasar culture, 23, 24, 34, 35
Atlantic period, 29, 35
atomic bombs, *see* nuclear testing site
Attila the Hun, 72, 87
Atyrau, 127, 168
*aul* (village), 139, 140, 141, 144
Aulye-Ata, *see* Taraz
Aurignacian man, 27
Avar (tribe), 88
Avesta, the, 59
Ayaguz fortress, *see* Sergiopol
Ayaguz River, battle of, 124
Ayteke Bi, 115
Azerbaijan, 168

## B

Babur, 122
Bactria, 43, 49, 56, 60, 75, 76
Bactria-Margiana Archaeological Complex (BMAC), 41, 42, 43
Baikal Lake, 16, 40, 42
Baikonur Cosmodrome, 155, 170
Baiterek Tower, 159
Baitursynov, Akhmet, 148, 150, 154
Bakyrgali, Suleiman, 104
Balasagun, 73, 84, 85, 90, 103, 108
Balasagun, Yusuf, 105
*balbals*, 8, 81, 83, 92
Balkan-Carpathian Metallurgical Province ((BCMP), 40
Balkh, 75, 102, 104, 106
Balkhash Lake, 26, 28, 69, 108, 109, 110, 118
Barak Khan, 110, 116
Barak Sultan, 136
Baranduk Khan, 117, 118
Barlas (tribe), 109
Bashadyr (burial site), 64, 76
Bashkir (tribe), 87, 111, 120, 135
Basmachi rebels, 149
Basmyly (tribe), 88, 89
Batu Khan, 97, 100, 107
Batur (Dzungar leader), 124
*batyr*, 115, 125, 128
Batyr Sultan, 136
*beg, see bek*
Begazy-Dandybai culture, *see* Dandybai culture

Eneolithic era, 21, 24, 27, 34, 35, 39, 45
Epipalaeolithic period, 33
Eraly Khan, 138
Ertis River, see Irtysh River
Esen Buga Khan, 113, 116
Esil River, see Ishim River
Esim Khan, see Ishim Khan
Eurasian Economic Community (EEC), 167
Eurasian Economic Union (EUU), 185
Eurasian forest-steppe belt, 16, 53
Eurasian Metallurgical Province (EMP), 40, 42, 43, 47
Euro-Asian Transport Links Project, 180
European Bank for Reconstruction and Development (EBRD), 185
EXPO-2017, see World EXPO-2017

## F

famine (1933-34), 150
Farab (Otrar), 74, 81, 82, 84, 104
"February Revolution", 148
Fedorovo culture, 37, 42, 44, 46, 49, 51
Fergana Oblast, 141
Ferghana Valley, 56, 68, 72, 76, 77, 85, 103, 115, 121
    mountain range, 51
financial crisis (global), 158, 171
Five-Year Plans, 150, 152
forced resettlement (Soviet), 19, 144, 151
foreign direct investment (FDI), 161, 177
Foreign Investors Council (FIC), 179, 185
free market economy, 156

## G

Gagauz (tribe), 87
Galdan Khan, 124
Gaugamela, Battle of, 60
Gayir Khan, 95
Genghis Khan, 18, 85, 94, 97, 102, 103, 104, 105, 107, 113, 115, 116
Georgia, 100, 103
Ghazan Khan, 97, 104
glasnost, 153
Gokturks, see Kok Turks
Golden Horde, the , 97, 98, 100, 107, 108, 109, 110, 111, 117
Golden Man, the, 17, 56, 58, 60, 61, 185
Gorbachev, Mikhail, 153, 154
Governorate General of the Steppe, 141, 149
Governorate General of Turkestan, 141, 149
governorate generals, 141
"Great Revolt", the, see Central Asian Revolt
Greco-Persian wars, 60
Green Bridge Initiative, 185
gulags, 19, 144
gunmo, 69
Guriyev family, 127

## H

Han Dynasty, see China
Haq Nazar Khan, 113, 115, 120, 123
Hazrat Sultan Mosque, 171
Hephthalites, 74, 88
Herat, 106
Herodotus, 53, 54, 55, 59, 76
History of the Northern Dynasties, 80
Holocene era, 21, 23, 27, 29, 31, 40
Holy Ascension Cathedral, 9, 132, 156
Homo
    erectus, 20, 21, 23, 27, 28, 30
    ergaster, 20, 27
    habilis, 20, 21, 23, 27
    sapiens, 20, 21, 23, 27
    sapiens sapiens (Modern man), 27, 31
Hordes (Kazakh), see Zhuzes
horse domestication, 24, 27, 35
House of Representatives, the, see Majilis
Hulagu (grandson of Genghis Khan), 107
Hulaguids, 107
Hunger Steppe, the, 98
Hunnic Empire, 72, 87, 92
Hunnoi (tribe), 72
Huns, the, see Xiongnu
Hurrian Mitanni state, 44

## I

Ibn Arabshah, 98, 102
Idanthyrsus, 54
Idrissov, Erlan A., 3, 184
Iki-Oguz, 73, 108
Ili Delta, 131
Ili River Valley, 62, 68, 69, 73, 77, 97, 103, 106, 108, 109, 128-129, 131, 150
Imamkuli Khan, 123
Imperial Russia, 14, 19, 111
Independence Square (Almaty), 123
Independent International Observer Mission, 172
India, 68, 77, 98, 109
Indo-Europeans, 42
Indo-Iranian language, 43, 44, 51, 53, 73
Indus Valley, 40, 41, 44
inflation, 158, 160
Inner Horde, see Bukey Horde
International Monetary Fund (IMF), 160, 161, 162, 180
intra-regional cooperation, 177, 179
Investor Protection Index, 185
Iranian Plateau, 40, 41
Iron Age, the, 14, 15, 16, 48, 50, 53, 66, 75
iron, development of, 37, 51, 53, 58
Irtysh Line, the, 127, 135
Irtysh River, 74, 76, 82, 85, 90, 102, 105, 107, 109, 110, 120, 124, 127, 134
    Black Irtysh, 90
Ishim Khan, 115, 123, 124
Ishim River, 35, 74, 103, 159, 166, 170
Islam, 77, 82, 84, 90, 93, 97, 104, 107, 108, 111, 117, 133
Islamic Development Bank, 180
Ispidzhab (Sayram), 18, 73, 74, 81, 103
Issedones (tribe), 59, 60
Issyk-Kul, 68, 69, 77, 103, 131
Issyk kurgan, 56, 60, 61, 62, 76, 78
Istanbul Process on Afghanistan, 184
Istemi Khagan, 80, 81, 88
Ivan the Terrible, Tsar, 127

## J

"Jade Road", 75
Jahangir (Salqam-Jangir) Khan, 124
Jamukat, 73, 77, 84
Janibeg Khan (son of Uzbeg), 98, 107
Janibek Sultan, 19, 110, 113, 116, 117, 119, 128
Janysh Sultan, 118
Jaxartes (Syr Darya) River, 55, 103
John of Plano Carpini, 103, 110
Juan-Juan, see Rouran
Juchi (Jochi), 95, 97, 100, 106, 107, 108, 109, 116
Juchid dynasty, 98, 116, 117, 118
Junggar, see Dzungar
Junggar Gate, 73
Junggarian Basin, 69, 107
Jurchen (tribe), 103

## K

Kaip Khan, 124, 135
Kaip Sultan, 138
Kalmakkyrgan River, 135
Kalmyk (tribe), 110, 124, 127, 135, 136
Kanay culture, 49
Kangju (tribal confederation), 56, 68, 69, 72, 73, 74, 76, 78, 87
Kangly (tribe), 85, 102, 109, 113, 114
Kapagan Khagan, 89
Karachay-Balkar (tribe), 87
Karaganda, 142, 144, 152
Karaites (tribe), 87
Kara Khagan, 89
Karakhan (ruler), 84, 85
Karakhanids, 18, 84
    Khanate, 84, 85, 87, 90
Kara-Khitan, see Karakitai
Karakitai, 85, 89, 102, 103
Karasuk culture, 37, 44, 49, 50, 51
Kara Suyek, 115
Karatai Sultan, 138

Mousterian tool industry, 28, 30, 31, 33
Movius Line, 30
Mughal India, 19
Mugodzhar, 32
Muhammad Haidar (general), 118, 120
Muhammad Shaybani Khan, 118, 119, 120
Mukan Khagan, 89
multi-vector policies, 3, 130, 159, 166, 167, 168, 181
Murghab Delta, 51
Mycenean civilization, 75

## N

Naiman (tribe), 85, 102, 103, 104, 105, 113, 114, 136
Narymsky Mountains, 47
nationalities policy (Soviet), 150
National Memorial Day, 147
national oil fund, *see* National Wealth Fund
National Programme of Denationalization and Privatization, 163
National Space Agency, 170
National Wealth Fund, 171
NATO, 166, 184
natural resources, 156, 168
Navaket (Red River city), 73, 84
Nazarbayev, Nursultan (President), 19, 130, 147, 154, 156, 157, 158, 159, 160, 161, 164, 165, 166, 167, 168, 172, 173, 176, 178, 179, 180, 181, 184
Nazarbayev University, 165
Neolithic era, 15, 21, 23, 27, 29, 30, 31, 39, 41
    archaeological sites, 31, 34
Nestorianism, 77, 79, 84
Nevada-Semipalatinsk Anti-Nuclear Movement, 147, 155, 166
New Silk Road, *see* Silk Road (New)
Nogai (tribe), 87, 110, 111, 114, 119, 120
nomadic pastoralism, 16, 37, 58
nongovernmental organizations (NGOs), 166
Novo-Ishim fortress, 137
nuclear disarmament/non-proliferation, 15, 159, 166, 184
Nuclear Non-Proliferation Treaty (NNPT), 167
nuclear testing site, 14, 19, 147, 152, 153, 155, 166
Nuraly Khan, 137, 138
Nur Otan (political party), 173
Nurinsky culture, 49
Nurzhol Boulevard, 166, 168, 174, 176
Nushibi (tribe), 89

## O

Obama, President Barack, 167
*oblast* (province), 141, 149, 165
Ob River, 107
Ogedei Khan, 95, 97, 106, 108, 109
Oghuz (tribe), 82, 88, 101, 102
oil deposits, 133, 146, 162
Oirat (tribe), 109, 120, 124, 135
*okrug* (administrative division), 139
Okunevo culture, 42, 49
Oldowan culture, 30
Omsk, 127, 141
Onoq (Ten Arrows), 82
*oquz*, 88
Orda-Balyk, 90
Orda-Edzhen, 109
Orda Khan, 100, 108
Orenburg, 137, 138, 139, 140, 141, 143
Organisation of Islamic Cooperation (OIC), 159, 184
Organization for Security and Co-operation in Europe (OSCE), 159, 180, 184
Orhon River Valley, 87, 88, 90, 92, 93
Orkhon script, *see Turuk bitik*
Orsk fortress, 136, 137
Orynbor, *see* Orenburg
Otrar, 18, 72, 73, 74, 78, 81, 84, 94, 95, 97, 100, 103, 104, 105, 106
Ottoman Empire, 19, 121
Otüken, 88
Oxus River, 55, 72, 103

## P

Palace of Independence (Astana), 170
Palace of Peace and Accord (Pyramid), 159, 172

Palaeolithic era, 21, 26, 27, 30, 31
Pamir Mountains, 45, 75
Panfilov, General Ivan, 151
Parliament of Kazakhstan, 164
Parthians, 59, 73, 78
*pax Mongolica*, 97
Pazyryk culture, 51, 55, 56, 64, 65, 66, 76
Pebble stone tool industry, 30
Pechenegs, 82, 85, 93, 102
*perestroika*, 147, 153
Perovsky, Governor General V.A., 140
Persepolis, 56
Persians, 59, 90, 98
Peter I (the Great), 127, 134, 135
petroglyphs, 15, 31, 48, 49, 50, 58, 89
Petropavlovsk, 137
Petrovka culture, *see* Sintashta-Petrovka culture
Pit Grave culture, *see* Yamna culture
Pleistocene era, 21, 27, 28
political reforms, 172
Polovians (aka Kipchaks), 102
Poltavka culture, 37, 42, 44
Pontic Steppe, 40, 54, 58, 82
Pre-Balkhash region, 28, 29, 30, 31, 32, 33
Presidential Cultural Centre (Astana), 17
presidential elections, 172
Presidential Palace (Akorda), 159, 166, 174-175
prison labour camps, *see* gulags
Privatization Investment Funds (PIFs), 162
proto-Dravidian, 41
proto-Finno-Ugrian, 41
proto-Indo-Europeans, 34, 37, 41, 42
proto-Levallois industry, 30, 32
"Proto-Silk Road", 75
proto-Turkic language, 50, 72
Ptolemy, 59
Pugachev, Yemelyan, 130
purges of "undesirables", 19, 150

## Q

Qaghan, *see* Khagan
*qatun*, 90
Qazaq, *see* Kazakh
Qianlong, Emperor, 128
Qing Dynasty, *see* China
*qiz*, 90

## R

Rabdan, Khuntay-shi Tsewang, 124, 135
railways, 147, 181
Raimbek Batyr, 125
Raim fortress, 140
Rashid al-Din, 102, 106, 109
religion, dissemination of, 77
religious tolerance, 159
repatriation policy, 160
Republic of Kazakhstan, 19, 156-185
Richthofen, Ferdinand von, 76
Rig Veda, the, 42
rock art, *see* petroglyphs
Rome, 68, 73, 77, 88
Rouran Khaganate (Empire), 74, 80, 88, 89, 93
Royal Scythians, 59
Russian Empire, 19, 113, 115, 120, 121, 125, 126-141, 143
Russian Federation, 154, 167, 171, 174
Russian Peasants' War, 130
Russian princes, 98, 107
Russian Revolution, 133, 148
Ryskulov, Turar, 150

## S

*Sacae, see* Saka
Safavid Empire, 109, 113, 121
Said Khan, 109
Saimaly Tash, 51
Saka culture, 3, 16, 51, 53, 59, 60, 62, 66, 67, 68, 73, 75, 76, 78, 92, 102, 185
    burial sites, 62, 63, 65
    Haumavarga, 56, 59, 60

Transoxiana, 68, 72, 74, 78, 79, 82, 95, 103, 109
Tsar, abdication of, 148
Tsarists (Whites), 143, 148, 149
Tuekty (burial site), 76
Tughluk Timur, 109
Tujiue (clan), 88
*Tumen*, 91
Tungusic language, 87, 88
Turfan, *see* Turpan oasis
Turgai Depression, 27
Turgai Oblast, 141, 149
Turgen, 73
Turgesh Khaganate, 82, 84, 87, 88, 89, 90, 93, 102
Turkestan-Siberian (Turk-Sib) Railway, 147
Turkic Khaganate, 18, 74, 81, 82, 87-93
    Eastern wing, 81
    Western wing, 81, 82, 84, 90
Turkic peoples, 14, 53, 80, 87, 102, 109
    administrative divisions, 91
    language, 69, 73, 89, 91, 93, 102
    military structure, 91
    period, 77, 80-93
Turkistan (town), 33, 74, 100, 101, 118, 122, 123, 124, 130, 141
*turk kara budun*, 91, 92
Turpan oasis, 79, 90, 124
turquoise trade, 42
Tursun Sultan, 123, 124
*Turuk bitik* (script), 92, 93
*Turuk Eli*, 87, 88, 89, 93
Tuul River Valley, 87, 93
Tuva, 54, 76, 93
Tuvan (tribe), 87, 91
Tyumen, 100

## U

Uch Elig Khagan, 89
*uezd* (district), 141
Uighur (tribal confederation), 80, 82, 87, 88, 89, 90, 105, 109
Uighurs (modern), 151
Uighur script, 93
Ukok (burial site), 64
Ulaanbaatar, 105
Ulandryk (burial site), 76
Ulugh Beg, 117
*Ulus* (appanage), 106, 111
Ulytau Mountains, 45, 47, 74, 113, 119, 130
United Nations (UN), 158, 166, 185
    Development Programme (UNDP), 170, 180
    Security Council (UNSC), 184, 185
    UNESCO, 67, 79, 185
    World Heritage site, 15, 49
Upper House, the, *see* Senate, the
Ural Mountains, 24, 36, 40, 42, 43, 45, 51, 59, 72, 75, 145
Ural River, 98, 106, 110, 111, 119, 122, 127, 130, 135
Uralsk, 127
    Oblast, 141, 149
urbanization, 165
Urgench, 95, 106
Urgenj, *see* Urgench
Urus Khan, 98, 110, 116
Ush Zhuz (political party), 148
Ust-Kamenogorsk, 127
Usun, *see* Wusun
Utemisuly, Makhambet, 130
Utigur (tribe), 88
Uygarak (burial site), 66
Uzbeg Khan, 97, 98, 101, 107
Uzbek Horde, 19, 100, 109, 110, 111, 113, 114, 116, 117
Uzbekistan, 93, 167
Uzgen, 85

## V

Vali Khan, 138
Valikhanov, Chokan, 33, 131
Vasilkovska, 35
Verevkin, Colonel P.L., 141
Verniy, Fort, 132, 140
vertical nomadism, 67, 79, 185

Virgin and Idle Lands Project, 19, 145, 151, 152, 153, 155, 170
Volga River, 59, 92, 98, 106, 107, 108, 109, 111, 120, 122, 130, 135
Volokolamsk Shosse, Battle of, 151
*volost* (administrative division), 139, 140, 141

## W

West Asian Metallurgical Province (WAsMP), 40, 42, 43, 44, 47, 49
Western China-Western Europe International Transit Corridor, 180
"Western Regions", the, 68, 75, 77
West Siberian General governorship, 139
White Horde, the, *see* Ak-Orda
William of Rubruck, 76, 103
World Bank, the, 146, 160, 161, 170, 180, 185
World Economic Forum, 185
World EXPO-2017, 173, 185
World Trade Organization (WTO), 173, 177, 185
World War I, 143, 148
World War II, 144, 145, 150, 151
writing (Kazakh scripts), 150
Wudi, Han Emperor, 68
Wusun, 16, 56, 68, 69, 72, 74, 76, 77, 78, 87, 92

## X

Xerxes, Persian Emperor, 59
Xian, *see* Chang'an
Xianbei (tribe), 74
Xinjiang, 75, 76, 84, 90, 93, 124, 144, 151
Xiongnu (tribe), 56, 68, 69, 72, 74, 76, 87, 88, 93, 102
Xi-Xia Empire, 105
Xuan Zang, 76, 82

## Y

*Yabghu*, 82, 90, 91
Yagma (tribe), 84, 90
Yaik River, *see* Ural River
Yakut (tribe), 87
*Yam* (Mongol postal system), 111
Yamishevsk, 127
Yamna culture, 41
Yancai (tribal confederation), 68, 72, 73
Yangikent, 18, 74, 81, 103
Yarkand Khanate, 109, 124
Yarkand River, 75
*Yasachnaya* tribute, 140
Yasawi, Khoja Ahmed, 124
Yassi (Turkistan), 74, 100, 101, 118
*Yduk Yer*, 92
"Years of great Distress", 19, 115, 124
Yeltsin, Boris, 154
Yenisei River, 41, 42, 44, 58, 90, 92, 105
*Yer su*, 92, 104
*Yogu* (rite), 92
*Yuan Shi* (History of the Yuan), 102
Yuezhi (tribe), 56, 68, 69, 72, 76, 87
Yunus Khan, 109

## Z

Zaghunluk (burial site), 76
Zaysan Lake, 33, 64
Zeravshan Valley, 42
Zhalauly treasure, 1, 12, 59, 63, 64
Zhanaozen, 172
Zhang Qian, 68, 69, 72, 75, 76
Zhantore Khan, 138
Zhayik River, *see* Ural River
zhaylau, 92
Zhaysan (burial site), 82
Zhetisu (Semirechye), 19, 49, 53, 56, 62, 68, 84, 90, 92, 140
*Zhety Zhargy* (Seven Rules), 115, 123
Zhoukoudian, 33
Zhuchi, *see* Juchi
Zhungar, *see* Dzungar
Zhuzes, origin of, 113
    Junior, 111, 114, 115, 124, 125, 130, 135, 136, 137, 139
    Middle, 110, 114, 115, 124, 125, 128, 130, 136, 137, 139
    Senior, 114, 124, 125, 141
*Zizhi Tongjian*, 80
Zoroastrianism, 59, 78, 79, 82, 84

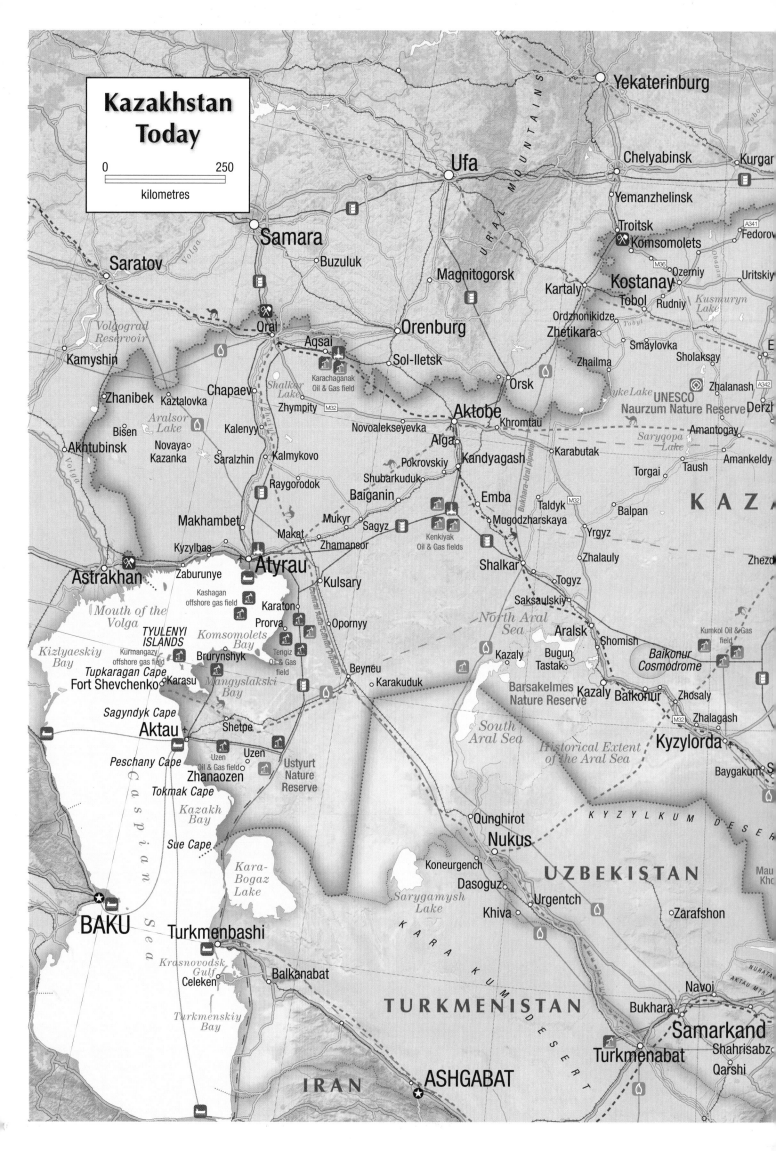

# Kazakhstan
# Today

0             250

kilometres

Yekaterinburg

Ufa

Chelyabinsk    Kurgar

Yemanzhelinsk

Troitsk    Fedorov

Komsomolets

Samara    Buzuluk      Magnitogorsk    Kartaly   Kostanay    Ozerniy    Uritskiy

Saratov        Tobol   Rudniy    *Kusmuryn Lake*

Ordzhonikidze

Qral      Orenburg      Zhetikara    Smaylovka

Aqsai      Sol-Iletsk      Zhailma    Sholaksay

Kamyshin    *Volgograd Reservoir*    *Shalkar Lake*    Karachaganak Oil & Gas field    Orsk    Zhalanash   Derzh

Zhanibek   Kaztalovka   Chapaev    Zhympity   M32      Aktobe      UNESCO

Bišen    *Aralsor Lake*    Kalenyy    Novoalekseyevka    Khromtau    Naurzum Nature Reserve

Akhtubinsk   Novaya Kazanka   Saralzhin   Kalmykovo    Alga    Karabutak    Amantogay

Pokrovskiy    Kandyagash    *Sarygopa Lake*    Amankeldy

Raygorodok    Shubarkuduk      Torgai   Taush

Makhambet    Baiganin    Emba    Taldyk   M32    Balpan    K A Z A

Mukyr   Sagyz    Mugodzharskaya    Yrgyz

Kyzylbas   Makat    Kenkiyak Oil & Gas fields    Zhalauly    Zhezd

Astrakhan   Zaburunye    Zhamansor    Shalkar

Atyrau    Kulsary    Togyz

Kashagan offshore gas field    Karaton    Saksaulskiy    *North Aral Sea*    Aralsk    Kumkol Oil & Gas field

*Mouth of the Volga*    Prorva    Opornyy    Shomish

TYULENYI ISLANDS    *Komsomolets Bay*    Kazaly    Bugun    *Baikonur Cosmodrome*

*Kizlyaeskiy Bay*   Kurmangazy offshore gas field   Brurynshyk    Tengiz Oil & Gas field    Beyneu    Tastak

*Tupkaragan Cape*   Karasu    *Mangyslakski Bay*    Karakuduk    Barsakelmes Nature Reserve    Kazaly   Baikonur    Zhosaly

Fort Shevchenko      *South Aral Sea*    M32    Zhalagash

*Sagyndyk Cape*    Shetpe    *Historical Extent of the Aral Sea*    Kyzylorda

Aktau    Uzen Oil & Gas field   Uzen    Baygakum

*Peschany Cape*    Zhanaozen    Ustyurt Nature Reserve

*Tokmak Cape*    *Kazakh Bay*

*Sue Cape*    *Kara-Bogaz Lake*    Qunghirot    K Y Z Y L K U M   D E S E R

BAKU    Nukus    U Z B E K I S T A N    Mau Kho

Koneurgench

Turkmenbashi    Dasoguz    Zarafshon

*Krasnovodsk Gulf*    *Sarygamysh Lake*   Urgentch

Celeken    Balkanabat    Khiva

*Turkmenskiy Bay*    K A R A   K U M   D E S E R T    Navoi

Bukhara    NURATA

T U R K M E N I S T A N    Samarkand

AKTAU MTS

Turkmenabat    Shahrisabz

I R A N    ASHGABAT    Qarshi

*Caspian Sea*    *Volga*    U R A L   M O U N T A I N S    *Tobol*    *AykeLake*    Bukhara-Ural pipeline    Central Asia-Center pipeline